Interpreting
the
NEW TESTAMENT TODAY

Interpreting
the
NEW TESTAMENT
TODAY

*an introduction to
methods and issues
in the study of the
New Testament*

R. C. Briggs

ABINGDON

Nashville

INTERPRETING THE NEW TESTAMENT TODAY

A Revision of

INTERPRETING THE GOSPELS

Copyright © 1969, 1973 by Abingdon Press

Fourth Printing 1979

ISBN 0-687-19327-3
Library of Congress Catalog Card Number: 73-8024

Scripture quotations unless otherwise noted are
from the Revised Standard Version of the Bible,
copyrighted 1946, 1952, 1971 by the Division of
Christian Education, National Council of Churches,
and are used by permission.

Scripture quotations noted American Bible Society
are from *Good News for Modern Man,* The New
Testament in Today's English, trans. Robert G.
Bratcher, copyright 1967 by the American Bible
Society.

MANUFACTURED BY THE PARTHENON PRESS AT
NASHVILLE, TENNESSEE, UNITED STATES OF AMERICA

To my wife
Elizabeth

preface to first edition

This book is the result of stimulation that has arisen in connection with my experiences as a teacher. These experiences have occurred largely within two contexts; in the structured setting of the classroom, and in the informal situation of discussion groups composed of inquiring churchmen. It may be surprising that many dimensions of the discussions in both groups have been remarkably similar. I take this opportunity to express my sincere gratitude for the insights which both groups have contributed as well as for the abiding friendships that have resulted from these relationships.

An introductory study of the methods and perspectives of current biblical scholarship can be both rewarding and baffling. The insights that arise through such a study may provide meaningful solutions for basic issues. At the same time, the scope and quantity of details toward which such a study points may seem to be prohibitive for the beginning student of theology or for the interested churchman. Furthermore, it soon becomes apparent that the study is not confined to the acquisition of additional factual information. The learner is confronted with the more demanding task of interpreting the implications of this information for his larger perspective concerning the Bible. The material in this book is not designed as a guide for the entire journey to understanding. However, it is hoped that it may serve to indicate some directions at one stage of that journey.

My personal gratitude is due the following persons who have made valuable contributions to the work: Peggy Briggs and Elizabeth Anne Barnes, for the preparation of the manuscript; Don and Kathy Daughtry, for valuable insights and suggestions concerning the form and content of the material.

R. C. Briggs

The Interdenominational Theological Center
Atlanta, Georgia

preface to revised edition

The need for the second edition of *Interpreting the Gospels* has provided a limited opportunity to respond to suggestions for correction and improvement. Apart from a thoroughgoing revision it has unfortunately been impossible to incorporate many valuable suggestions. I take this occasion to express grateful appreciation to those who have expressly indicated their evaluation of the work, including the nature and extent of its limitations.

This work largely reproduces the text of *Interpreting the Gospels* with certain minor revisions. These revisions involve the following changes. First, bibliographical references and lists have been updated, enriched, and expanded, primarily with reference to the needs of students at the level of introductory study. Second, Chapter 1 has been revised. Third, certain inadequate or incorrect assertions have been restated or deleted where the format of the earlier work has allowed.

In addition to the revisions noted above, the present work represents a twofold expansion of *Interpreting the Gospels*. First, two additional chapters dealing with Pauline literature (Chapter 6) and the Gospel of John (Chapter 7) have been added. Accordingly, a change of title—*Interpreting the New Testament Today*—seems appropriate. Second, a brief Excursus has been appended to each of four chapters (2–5).

Two agencies have made indispensable contributions toward

the completion of the work: The Interdenominational Theological Center which granted a leave of absence from normal classroom duties and the American Association of Theological Schools which administered the Faculty Fellowship Grant provided by the Sealantic Fund, Inc. Special words of gratitude are also due Professors Hendrikus W. Boers and John E. Steely for valuable suggestions concerning the format and content of the material. Finally, words of appreciation are due numerous other persons, including colleagues, students, and members of my own family.

The Interdenominational Theological Center
Atlanta, Georgia

Contents

Introduction   15

1 Problems in Biblical Interpretation   18
   Historical Methodology and Biblical
     Interpretation   19
   Scientific Methodology and Protestant
     Understanding of Scripture   21
   Areas of Critical Research   25

2 The Problem of the Text: Textual Criticism   30
   The Materials and Procedures of
     Bookmaking in Antiquity   32
   The Nature and Sources of Manuscript
     Errors   33
   The Materials of Textual Criticism:
     The Manuscript   37
   The Methodology of Textual Criticism . .   44
   The Present Status of the Text of the
     New Testament   50

   Excursus: The Practice of Textual Criticism   53

3 The Problem of Sources: Source Criticism   59
   Theories of Indirect Relationship of
     the Gospels   65
   Theories of Direct Relationship of the
     Gospels   70

Additional Problems for Investigation . 73
Conclusion 79

Excursus: The Practice of Source Criticism . 81

4 The Problem of Oral Tradition: Form
Criticism 87
The Foundations of Form-Critical
Research 90
Assumptions of Form Criticism 92
Forms of Oral Tradition 94
Conclusion 101
Excursus: The Pronouncement Story and
the Miracle Story 104

5 The Problem of Theology:
Redaction Criticism 110
Redaction Criticism: Its Origin and
Methodology 112
The Results of Redaction Criticism: The
Theology of the Gospels 118
Conclusion 131
Excursus: The Practice of Redaction
Criticism 133

6 Pauline Literature 138
Paul the Apostle 140
History of Pauline Research 145
The Crisis: Jesus or Paul? 155
History and Theology: The Quest for
Synthesis 157

The Center of Paul's Theology 160
Conclusion 172

7 Johannine Literature 174
The Johannine Corpus 178
*Historical Tradition in the Fourth
Gospel* 179
Johannine Sources 183
*The Literary Structure of the Fourth
Gospel* 190
*The Religious-Historical Heritage of
John's Gospel* 193
The Johannine Intention 201
Conclusion 206

8 The Bible: The Problem of the Canon 208
Scripture and the Canon 209
The Gospel in the Early Church 212
The Development of the Canon 216
The Nature and Authority of the Canon 219
Scripture and Tradition 222
The Limits of the Canon 224

9 The Problem of History: Jesus of History or
Christ of Faith? 227
*The Origin of the Problem of History in
New Testament Research* 228
Theology and History 235
*The Crisis of the Problem: Jesus of
History or Christ of Faith?* 238
Conclusion 246

10 The Problem of Interpretation: The Function
of Biblical Language 250

*The Modern Crisis in Man's Self-
understanding* 251

*The Modern Perspective and Biblical
Interpretation* 254

The Nature of Biblical Language 260

Conclusion 269

11 The Scriptures: The Problems of Unity and
Authority 271

*Critical Research and Biblical
Interpretation* 272

The Unity of the Scriptures 273

The Authority of the Scriptures 276

Conclusion 282

Scripture Index 284

Author Index 287

introduction

The number of Bibles sold each year in the United States exceeds that of any other single book. The publications that appear purporting to contribute to a better understanding of its contents have reached such proportions that it has been suggested that a five-year moratorium on publication of such literature would be helpful. At the same time, it is widely recognized that there is a dearth of understanding of the essential message of the Bible even among those who maintain some identification with the church. If justification for the appearance of another book on the subject is required, it is to be found in this paradoxical situation.

The annual sale of millions of copies of the Bible may be explained in various ways. It is doubtless true that reverence for the Bible as a sacred book plays a certain role. It is frequently presented as a gift by those who have a minimal knowledge of its meaning and who have little genuine commitment to its message. Numerous families who seldom read its pages would be uncomfortable if there were no family Bible in the home. At the same time, there are countless persons who read the Bible daily with a genuine desire for understanding. The eagerness with which recent readable translations are received attests to this fact. Undoubtedly, there is genuine widespread interest in the meaning and content of the biblical message.

In spite of noteworthy advances in the field of biblical interpretation, there is a growing sense of estrangement from the Bible itself. Many readers candidly confess that they cannot "understand" it. In many cases this lack of understanding is not so much a result of unfamiliarity with the literal content of

15

biblical material as it is the consequence of the reader's perspective. The biblical message is expressed in language and concepts that are strange and obscure to modern man. Although the problems posed by these unfamiliar perspectives have been treated exhaustively in theological circles, this knowledge is largely confined to the libraries of theological specialists. The average reader feels isolated from those who possess this specialized information and frequently refers to them as "scholars" and the "clergy." The task of communicating this information to nonspecialists who read the Bible has been frequently neglected. Meanwhile, this failure of the specialists to share their insights with the average reader has created a major barrier to his meaningful use of the Bible.

The trained theologian confronts a major problem when he attempts to convey his understanding of biblical truth to the average reader; namely, the reader's limited insight into the nature of biblical literature as a whole. Such readers are often hampered by ideas which they have learned from those who were unprepared to instruct them. The theologian feels that he is unable to impart his mature ideas, and the uninstructed reader interprets the theologian's statements as meaningless and irrelevant. It is at this fateful juncture that the importance of presuppositions is often overlooked. The discussion "makes sense" to the theologian because it arises out of assumptions which are consistent with his training. It is "senseless" to the nonspecialist because it is the product of assumptions that are totally unknown and alien to him. Thus, the fundamental problem of communication is a reflection of diverse perspectives. This diversity comes to its sharpest focus in relation to the nature and function of biblical literature as a whole. The solution is not to be found in a simple exchange of presuppositions, a procedure which is impossible, but rather by a meaningful analysis of biblical material by those who are able to interpret the nature of the problem which the reader has already discovered to some degree.

The discussion between specialist and nonspecialist is often encumbered by the demand that the nonspecialist become in fact a specialist. This is in principle impossible and unnecessary. To be sure, the trained thinker has reached his viewpoint through a long and arduous journey. However, the average reader is not obligated to become a trained theologian in order to achieve his purpose. His concern is for understanding at a less technical level, and his case raises a question for the specialist regarding the nature of his own information: Has he become so enslaved to the technical language which he uses that he is unable to express his knowledge in any other form? As with all specialized knowledge, the nonspecialist must continue to be dependent to some extent upon his better-informed colleague. Religious truth cannot be packaged in the manner of a prescription in the corner drugstore. It involves a degree of understanding which enables man to appropriate its meaning for his own existence.

The thesis of this work is that it is both necessary and possible for the nonspecialist to understand and use the basic tools of biblical interpretation, without at the same time facing the necessity of acquiring the mass of detailed and technical information which the specialist has at his disposal. Consequently, this work is motivated by a twofold purpose. First, it intends to provide a brief, analytical description of the basic tools which are necessary for meaningful interpretation of the New Testament, with specific reference to the first three Gospels, Paul's letters, and the Gospel of John. Subsequent discussion will indicate the reasons for selecting these segments of New Testament literature as the primary points of reference. Second, it attempts to indicate some implications of the use of these tools which contribute to meaningful understanding of the biblical message, both in private reading and in the experience of listening to pulpit proclamation. This information may also serve as a basis for further theological study.

1

Problems in Biblical Interpretation

The course of modern biblical scholarship can be described as a journey in search for appropriate methodology for interpreting the Bible. The character of this journey is reflected in the complicated issues that have arisen in theological circles since the time of Martin Luther (1483-1546).

18

HISTORICAL METHODOLOGY AND BIBLICAL INTERPRETATION

Contemporary biblical interpretation is almost universally based upon the principles of historical-critical research. The extent to which biblical interpretation involves historical issues can be seen through a review of biblical scholarship during the past two centuries.

Although the ultimate goal of biblical interpretation concerns the meaning of the biblical message for the present, biblical writings arose in circumstances that differed in important respects from those of modern readers. For example, the apostle Paul wrote his letters to Corinth in response to existing problems in the Corinthian church (*ca.* A.D. 54-56). Certain sections of these letters contain the Apostle's reply to specific questions (I Cor. 7:1; 8:1; 12:1; etc.). Likewise, other New Testament writings must be understood in the light of conditions and issues in various first-century Christian communities. Therefore, understanding these writings involves the attempt to determine the authors' intended message for the original readers within the context of their first-century experiences. As is the case with other literature of the past, the search for the original meaning of the scriptures represents a historical endeavor that calls for the use of the tools of historical investigation. Hence, the biblical interpreter's involvement in historical procedures arises out of the nature of the scriptures as historical documents of the past. To be sure, historical research does not encompass the total work of biblical interpretation, but it does define an indispensable point of departure. When biblical interpretation is undertaken without regard for the historical character of the scriptures, a fundamental point of reference for testing conclusions has been surrendered. Subsequent chap-

19

ters in this work deal with the nature and function of the tools of historical-critical research, with particular reference to their application to biblical interpretation.

Historical questions are investigated by use of methodology appropriate to historical truth. The development of these scientific principles constitutes one of modern man's crowning achievements. However, contrary to sporadic claims, historical research does not represent an instrument for obtaining exact and final answers to all questions concerning the past. Rather, historical evidence points to the "degree of probability" for its conclusions. Consequently, historical-critical research—in the area of biblical investigation, too—does not provide final and exact answers for all questions. Its conclusions arise out of evidence available at a specific point in time, viewed from the perspectives of the era. Hence, such conclusions are subject to continuing appraisal and correction, as the history of modern biblical scholarship abundantly demonstrates. This fact has been understood as both strength and weakness in biblical research.

It is not surprising that the proponents of historical-critical methodology have not reached identical conclusions, even though they may be equally committed to its basic principles. This situation, too, arises out of the character of historical truth. For example, although the cause(s) of the Civil War in the United States is subject to historical investigation, more than a century of study has failed to provide an answer to the question that is convincing to all historians. Likewise, vigorous debate continues concerning numerous historical issues in biblical research.

In spite of evident progress resulting from general acceptance of historical-critical methodology, contemporary biblical interpretation is marked by a certain degree of ambiguity. On one hand, some degree of reservation regarding the methodology is evident. Outright opponents of critical methodology occasionally reverberate the earlier accusation that this approach destroys the Bible as the Word of God. Others—notably the so-called "Jesus" adherents and some segments of the pentecostal movement—utilize the scriptures in ways that overlook or deny the relevance of critical questions. Finally, some groups tacitly approve historical-critical methodology in the "spirit of the times," but the theological conclusions at which they arrive contain meager evidence of genuine allegiance to the approach. On the other hand, those who adhere rigidly to the application of historical-critical principles face vexing questions. What justification can be given for the use of principles that lead to such divergent conclusions? Are conclusions understood in terms of "probability" adequate in religion where certainty is a primary consideration? Also, if—as Protestants have contended—the Bible is accepted as the Word of God, is it possible to devise a scientific instrument to *investigate* that Word? Although such rigid formulations of the problems may not exhaust the alternatives, they should at least alert the cautious reader to the fact that crucial issues are involved in the discussion of methodology.

SCIENTIFIC METHODOLOGY AND PROTESTANT UNDERSTANDING OF SCRIPTURE

The scientific approach to interpretation of the scriptures is of relatively recent origin, having achieved its cogent formulation first in the nineteenth century. The recent origin of this approach has sometimes been used as an argument against its validity. However, such arguments oversimplify the issue. To be sure, the scriptures did serve as a source of

21

authority and guidance for the church for more than seventeen centuries, apart from the insights which scientific methodology has subsequently provided. However, return to this precritical understanding of the scriptures is not possible. When the church confronted questions raised during the modern revolution in thought, its traditional understanding of the scriptures proved to be inadequate, resulting in a diminishing role for the scriptures in the life of the Christian community. It should be noted that the problem centered upon the church's *understanding* of the scriptures, an understanding that had been developed within the framework of a world view that has now been superseded. Hence, the development of scientific methodology for interpretation of the scriptures represents the church's effort to expand and correct its own understanding within the context of its experience in a changing world. Consequently, the question now is this: "Can the scriptures continue to function effectively in the life of the church apart from the contributions of scientific methodology?" The material in this book is intended as a negative reply to this question.

Problems arose in the life of the early church which pointed toward the necessity of critical tools for the interpretation of scripture. The conflict with Gnosticism (a philosophy based upon a rigid dualism between spirit and matter) actually raised historical issues that called for critical analysis, particularly of the formation of the New Testament canon. However, the spirit of scientific inquiry in all areas of human thought had not been born. In the absence of insights created later by the Renaissance and Enlightenment, the church used a kind of proof which maintained its influence for fifteen centuries—the principle of tradition.[1] In this

[1] It is difficult to indicate the meaning of tradition by a brief statement. Prior to the middle of the second century, tradition referred primarily to

usage, tradition designated as Christian such material outside the Bible which sheds light upon the meaning of biblical
literature. The early-church father Irenaeus used this principle effectively before the close of the second century, and
later leaders of the church built upon and expanded his
arguments. This principle of tradition exercised definitive
influence upon the interpretation of scripture until the time
of the Protestant Reformation.

Martin Luther, the inaugurator of the Protestant Reformation, challenged the principle of tradition as a norm for
scriptural interpretation. Tradition, supplemented by the
use of allegory, constituted the norm for interpretation in
Luther's day. The sayings of the fathers (tradition) represented the primary source for understanding the meaning of
scripture. The allegorical method provided the basic tool
for interpreting its threefold meaning; namely, the literal,
the moral, and the eschatological (eschatology refers to final
things or the consummation of history). Luther announced
his rebuttal to these presuppositions in terms of the principle
of *sola scriptura* (scripture alone, i.e., scripture as the only
source of authority for the church). He insisted that scrip-

---

statements attributed to the apostles. The scope of this reference was
gradually expanded to include pronouncements made by recognized
representatives of the church. At the time of the Reformation, tradition
was often identified with extrabiblical material, either oral or written.
This concept of tradition was foreign to the earliest Christian meaning
of the term which served to distinguish authentic (apostolic) material
from false or invalid material (cf. Chapter 8, pp. 220 ff.). The larger historical issue is obscured when tradition is understood in terms of
formal categories, such as specific oral or written material. The larger
historical issue concerns the nature of tradition as *phenomenon*. In the life
of the Christian community, two questions arise in this connection: (1)
What is the nature of the later (post-first generation) church's dependence upon original proclamation of the gospel? (2) How does the
later church appropriately propagate the gospel proclaimed initially in
the first-generation community, without at the same time reducing it to a
historical phenomenon of the past?

ture is to be interpreted in the light of other scripture rather than by reference to tradition *(sui ipsius interpres est),* and furthermore, that the scriptures are marked by clarity *(perspicuitas)* of content and essential meaning and that the use of allegory is not necessary to discover their meaning. Luther formulated his claims in view of the problems of his own day, and he should not be expected to have anticipated those of the modern era. Some Protestants in succeeding generations have exhibited a limited understanding of Luther's basic concept. Nevertheless, his motto of *sola scriptura* expressed an understanding of the nature of scripture which has been affirmed by Protestants to the present time.

The Protestant principle of *sola scriptura* played a decisive role in the rise of historical-critical methodology for the interpretation of scripture. Obviously, scientific mentality has both contributed to techniques and influenced the form which the method has assumed. To be sure, Roman Catholic scholarship has not remained silent, although it has been noticeably reticent to apply the method consistently, particularly with respect to the implications of this approach for certain areas of polity and theology. It should be noted, however, that current Roman Catholic biblical scholarship contains substantial evidence of more serious involvement with the issues raised by critical methodology, a fact which holds great promise for the future of biblical interpretation as a whole. Nevertheless, Protestantism's contributions to the development of critical perspectives are substantial, a fact that is to be understood in the light of its traditional claims for the scriptures. If the Protestant remains loyal to his traditional principle of biblical authority, no easy solutions are possible for issues that arise in the areas of science, history, and theology. According to this basic claim, the answers must be sought *within scripture,* and no appeal to

24

another norm is permissible in order to alleviate difficulties. This fact has stimulated Protestant scholars to approach the task of scriptural interpretation with a seriousness that would not have been otherwise possible. Concisely stated, historical-critical methodology represents the techniques that have been developed to answer questions which are raised by adherence to the principle of *sola scriptura*.

The remaining discussion in this chapter is concerned with the issues that have stimulated the development of methodological tools. Each specific discipline is heir to an extended and complicated heritage, and no effort will be made in this chapter to include a treatment of that history. Some indication of the character of the problems may serve to provide a background for understanding the discussion in the following chapters.

AREAS OF CRITICAL RESEARCH

Protestant emphasis upon the centrality of the scriptures raised the problem of the text (the text of the original manuscripts of the books of the Bible) with new urgency. Even though some attention had been previously given to the subject, as late as 1689 Richard Simon used the hopeless state of confusion regarding the exact text as an argument against the Protestant position.[2] Simon did little more than call attention to the confusion, but the evidence he produced pointed to the necessity of textual research. The rise of textual criticism as a critical discipline represented the response of biblical scholarship to this problem. This discipline is described in Chapter 2.

[2] Richard Simon, *Histoire critique du texte du Nouveau Testament* (Rotterdam: R. Loers, 1689).

Current methodology for interpreting the scriptures is generally described as historical-critical methodology. This is one way of indicating the centrality of the problem of history in biblical interpretation. Even though some aspects of the problem were recognized as early as the second century, history did not emerge as a primary question until the nineteenth century. The roots of this development can be seen in the movement of Deism in England, in the circle of thinkers known as the Encyclopedists in France, and in the movement of Rationalism in Germany. The latter movement provided the decisive stimuli for modern concern with the subject of history. Ferdinand Christian Baur (1792-1860) created an awareness among theologians of the focal significance of the subject of history for biblical interpretation. In many respects, biblical scholarship since his day has been involved in finding answers to problems which he raised. These problems have played an important role in the critical analysis of biblical texts. They are related in some way to each of the following chapters but more specifically to Chapter 9.

The Synoptic Gospels (Matthew, Mark, and Luke) have represented an area of uncertainty in New Testament research. Early in the history of the discussion, it became evident that John's Gospel presents a distinctive tradition. However, even the relationships among the Synoptics proved to be more complicated than could have been anticipated. Clarification of these relationships necessitated historical and analytical reconstruction of the total history of the material from the time of its origin until its incorporation in the present forms of the Gospels. This task involved analysis of the material in its earliest oral from (form criticism), the description of the circumstances in which one or more of the Gospels in their present form had been used as a source for the others (source criticism), and determination of the specific contribution which each author made to the present structures and contents of the works (redaction criticism). The search was stimulated by the presence of *likenesses* and *differences* in the Synoptics, i.e., it was necessary to discover a single explanation for the presence of both. This problem, called the synoptic problem, has called forth more effort than any other single question in New Testament research. The description of the techniques it has produced appears in Chapters 3 through 5.

The letters of Paul constitute one of three primary points of reference for discerning the focus and scope of New Testament thought (the Synoptic Gospels and the Gospel of John complete the triad). Throughout the modern era of biblical scholarship the Apostle's letters have provided a fertile field of research. During much of this period historical questions have claimed the attention of interpreters (Paul's role in the development of the early Christian movement, his relation to Jesus and the earliest Christian community, his relation to first-century Jewish and Hellenistic culture, etc.). However, theological issues have also played an important part in Pauline research (the extent to which Paul's thought is determined by Jewish or Hellenistic presuppositions, the essential focus of his thought, etc.). Chapter 6 describes the general pattern of historical-critical investigation of Pauline literature.

Although the importance of the Gospel of John is acknowledged in all quarters, it occupies a peculiar position within the New Testament canon. On the whole, it must be admitted that historical-critical research has served to emphasize the distinctive and, in some respects, isolated character of the Fourth Gospel. Investigation has shown that it is separated from the Synoptic Gospels by certain basic

27

differences, even though its form as historical narrative relates it to them. Paradoxically, historical-critical research has not succeeded in resolving the historical enigmas regarding this work, namely, the locus of the tradition, the relation of the Johannine tradition to other strata of New Testament thought, the historical development of the segment of Christianity represented by the Fourth Gospel, etc. Due to the absence of external evidence for John's Gospel, particular attention has been devoted to analysis of the form and structure of the work. Chapter 7 indicates the course of Johannine research in the modern era.

Modern biblical investigation has focused attention upon two issues related to the historical character of the scriptures. First, basic differences among New Testament writings have been identified and more carefully defined. Contrary to earlier assumptions, these differences relate not only to the writers' style and vocabulary but involve their fundamental motifs and structures of thought. Second, modern research has also shown that the decisions by which the church brought together selected early Christian writings into a single collection (canon) were historically conditioned. These decisions, like other historical decisions, were tentative in character. These insights pose crucial questions with respect to the nature and authority of the scriptures. What is the nature of the unity of the scriptures, and what implications does the answer to this question have for understanding the authority of the scriptures (Chapter 11)? Furthermore, what is the meaning of the canon for the interpretation of the nature and authority of the scriptures (Chapter 8)?

Christians claim that the words of the scriptures mediate the Word of God. This claim for present relevance and authority of the scriptures stands in some degree of tension with the acknowledged historical character of the scriptures as historical documents of the past. Biblical interpreters have expended great energy in the attempt to supply a viable interpretation of this claim. For example, if Paul's letter to the Galatians was originally intended to be understood within the structures of the situation of the Galatian Christians, what are the dimensions of its authority for twentieth-century men? The answer to this question is complicated by a series of revolutions in modern thought which prohibit a simple transfer of Paul's specific instructions to the modern situation. The historical, philosophical, and scientific dimensions of this problem have presented an imposing challenge to biblical interpreters in this century. It is understandable that hermeneutics (the principles of interpretation), an area largely neglected for half a century, now stands in the forefront of theological discussion. Chapter 10 is devoted to the treatment of some aspects of this problem.

This survey has called attention to areas of biblical interpretation in which historical-critical methodology has proved fruitful, with particular reference to the Synoptic Gospels, Paul's letters, and the Gospel of John. In addition, reference has been made to certain subjects (the Bible, history, hermeneutics) related to interpretation of the scriptures for which critical procedures have profound implications. Accordingly, Chapters 1–7 may provide some basis for the treatment of more general subjects in Chapters 8–11.

2

The Problem of the Text:
Textual Criticism

Textual criticism is a scientific discipline that attempts to restore the original text of a document which has perished. Its conclusions provide the basis for editing, translating, and interpreting important ancient texts. New Testament study is entirely dependent upon the work of the textual critic since all original manuscripts perished early in the history of the Christian movement. Existing manuscripts represent copies of copies which have arisen through an extended process of transmission. One aspect of the work of textual criticism involves the description of that process. Stated precisely, the task of New Testament textual criticism is to restore the original text of the New Testament documents.

The importance of the work of the textual critic is often overlooked outside scholarly circles where the work is carried on. The average reader of the Bible is frequently more concerned with the beauty and familiarity of the language of a translation than with the accuracy of the text upon which it is based. Because the King James Version has been read traditionally in the pulpit, many readers are reluctant to accept a more recent version. Nevertheless, textual criticism has shown conclusively that it contains extended sections which did not appear in the original manuscripts (Mark 16:9-20 and John 7:53–8:11 are noteworthy examples). Sectarian movements have arisen in Christianity whose basic claim to distinctiveness has been based upon ideas contained in these and other texts which did not appear in the original manuscripts.

The work of textual criticism is often assumed to have been accomplished with such precision that any critical edition is final. This assumption conceals the tentative character of textual reconstruction, including the most recent works. If the scriptures are accepted as the norm for the life of the church, the search for the best text must be carried on continuously. The purpose of this introductory discussion does not require a detailed description of the discipline of textual criticism. Rather, it is designed to call attention to the problems which the textual critic faces. This information provides a basis for understanding the goals of investigation and at the same time prepares the reader for a sympathetic evaluation of the results of scholarly work.

THE MATERIALS AND PROCEDURES
OF BOOKMAKING IN ANTIQUITY

Knowledge of the process by which written material was produced in the first and succeeding centuries clarifies many problems of textual criticism. The ease, speed, and precision of modern printing represent a recent development. Prior to the invention of the printing press in the fifteenth century, written material was copied by hand. The invention of the printing press resulted in the introduction of paper as the common material for writing. Various kinds of material were used for writing in the first century. Although clay, stone, ivory, wood, and even steel had been used earlier, papyrus and vellum had largely supplanted them by the first century. The methods by which these materials were produced and used are of interest to the student of textual criticism, since they made it possible to circulate and preserve New Testament documents.

Papyrus was used as a material for writing in Egypt as early as 3000 B.C., but it came into general use at a much later date. There is evidence that it had been introduced into Greece by 600 B.C. It was widely used in the first century, the period in which the majority of New Testament books were written. Papyrus was a reedlike plant which flourished in the first century along the banks of the Nile River. It reached the normal height of twelve to fifteen feet and attained a thickness of three to four inches. It was prepared as writing material by a simple but tedious process. The bark was cut lengthwise into narrow strips and laid side by side. Other strips were then laid horizontally across them, and they were glued together by water from the Nile River. After they had dried, these sheets were attached to one another until they reached the desired length which seldom exceeded thirty-five feet. Using a spindle, the material was made into a roll or scroll. Scribes used a quill and a primitive form of ink made of soot and glue to write upon these scrolls. It is amazing that some of these texts are still legible after two thousand years.

Vellum, a material for writing made from the skins of animals, was also used before the time of Christ. It was prepared for use by removing the hair, scraping away the fatty substance, smoothing it with pumice, and dressing it with chalk. It was superior to papyrus for possessing greater durability. It resisted moisture for longer periods of time and was better adapted for use in the codex (book) form. It gradually supplanted papyrus and, by the fifth century, became the primary material for manuscripts and significant documents.

THE NATURE AND SOURCES
OF MANUSCRIPT ERRORS

Errors in the transmission of texts have been greatly reduced by the use of the printing press. No such safeguard existed in antiquity when professionally trained scribes copied the materials by hand. Knowledge of the methods, customs, and habits of these scribes enables the textual critic to explain many errors that arose in the reproduction of manuscripts. Scribes sometimes served as private secretaries who copied from dictation (cf. II Thess. 3:17). When several copies were desired, a reader read aloud to a group who copied simultaneously. Many errors in New Testament manuscripts can be traced to this method of copying.

33

In addition to individual styles, two main types of writing were used in the first century. There was the *cursive* style by which letters were written small, joined together, and written rapidly. This style was used mainly for business and nonliterary correspondence. A second style, the *uncial,* was used for documents of greater importance. In the uncial style letters were written larger and more deliberately and were separated one from another. Most of the important New Testament manuscripts were written in this style. After the ninth century it proved to be too clumsy and expensive. It was then replaced by the *minuscule* style, a variation of the cursive. The style of writing can serve as one basis for classifying and dating New Testament manuscripts.

The customary format of papyrus manuscripts was conducive to error. The writing on scrolls was arranged in parallel columns of two to three inches in width. The height of the columns was determined by the width of the papyrus sheet. This format was retained even when the scroll was replaced by the codex or book form. The work of the scribe was complicated by many factors when he copied by sight directly from a scroll: words were not separated from one another, no marks of punctuation were used to separate verses, paragraphs, and chapters, and other marks of punctuation used in modern Greek had not been devised. Since space was a precious commodity on papyrus scrolls, numerous symbols and abbreviations were used. In addition to these technical problems, scribes often worked long hours in unheated, poorly lighted rooms. In contrast to modern custom, the title of a work was normally placed at the close of the text. Damage due to usage and moisture often destroyed the end of the scroll, thereby making identification of the work difficult. Under these circumstances, accuracy was not easily achieved. (A simple practice exercise will

34

provide the reader with an opportunity to discover many types of errors which arose in the process of copying. First, paste three sheets of typing paper together, end to end. Copy the text from any translation of the early chapters of Mark's Gospel using the method described above, i.e., use only capital letters, omit all marks of punctuation, and do not separate words, paragraphs, or chapters. Second, repeat the process on a second scroll. Finally, compare the text of the last copy with the text of Mark from which the first copy was made. This procedure normally provides concrete examples of the types of errors which arose in copying the text of the New Testament.)

Errors that arose in copying from sight or from dictation are classified as *unintentional* errors, i.e., they do not represent deliberate alterations of the original texts. As has been indicated, copying by sight was complicated by the basic format of scrolls. Letters written similarly could be easily misread, especially when moisture or frequent handling had damaged the manuscript. Words, parts of words, or even entire lines were omitted or repeated when the eye chanced to return to a different section of the manuscript. Unintentional errors of a different sort occurred when copying was done from dictation. Many Greek vowels and diphthongs sounded alike (compare wood and would, see and sea, bored and board, etc.). Long and short e and o indicate the indicative and subjunctive modes in Greek, but it was often impossible to distinguish the sounds. There are many examples of these types of errors in New Testament manuscripts. Finally, the human factor also contributed to unintentional errors. Scribes did not bring the same level of competence to their tasks. Early Christian writers called attention to instances where a poor text was produced by an indifferent or lazy scribe. But the arduous nature of the work

35

should not be overlooked. It is unreasonable to suppose that a scribe would copy with the same precision at the close of the day as at the beginning, particularly in uncomfortable working conditions. The mercenary motive for rapid production could have played a role in isolated circumstances. However, in spite of Origen's complaint concerning "sleepy-headed and lazy scribes," on the whole they seem to have been dedicated workers. This may have been related to the fact that they were often Christians who did their work as a labor of love. Numerically, unintentional errors constitute the majority of those which appear in New Testament manuscripts. However, their collective significance is not so great as those which resulted from the deliberate efforts of scribes to improve the text.

Scribes sometimes deliberately attempted to improve or correct a text (*intentional* errors). These deliberate alterations arose out of many kinds of motivations, some of which can never be reconstructed. In minor alterations the scribe intended only to improve grammatical construction or spelling, correct historical errors, or rectify a scriptural quotation. This procedure can be seen in the Gospels. For example, in Mark 1:2 ff. the author attributes a statement to Isaiah which actually derives from Malachi. The author of Matthew's Gospel apparently noticed the error and omitted it. The case does not represent a perfect parallel with scribal correction, but it does point toward an attitude toward written scripture which differs from the modern perspective. Comments, alterations, and supplementary remarks were often written in the margin and later added to the actual text by other scribes. Theology also played a major role in these intentional alterations. Professor Ernest C. Colwell has suggested that precisely because the text had become scripture to the scribe, error, particularly theological error, could not be tolerated.[1] We should not forget, however, that biblical documents were not looked upon with the same reverence and respect during the early period of Christian history as at the present time. Church leaders sometimes corrected texts that did not agree with the one used in their geographical area. (This was Lucian's procedure before 312 in Antioch.) This practice of correcting texts has created many problems in the work of restoring the original texts.

THE MATERIALS OF TEXTUAL CRITICISM: THE MANUSCRIPT

Evidence for the New Testament texts is divided into three general groups or categories: Greek manuscripts, versions (translations), and quotations of scripture which appear in the writings of the early church fathers. These categories must be defined further for purposes of precise reference. Some attention will be given to them in the following paragraphs, but detailed information can be found in handbooks on textual criticism.[2]

The rapid advance of textual criticism in the past two centuries has been stimulated by unprecedented discoveries of important manuscripts. The classification, evaluation, and interpretation of this material was carried on by many scholars in different parts of the world, often without direct communication with one another. It soon became necessary to develop a common system of notation for manuscripts. In the beginning, a manuscript was often named after the person or library with which it had been closely associated.

[1] Ernest Cadman Colwell, *What Is the Best New Testament?* pp. 52 ff.
[2] Bruce M. Metzger, *The Text of the New Testament;* Leo Vaganay, *An Introduction to the Textual Criticism of the New Testament;* Vincent Taylor, *The Text of the New Testament* (New York: St. Martin's Press, 1961).

When this procedure became impractical, various attempts were made to devise a universal system. Following these earlier attempts, C. R. Gregory proposed a simplified system that has come to be widely used.[3] According to Gregory's system, evidence is classified in the following manner: (1) Uncial manuscripts are designated by letters of the Greek, Hebrew, and Latin (capital) alphabets. When these letters were exhausted, an Arabic number preceded by zero was used. (2) Papyrus manuscripts are designated by P with an Arabic number at the upper right hand. (3) Minuscule manuscripts are designated by numbers. (4) Old Latin manuscripts are designated by small letters of the Latin alphabet. (5) Other versions, Coptic, Syriac, Ethiopic, etc., are designated by abbreviations of the word. It should be noted that this system of notation does not strictly correspond to the general categories listed earlier but is based upon the necessity of more precise designation. For example, Greek manuscripts appear under notations for uncial, papyri, and minuscule categories. In the classification of evidence, language is not the decisive consideration. In the following discussion, individual notations indicate the particular class of evidence to which a manuscript belongs.

Greek Manuscripts

Uncial Manuscripts

ℵ (CODEX SINAITICUS). Konstantin von Tischendorf discovered this uncial manuscript in a monastery on Mt. Sinai in 1841. Tischendorf, a professor of New Testament at the University of Leipzig, immediately announced the importance of his discovery. He thought that it was the oldest

---

[3] C. R. Gregory, *Die griechischen Handschriften des Neuen Testaments* (Leipzig: J. C. Hinrichs, 1908).

known manuscript of the New Testament and named it ℵ (aleph), the first letter of the Hebrew alphabet. Tischendorf's judgment concerning its importance has been confirmed by further study; even at the present time, it is recognized as one of the most important manuscripts in existence. It originally contained the entire Old and New Testaments, but sections of the Old Testament have perished. (It is interesting to note that it also contains two books not found in the present canon of the New Testament, The Epistle of Barnabas and The Shepherd of Hermas.) It probably originated either in Palestine or Egypt, but no absolute evidence is available. Scholars generally date it in the middle of the fourth century. Since 1933, it has been the property of the British Museum in London where it is displayed publicly.

B (CODEX VATICANUS). This excellent manuscript is located in the Vatican library in Rome. Nothing is known of its history prior to 1481 when it was listed in the catalogue of the library. For reasons never fully explained, only limited access was permitted to this manuscript prior to the close of the nineteenth century. Tischendorf tried unsuccessfully to gain permission to make it available for study. The text is written in small uncial letters and has been corrected by two editors. Some sections of the Old Testament and the section following Heb. 9:14 (i.e., I and II Tim., Titus, Phil., and Rev.) are missing. Westcott and Hort, two renowned British scholars, used this manuscript as the primary basis for their edition of the New Testament. Although they overestimated the purity of its text, its importance is recognized by all scholars. Like ℵ, it was produced either in Egypt or Palestine in the middle of the fourth century.[4]

---

[4] For the discussion of other Greek uncial manuscripts, see Bruce M.

Papyrus Manuscripts

It would be logical to assume that all papyrus manuscripts perished early. However, unexpected discoveries in the sands of Upper Egypt have produced documents of great importance. Two recent discoveries of sensational significance have been made at the Qumran caves near the Dead Sea, and at Nag Hammadi in Egypt. They are of great importance for the interpretation of early Christian history, but they do not contribute significantly to the restoration of New Testament texts. (The discoveries in Qumran contain Old Testament and other Jewish texts.) Grenfell and Hunt had made important discoveries of papyrus manuscripts at the beginning of the twentieth century which raised hopes that New Testament documents might be recovered also. These hopes were realized half a century later. Two recent discoveries are especially important: the Chester Beatty biblical papyri, and the Bodmer group. Sir Chester Beatty collected a very important group of manuscripts during the decade following 1930. M. Martin Bodmer obtained the first in a series of fragments in 1955. Although most of them contain already known small sections of the New Testament, their age makes them extremely important.

P[45] (CHESTER BEATTY). This papyrus codex seems to have originally contained most, if not all, of the four Gospels and Acts. Less than thirty of the original two hundred leaves have been recovered, half of which contain texts from Acts. Its importance is based on the fact that it is dated in the first half of the third century, almost a century earlier than ℵ and B.

P[46] (CHESTER BEATTY). This codex originally contained

Metzger, *The Text of the New Testament,* pp. 42 ff., or B. H. Throckmorton, Jr., ed., *Gospel Parallels* (New York: Thomas Nelson & Sons, 2nd ed., 1957), pp. VII ff.

ten Pauline epistles, including Hebrews but excluding the Pastorals. Eighty-six of the original one hundred four leaves have been recovered. Like P[45], it is dated in the middle of the third century.

P[52] (JOHN RYLANDS). This tiny fragment measures only 2½ by 3½ inches, but its importance is not determined by its size. It is the oldest recovered copy of any fragment of the New Testament. It lay unnoticed among other papyri fragments for almost fifteen years following its discovery by Grenfell and Hunt. It contains parts of four verses from John's Gospel (18:31-33 and 18:37-38). It is generally dated in the first half of the second century. Based upon the evidence of this fragment, it is now possible to establish a date early in the second century for John's Gospel. This does not mean that the Gospel must be dated as late as the second century, but it does eliminate the possibility that it may have been composed near the middle of the second century, as has often been suggested.

P[66] (BODMER). This manuscript, dated near the beginning of the third century, contains the entire Gospel of John. In addition to its importance as an early manuscript, it preserves an interesting example of correction of one type of text by another (cf. later discussion of families of texts).

P[75] (BODMER). One hundred of the original one hundred forty leaves of this manuscript have been recovered. Its importance is based on the fact that it is the earliest copy of any part of Luke's Gospel which has been recovered (ca. 200). Like P[66], its text shows a kinship with that which is preserved in B.

Minuscule Manuscripts

Minuscule manuscripts, designated by Arabic numbers, represent a considerable collection. They are classified ac-

41

cording to their style of writing, the minuscule, which appeared at the beginning of the ninth century. The style used earlier for biblical manuscripts, the uncial, had become burdensome and expensive for the production of increasing numbers of manuscripts. The use of the cursive style would have made it possible to produce manuscripts more rapidly, but it had not been used for literary and important documents. The minuscule, a style that enabled the scribe to write more rapidly since letters were often joined together, arose as a compromise between the two earlier styles. Minuscule manuscripts preserve a later stage of the textual tradition and have been frequently neglected by textual critics. In more recent years attention has been given to the classification and evaluation of this material. This work requires precise and accurate analysis of the various strains of textual tradition which appear in these manuscripts. Individual manuscripts have not been mentioned here but, again, are listed in handbooks on textual criticism.

Lectionaries

Lectionaries, designated by the letter l, contain brief passages of scripture which were read in the church. They appeared in the same general period as the minuscules. There are more than 1500 of these manuscripts, but, like the minuscules, they require careful evaluation. The minuscule and lectionary manuscripts contain valuable historical evidence for the history of the textual tradition.

Versions

Sometime after the close of the first century it became necessary to translate the scriptures into the various languages of the people who were coming into the church. Although these translations represent important links with the text at an early stage, it is difficult to determine the date and location of a translation. In addition to this problem, there are questions that concern the purity of the text of the translation, prior corruptions of the text translated, etc. Textual critics have exercised great caution in the use of the versions. At the same time, evidence appearing in the versions often supports other evidence that appears elsewhere and serves to confirm that testimony. The Latin, Syriac, and Coptic or Egyptian versions are most important.

The Church Fathers

The writings of the church fathers in the first three centuries contain numerous quotations from the New Testament. Although they are not separated from the originals by an extended period of time, other factors must be considered in the evaluation of the evidence. In some cases the text of the fathers has been corrupted. The sayings of the fathers were valued as highly as the text of the New Testament in some circles. Consequently, the attitudes that led to alteration of the New Testament material exercised similar influence upon the sayings of the fathers. Furthermore, it is often impossible to determine whether the fathers intended to quote a text exactly or whether they were using a paraphrase. Taken as a whole, even quotations from important writers like Irenaeus, Tertullian, and Origen may do no more than provide evidence for the type of text used in a given geographical area at the time the author wrote. (Cf. the discussion, below, of families of texts.)

43

THE METHODOLOGY OF TEXTUAL CRITICISM

The actual work involved in evaluating the mass of textual evidence which has been described above requires detailed knowledge of the materials and principles of textual criticism. At the same time, general information concerning these materials and principles can provide a basis for interpreting many issues that are indicated in critical editions of the New Testament text.

The scholar may seem to occupy a favored position because he possesses such a wealth of manuscript evidence. Some of these apparent advantages disappear when the attempt is made to classify and organize this material. There are more than five thousand available Greek manuscripts in which there are approximately one hundred fifty thousand variant readings. Confronted with this mass of evidence it is difficult to establish a point of departure for interpreting any segment of the testimony. The problem of methodology has been the primary issue in the history of textual criticism. Permanent progress has been possible only when mature principles of procedure have been developed. Although unanimous agreement has not been achieved even in all areas of methodology, the serious work of two centuries in this area has provided significant insights not likely to be disproved. In the first place, it has become clear that textual criticism must be carried on in close cooperation with the historical sciences. In order to determine the genuine text, the entire historical tradition represented by available manuscripts must be reconstructed, i.e., in order to demonstrate the original text it is necessary to show how the spurious texts arose from it. Secondly, it has now become clear that there is no pure or uncontaminated text preserved by any manuscript or group of manuscripts. This means that the task of reconstructing the text is more complicated than it was previously assumed to be. These results may appear to represent a small reward for two centuries of effort. Obviously, there are many technical methods of procedure which are used by all textual critics. A mass of information is the common property of all students. However, previous work remains subject to continuing evaluation and assessment. The basic errors of the past have arisen out of the tendency toward oversimplification and generalization. With such a tremendous body of evidence at his disposal, the textual critic must labor incessantly in testing a single hypothesis or principle of explanation.

Classification of the Evidence: The Families

New Testament manuscripts can be classified according to certain major types or families. A family is the name given to a group of texts with a common ancestor. These texts are discovered through the deviations common to a group of manuscripts. For example, the errors made in copying the text in Alexandria were perpetuated in later reproductions. Classification according to families is the basic point of departure in the actual work of textual reconstruction. One reading of a text that represents a good family may provide more support for the original text than a dozen readings from a poor family. Caution is required at this point lest a generalization become misleading. Families are not represented by entire manuscripts but often only segments of them. The modern practice of copying an entire manuscript of the New Testament at once was seldom followed in antiquity. Thus, several families of texts may be represented in a single manuscript. Four types of families of texts have been sufficiently defined to merit discussion.

45

THE ALEXANDRIAN TEXT (named "neutral" by West-cott and Hort to indicate that in their judgment it was a pure text that preserved the original reading most adequately). This text arose in Egypt and is generally conceded to be the most important one. Westcott and Hort thought that ℵ and B had preserved a pure form of the Alexandrian type of text. It is now evident that these manuscripts had been corrected by later scribes, but they are the most ancient uncials and preserve the Alexandrian text at an early stage. Some of the important papyrus manuscripts also represent this family.

THE BYZANTINE TEXT. This family has been designated by many names. It is called Byzantine because it was adopted in Constantinople and used as the common text in the Byzantine world. It was produced in Antioch, Syria, under the direction of Lucian near the beginning of the fourth century and has been called the Syrian or Antiochene text. It was used almost universally after the eighth century. Both Erasmus, who created the first printed Greek text, and the translators of the King James Version of the Bible used this type of text. It was produced by combining earlier texts and has less value than the Alexandrian text. A (Codex Alexandrinus, fifth century) and C (Codex Ephraemi, fifth century) are the oldest representatives of the Byzantine family. A great majority of late uncials and minuscules belong to this group.

THE WESTERN TEXT. This family of texts was closely related to the church in the west, particularly in North Africa. Although it can probably be traced to the second century, its value has been disputed. It was used by the early church fathers. Its age would seem to suggest great importance, but there are clear indications that it was not carefully preserved. It is best represented by the Old Latin translations, by the Syriac versions, and the church fathers. Its most famous representative is manuscript D for the book of Acts.

THE CAESAREAN TEXT. This family of texts was widely used in Caesarea from which it derived its name. It seems to have arisen out of the Alexandrian text but was also mixed with the Western text. Consequently, its value is limited. Metzger suggests that it is necessary to distinguish between two stages in its development, the pre-Caesarean and the Caesarean.[5] Some of its more prominent representatives are W (Washington Codex, fifth century), P[45], and two groups of minuscules and lectionaries.

The Interpretation of the Evidence:
(1) External Evidence

Variant readings which occur in manuscripts are classified according to the families described above. This evidence contained in the manuscript is called *external evidence*. Reference is made to the manuscript by means of notations or symbols which have become a kind of scientific language in textual criticism (cf. Gregory's system). In order to be able to use these symbols in the work of evaluation of variant readings, it is necessary to know the manuscript to which a symbol refers, the general character of the manuscript, the family to which it belongs, and the relative value of the text preserved by this family. Important external evidence is given at the bottom of each page in critical editions of the Greek New Testament. Limited evidence is sometimes given in English translations.[6] The following basic considerations are involved in the evaluation of the testimony of external evidence.

[5] Bruce M. Metzger, *The Text of the New Testament*, p. 215.
[6] B. H. Throckmorton, Jr., ed., *Gospel Parallels*, p. 8.

THE DATE OF THE WITNESS. The period of time which intervened between the original copy and the creation of a manuscript is an important factor in the value of a manuscript. The shorter the period of time that had elapsed, the fewer were the opportunities which occurred for errors in transmission. However, it is the *age of the text* that is important rather than the age of the manuscript. For example, an eighth-century manuscript taken directly from a good third-century one is superior to a sixth-century manuscript that is a poor third copy of a fourth-century manuscript. Nevertheless, the age of the text is not the sole point of consideration since poor copies also arose early (cf. the Western text).

INDEPENDENCE OF WITNESSES. It is important to determine whether or not two readings are related to the original through the same or independent lines of transmission. If ten manuscripts all belong to the Byzantine family, they actually bear witness to only one line of transmission. If it is shown that one other manuscript preserves the Alexandrian type of text, the testimony of that reading may outweigh that of the ten Byzantine witnesses. Since the textual critic does his work by reference to the variant readings (if all the readings concur there is no problem), independence of witnesses refers to independent origins and lines of transmission for these variant readings. It was once thought that readings appearing in separate, isolated geographical areas should be accepted as independent witnesses. This is not always the case since early Christians traveled widely. The textual critic must solve the problem created by the practice of standardizing texts during the early centuries of Christian history. Thus, care must be exercised lest a tradition be traced to a later standard text rather than to the original text.

The Interpretation of the Evidence:
(2) *Internal Evidence*

Since not all manuscripts of the New Testament have been recovered, external evidence provides material for a partial and fragmentary reconstruction of the total textual tradition. Many questions cannot be answered on the basis of external evidence alone. In seeking to answer questions that arise from external evidence, some basis must be found beyond manuscript evidence. This approach is called *internal evidence* and involves questions related to the transmission of the text (the habits and practices of the scribes, etc.) and the grammatical style, habits of thought, and ideas of the author. Thus, internal evidence often serves to confirm the testimony of external evidence.

Tentative judgments must often be made concerning errors that arose in the process of copying the text. Scribes sometimes corrected a text that appeared to be incorrect or illogical. It has therefore been suggested that the more difficult reading is to be perferred, i.e., a scribe would not correct a simple reading to a more difficult one, but he would seek to make an illogical one understandable. Obviously, the judgment of the textual critic is involved in these decisions. The exercise of this type of judgment requires intimate acquaintance with the habits and practices of ancient scribes in general, plus specific knowledge of the peculiarities of the scribe who copied the manuscript under consideration.

Finally, the thought and style of the author himself may provide clues to the original text. The ability to read the Greek New Testament with sensitivity for unusual stylistic patterns is prerequisite for this kind of judgment. Where the New Testament contains a sufficient quantity of material

49

by a single author, considerations relating to the author's theological ideas may be relevant. In the use of internal evidence one must guard against the temptation to create a stereotype and force the evidence into this pattern.

THE PRESENT STATUS OF THE TEXT OF THE NEW TESTAMENT

Viewed from the present perspective, printed editions of the Greek New Testament had an inauspicious beginning. The first issue, edited by Erasmus, appeared in 1516. It was a poor text even when judged by sixteenth-century standards, having been created in haste from two late minuscule texts. Where the evidence was inadequate, Erasmus used his own judgment. Erasmus' third edition (1522) served as the basis for Stephanus' edition (1550) which became the standard text in Great Britain. Other revisions of Erasmus' text were produced on the continent, culminating in the so-called Stephanus-Beza-Elzivir text. This text (1633 edition) became the standard text on the continent (Textus Receptus, received by all). Thus, Erasmus' work provided the basis for the texts which were used in Great Britain and on the continent for almost four hundred years. It is interesting to note that both Martin Luther and the translators of the King James Version used texts based upon Erasmus' edition.

Many modern editions of the Greek New Testament have been created. The names of Tischendorf, Westcott and Hort, von Soden, and Nestle represent a few of the better-known ones. International cooperation among scholars has contributed to a recent edition published by the American Bible Society.

50

Research in textual criticism may seem to have created a situation characterized by unresolved confusion. To be sure, a great deal of uncertainty still exists in matters of detail. Nevertheless, textual study during the past century has provided a much clearer picture of the history of the text. This information has contributed to a reliable degree of certainty regarding more than ninety-five percent of the New Testament text.

One result of critical investigation of the text of the New Testament can be stated precisely: *The* New Testament does not exist, i.e., the actual text of the original New Testament documents is not preserved by any critical edition. The New Testament is available in the forms created by individuals or groups of scholars. Each edition represents the results of thousands of critical decisions. No one of them claims to reproduce the exact text of the original documents. It is frankly recognized that final evidence is not available in some cases. The goal of textual criticism, the recreation of the original text, has not been realized but still lies in the future.

We must remember that no translation is better than the text upon which it is based. Simplicity of language, beauty of expresssion, or material in footnotes may have their appeal, but the critical value of the text must constitute the final criterion. Information concerning the relative value of the text used for a translation can be obtained from those acquainted with textual criticism or from numerous handbooks on the subject.

Books for Additional Reading

1. Ernest Cadman Colwell, *What Is the Best New Testament?* (Chicago: The University of Chicago Press, 1952).

2. Bruce M. Metzger, *The Text of the New Testament* (New York: Oxford University Press, 2nd ed., 1968).
3. Leo Vaganay, *An Introduction to the Textual Criticism of the New Testament,* trans. B. V. Miller (St. Louis: B. Herder Book Co., 1937).

Excursus: The Practice of Textual Criticism

The purposes of this discussion do not require detailed explanation of the technical processes of textual criticism. At the same time, it is hoped that a simplified exercise, based upon the more important readings in the history of the text, may provide the nonspecialist with clues to the nature of the

53

work which will equip him to understand and appropriate the results of specialized research. The following example concerns a textual problem regarding the ending of Mark 1:1, based upon the critical apparatus provided in *Gospel Parallels* (p. 8, par. 1, n. u). Although references are taken from the English edition, it is necessary to reproduce the Greek text in order to indicate the textual problem.

1. *Mark 1:1* Ἀρχὴ τοῦ εὐαγγελίου Ἰησοῦ Χριστοῦ [υἱοῦ θεοῦ]. *The beginning of the gospel of Jesus Christ, (the Son of God).*

The problematical segment of the verse is indicated by brackets. As subsequent discussion will explain, extant manuscripts preserve conflicting testimony regarding the presence of υἱοῦ θεοῦ at the conclusion of the verse. Accordingly, the issue can be formulated in this fashion: Does the original text of Mark 1:1 conclude with Ἰησοῦ Χριστοῦ, or does it also contain the additional phrase υἱοῦ θεοῦ? It is the goal of textual criticism to provide a reasonable answer to this question.

2. *The Critical Apparatus.*

Biblical manuscripts are designated by symbols (sigla) which have come to be recognized by those engaged in the work of textual criticism. These sigla serve as a kind of shorthand that facilitates discussion and classification. The following abbreviated explanations will provide the reader with information regarding the meaning of the sigla, plus additional indications of the date of manuscripts and the type or family of text to which they belong.

According to the critical apparatus, the following manuscripts (or group of manuscripts) read Ἰησοῦ Χριστοῦ υἱοῦ θεοῦ.

A (Codex Alexandrinus). Fifth century. Byzantine text (in the Gospels).

B (Codex Vaticanus). Fourth century. Alexandrian text (in the Gospels and Acts).

D (Codex Bezae). Fifth or sixth century. Western text.

W (Washington Codex). Fifth century. Western text (in Mark 1:1–5:30).

ℜ (koine). Group of late uncial and minuscule manuscripts dating from the seventh century. Western text.

λ (Family 1, Lake Group). Twelfth century and later. Akin to fourth and fifth-century Caesarean text.

φ (Family 13, Ferrar Group). Twelfth century and later. Akin to Caesarean text.

it (Itala or Old Latin). Eleventh century and later. Text is early Western (prior to date of Vulgate).

vg (Vulgate). Authorized Latin translation, completed by Jerome in A.D. 405 (Gospels A.D. 385). Western text.

syᵖ (Peshitta). Authorized fifth-century Syriac translation. Akin to the Byzantine text (in the Gospels).

sa (Sahidic). Fourth-century Coptic (Egyptian) translation. Alexandrian text, with Western influence.

bo (Bohairic). Coptic translation, later than Sahidic. Western text.

The critical apparatus also lists two significant manuscripts which preserve the shorter reading,

S also designated ℵ (Codex Sinaiticus). Fourth century. Like B, a primary representative of the Alexandrian text.

Θ (Codex Koridethi). Ninth century. Text akin to third and fourth-century Alexandrian text.

3. *Evaluation of External (Manuscript) Evidence.*

The raw material for the work of textual criticism is found in the critical apparatus, i.e., it provides the elementary classification of extant manuscript readings. Textual critics have developed norms or criteria which enable them to assess the relative value of the variant readings of the manuscripts.

In Mark 1:1 the overwhelming number of witnesses support the longer reading, Ἰησοῦ Χριστοῦ υἱοῦ θεοῦ. The number of manuscripts that preserve this reading might appear to be decisive evidence in favor of this text. However, this judgment contradicts a fundamental principle of textual criticism, namely, in evaluation of evidence *manuscripts are to be weighed, not counted.* This criterion is grounded in the insight that the *date* and *type* of the text are more important than the number of witnesses. (Ten witnesses may all be descendants from a single manuscript. Hence, the ten manuscripts actually only preserve the evidence of one manuscript that may have been corrupted in the process of transmission.) In the case of Mark 1:1, the reading of B is highly significant, since the manuscript is dated in the fourth century and represents the superior Alexandrian type text. Thus, the importance of the reading preserved in B is grounded both in the type of the text and in the date of the manuscript. Other evidence is to be evaluated in the light of its date, geographical distribution, and genealogical independence. It is also important that representatives of the Western text (D and W, particularly) lend corroborative support, even though the Western text is marked by tendencies to expand the text. In this instance, the inferior Byzantine readings (A, sy^p) and the mixed Caesarean testimony (λ, φ) can be explained in terms of their genealogical relation to the Alexandrian and Western text, i.e., they provide no independent evidence. Accordingly, even though numerous witnesses support the longer form of the text, primary evidence appears in B, with corroborative support from D and W.

The nature of the conflicting evidence for the ending of Mark 1:1 creates a difficult problem. Two important manuscripts (S and Θ) preserve the shorter reading, Ἰησοῦ Χριστοῦ. The witness of S, a fourth-century manuscript representing the Alexandrian text, must be accorded equal importance with the testimony of B. Furthermore, although Θ is dated in the ninth century, its text represents the type used in Alexandria during the third and fourth centuries. Hence, the textual critic is confronted by variant readings each of which reflects the Alexandrian text used during the fourth century. No further appeal beyond this evidence is possible: The external evidence is ambiguous and cannot, therefore, provide the basis for decisive judgment.

4. *Evaluation of Internal Evidence.*

In addition to the evidence contained in the manuscripts themselves, variant readings are further evaluated in the light of internal evidence. Some aspects of this type of evidence can be illustrated by reference to the problem in Mark 1:1.

The absence of υἱοῦ θεοῦ in some manuscripts can be explained as a scribal omission occasioned by similarity of endings of the words Ἰησοῦ Χριστοῦ υἱοῦ θεοῦ, i.e., the scribe inadvertently thought he had finished copying the verse. On the contrary, assuming the shorter reading is original, scribes sometimes made explanatory additions to the text before them, especially with reference to titular sections of a work. υἱὸς θεοῦ (Son of God) appears frequently in Mark's Gospel (1:11; 3:11; 5:7; 9:7; 15:39) as a designation of Jesus'

57

person and mission. Is it possible that υἱοῦ θεοῦ in Mark 1:1 reflects the scribe's knowledge of the importance of the concept in the Gospel and, therefore, represents an addition to the original text? Also, one canon of textual criticism claims that the shorter text is to be preferred to the longer reading, unless there is conclusive evidence to the contrary. These and kindred considerations weigh heavily in favor of the shorter text for Mark 1:1. At the same time, what explanation is available for the presence of the longer reading in early manuscripts that represent the Alexandrian text?

The evidence has been used to support both the longer and the shorter readings for Mark 1:1. (The English translation in *Gospel Parallels* preserves the longer reading, while the Greek text preserves the shorter reading. The American Bible Society's cooperative edition [1966] includes a notation that there is considerable doubt regarding the correct reading.) The evidence in this case is ambiguous. It is impossible to render more than a conjectural judgment regarding the original text of Mark 1:1.

3

The Problem of Sources:
Source Criticism

The first three books of the New Testament have been called "Synoptic Gospels" since the beginning of the nineteenth century. The term "synoptic" calls attention to the material that is common to all of them and indicates that they are to be understood by looking at them together

(Greek, *sunorao*, to look at or view together).[1] "Gospel," used since the middle of the second century, refers to the content of the books.

It is impossible to determine the circumstances in which the church first affixed titles to these books. Early evidence suggests that it occurred before the middle of the second century. These superscriptions (the Gospel according to Matthew, Mark, and Luke) may represent traditions which began to develop in the latter part of the first century. During the second century they were preserved, interpreted, and expanded as weapons against the Gnostics.[2] In order to refute Gnostic claims for superior revelation given to "spiritual" men in visionary experiences, Christian apologists appealed to the historical dimensions of their tradition. This apology included a claim for direct historical connection between the Gospels and authentic apostolic teaching. The works of Irenaeus, written in the last quarter of the second century, represent a good example of the nature of this apologetic defense. Even though this early tradition concerning authorship must be examined in the light of the motives that created it, it reflects an interest in the question of authorship which has continued until the present time.

Second-century Christians were less concerned about preserving the meaning of the term "Gospel" than about establishing the certainty of apostolic authorship of the Synoptic Gospels. Some indication of its early meaning (Greek, *euaggelion,* good news) can be seen in Mark 1:1 where it

---

[1] Cf. B. H. Throckmorton, Jr., ed., *Gospel Parallels,* as an example of such an arrangement of the material.

[2] The Gnostics, who first created literary works in the second century, represented a syncretistic system of thought. They taught that matter was evil and that God (the All, the Unknown, Father, etc.) was pure Spirit, unknown and unknowable. Since matter was said to be evil in itself, various ways were used to deny Jesus' humanity. They first raised the problem of history for Christian thought.

interprets the function of the entire book. The author understood his work as the extension of the proclamation initiated by John the Baptist and brought to full fruition by Jesus. Even Matthew and Luke, writing a quarter of a century later, overlooked this Markan emphasis. Luke, using Mark as one of his sources, eliminated the word "Gospel" from his book. Matthew, likewise using Mark, repeated it only four times. In three of these instances he revealed his misunderstanding by adding "Kingdom" or "kingdom of heaven." The word occurs frequently in Paul's letters, generally bearing some relationship to the idea of proclamation.

When the word "Gospel" was used as a title for the Synoptics it designated the content of the material, thereby expressing a subtle shift in meaning from Mark's original emphasis upon proclamation. This shift in emphasis was reflected in some later periods of church history when the Gospels were understood as books that contained information to be accepted by faith. This ambiguity in usage has persisted to the present time: At times "Gospel" refers to books that give information about the life of Jesus; in other instances it refers to the total Christian message that is centered in Jesus Christ; and in some cases it refers to the Word of God which comes to expression in the act of proclamation.

Although the term "synoptic" does not indicate how the first three Gospels are related to one another, it raises the possibility of a literary relationship, i.e., the possibility that one or more of the Gospels in their present form have influenced the others. If this possibility can be shown to have been the case, then expanded knowledge of each book contributes to larger understanding of the others. Thus, synoptic source criticism seeks to clarify the literary relationships of the first three Gospels. At the same time, it serves to create the foundation for further consideration of the nature and scope of their mutual influence upon one another. In order to facilitate this method of study, helpful editions of the Gospels have been created which present related texts in parallel columns.

Since the Gospel of John has often been included in a synoptic arrangement, some justification here of its exclusion is appropriate. Even though John's Gospel appears to deal with the same subject as the first three Gospels (the life of Jesus), careful investigation reveals basic differences in the nature of the works. The fundamental clue to these differences is seen in the divergent descriptions of Jesus' ministry. To be sure, there are variations in the synoptic accounts, but the general outline is the same. Beginning with the accounts of baptism and temptation, they describe the Galilean ministry, the journey to Jerusalem, the final week in Jerusalem, the arrest, trial, crucifixion, and resurrection. John's Gospel presents a sharp contrast to this outline with a single exception—the description of the final events of Jesus' life. The accounts of baptism and temptation are missing, Jesus is said to have begun his ministry in Judea at the same time that John was active there, he is purported to have visited Jerusalem three or four times instead of once as suggested by the Synoptics, and he is said to have concluded his public ministry in Perea prior to the crucifixion. Even the apparent unity in the descriptions of the final events is deceptive; while Matthew reports Galilean resurrection appearances only and Luke refers to appearances in Judea only, John seems to have combined the sources he shared with the Synoptics and reports appearances in both localities.

John and the Synoptics describe the details and character

of Jesus' ministry also in different ways. The synoptic accounts describe Jesus as preacher, teacher, and healer who expressed his message in parabolic form (Matt. 13:34; Mark 4:33-34). According to John, Jesus did not use parables to proclaim his message but resorted to extended allegorical discourses. Furthermore, the Synoptics describe Jesus as an apocalyptic preacher who promised that he would return on the clouds of heaven and usher in God's Kingdom. Quite to the contrary, according to John, Jesus preached that judgment and eternal life are realities known in the present rather than in a future time. Finally, John and the Synoptics differ in their basic Christology (teaching about the person of Jesus Christ). Mark, and to a lesser degree also Matthew and Luke, interpret Jesus' person in terms of the "messianic secret" (the notion that Jesus attempted to conceal his personal identity until after the resurrection, Mark 9:9). But, according to John, Jesus' identity was known and proclaimed from the beginning: John the Baptist proclaimed him as Lamb of God, Son of God, etc., at the beginning of his ministry (John 1:21 ff.). These illustrations are sufficient to indicate the essential differences between the Synoptics and John. The conclusion is evident: The synoptic approach to the study of the first three Gospels is grounded in their common perspectives, and the inclusion of John in this arrangement confuses the issues.[3]

The point of departure for the interpretation of the first three Gospels lies in the recognition of their basic agreements. However, these likenesses are not to be understood as identities. Important differences appear within similar structures. It is this combination of likeness and difference which constitutes the problem in source analysis. The differences are

[3] Cf. Chapter 7 for more extensive treatment of John's relation to the Synoptics.

so extensive that some interpreters have concluded that the similarities represent illusions. The extent and nature of the differences can be seen from the following illustrations: (1) Matthew describes Jesus as a teacher who observed the law of Moses and who even commanded his disciples to follow his example (Matt. 5:17). The Sermon on the Mount appears near the beginning of his Gospel as an indication of the nature of Jesus' mission. Mark's Gospel does not contain a single reference to the Sermon on the Mount. Luke places it in a different context and uses only twenty verses to report it. (2) According to Mark, Jesus, the divine Son of God, came into the world as God's challenge to the demonic lordship of the universe. Again, Matthew preserves few traces of this perspective but interprets Jesus as the fulfillment of Jewish messianic hopes in gathering together the New Israel. (3) Luke's Gospel is concerned with the problems that arose for Christians when the promise of Jesus' early return did not materialize. His interest in the universal gospel for all men is difficult to reconcile with Matthew's Jewish emphasis, particularly in such passages as 10:5-6.[4] (4) Although ninety percent of Mark's Gospel reappears in Matthew and Luke, their structure, order, arrangement, and emphasis vary greatly. (5) Matthew and Luke provide different frameworks for Markan material; Luke isolates it, together with his special material, in extended sections (6:20–8:3; 9:51–18:14), while Matthew generally incorporates his own interpretations into the structure of his sources.

Finally, these differences extend to such an important subject as the resurrection accounts; Matthew limits the ap-

[4] However, Matthew also emphasizes the universal mission of the church (cf. Matt. 28:16-20). This tension between exclusive and universal emphases in Matthew constitutes a basic problem in interpretation.

pearances to Galilee, Luke reports Judean appearances only, and Mark records only the promise of a future appearance (Mark 16:9-20 is a spurious passage).

It is obvious that the magnitude and scope of differences and likenesses raise difficult problems concerning the relationship of the Synoptics. Stated concisely, this is the "synoptic problem": What is the literary relationship between the first three Gospels? The answer must be given in a single explanation that recognizes the full dimensions of the likenesses and differences and that does not emphasize or minimize either at the expense of the other. The clue to the failure of many attempts to solve the synoptic problem lies in the inability to fulfill both these conditions.

THEORIES OF INDIRECT RELATIONSHIP OF THE GOSPELS

The problem of the differences in the Synoptic Gospels was evident as early as the middle of the eighteenth century. At that time critical methodology was still in its infancy, if indeed it had been born. Since no techniques were available for analyzing the total scope of the problem, attention was generally focused upon obvious differences in limited sections of the material. The importance of the oral form of the earliest tradition had not been recognized, nor had the possibility been considered that the authors of the Gospels had reinterpreted and restructured their sources. Thus, the principal differences in the Gospels had not even been defined as areas requiring analysis. Furthermore, the prevailing eighteenth-century viewpoint concerning scripture assumed that there was an underlying unity in all scripture. Where apparent differences existed, biblical scholarship attempted

65

to reconcile them by rational or allegorical methods. Thus, both critical and theological immaturity combined to hinder progress in solving the problems involved in the differences in scripture.

Most early formulations of the synoptic problem were based upon the assumption that the first three Gospels arose independently. While this assumption reflects awareness of the problems raised by the presence of differences in these writings, it also contains an indirect challenge to the claims for the apostolic character of the synoptic tradition. Where this challenge was recognized, an attempt was made to defend the tradition by asserting that the Gospels contain eyewitness reports. (This effort illustrates the tendency to defend the tradition by minimizing the differences.) Nevertheless, research soon refuted this position. In the first place, Christians of the second century who dealt with the problem of authorship did not claim that the Gospels contain eyewitness reports. Papias (A.D. 125–150), referring to the Gospel of Mark, asserted only that it represented a poor arrangement of what Mark remembered from his conversations with Peter.[5] Papias also mentioned the name of Matthew in the same passage, but the reference is ambiguous. (Papias said that Matthew had collected some of the sayings [logia] of Jesus and had written them in the Hebrew language. It is generally conceded that he was not referring to the Gospel of Matthew in its present form. At least, the reference cannot be used to establish the claim that Matthew's Gospel was written by an apostle or by an eyewitness.) Second, it is illogical to suggest that the Gospels preserve eyewitness (apostolic) reports. No single person could have been an

---

[5] Eusebius, *The Ecclesiastical History,* trans. Kirsopp Lake, Loeb Classical Library No. 153 (Cambridge, Mass.: Harvard University Press, 1953), III:39:16.

eyewitness to all the events reported in the Gospels, particularly in those circumstances where Jesus is explicitly said to have been alone. The most that could be claimed would be that some sections of the Gospels contain eyewitness reports. However, there is no method by which these reports can be clearly distinguished from secondary accounts. Thus, the claim that the Synoptic Gospels preserve eyewitness accounts of Jesus' life and ministry cannot be sustained. Furthermore, the theory of independent origins of the Synoptics fails to take proper account of agreements in the Synoptics. It is extremely difficult to explain minute agreements in vocabulary, style, word order, etc., if the Gospels exercised no direct influence upon one another. In retrospect, it is clear that many failures and frustrations in early synoptic research were rooted in the attempt to reconcile two conflicting assumptions—the independent origins of the Synoptics and the apostolic character of synoptic tradition—both of which have subsequently been shown to be erroneous. The theory of independent origins of the Gospels sought to explain the differences but was unable to deal with the problems posed by the likenesses in the Synoptics. When the effort was made to explain the likenesses by the theory of apostolic authorship, it was impossible to account for the differences.

Even though it became impossible to show that the Gospels were written by eyewitnesses, repeated attempts were made to discover apostolic strata in them. The authors of the Gospels were said to have used a body of well-defined tradition that could be traced to the apostles' preaching. While conceding that the original tradition existed in diverse forms, these proponents of apostolic tradition attempted to prove that the apostles had unified the original tradition in their preaching. They conceded that this apostolic material assumed different forms in the early Christian mission, but they found evidence of a core of authentic material in the Gospels. Source criticism was supposed to function in isolating this body of authentic material. The strength of this hypothesis lay in its willingness to admit that the literary stage of the Gospels had been preceded by a period of oral tradition. This discovery enabled its defenders to deal realistically with the presence of dissimilarities in the Gospels. Nevertheless, it is apparent that the proposal was based on hidden assumptions regarding apostolic authority. Some direct connection between the literary Gospels and the reports of the apostles was thought to be a necessary support for the authority of the Gospels. The failure of this attempt showed that the problem of sources could not be subordinated to the problem of authority. Again, the presence of marked differences in such crucial places as the accounts of the Lord's Supper and the resurrection demanded some better explanation. In retrospect it is evident that the failure of these early attempts pointed toward some solution that involved literary dependence.

The hypothesis of an early-written Aramaic document represented an attempt to solve the problem of sources by positing literary documents earlier than the Gospels. According to this hypothesis, the Gospel tradition assumed a written form in Aramaic at an early date, perhaps within the period of the Palestinian-Jewish church in Jerusalem. The Synoptics were said to represent the last in a series of translations of this Aramaic document. The weakness of this hypothesis lies in its inability to explain detailed agreements in the Gospels in such minute areas as style, grammar, and vocabulary. Such kinds of agreement are not preserved in independent translations into a foreign language. The theory served only to banish the problems into an elusive hypothetical document of antiquity whose existence could not be proved and to which no access was possible.

Each attempt to solve the problem of sources posed by the presence of likenesses and differences in the Synoptics seemed to pursue an independent course. However, all shared one or both of two assumptions: either the assumption of independent literary origins of the Gospels, or the assumption that the Gospels shared a common dependence upon a unified body of tradition (oral or written). Herein lay the cause of their common failure. But in spite of their failures, these early attempts pointed toward some significant facts: (1) It became clear that an adequate formulation of the problem of sources in the Synoptics must reckon with a period of oral tradition preceding the literary stage. (2) The possibility, indeed the probability, of written sources for some of the Synoptics became obvious. (3) The results of study pointed toward the likelihood of a plurality of sources, both oral and written.

An analysis of the results of investigation indicates two evident conclusions: First, it is unlikely that a theory which assumes a common synoptic dependence upon a unified body of oral or written tradition is able to explain the differences in the Gospels. Second, a theory which assumes independent literary origins of the Synoptics is incapable of explaining the likenesses in the Gospels.

Thus, early in the history of synoptic research the evidence began to suggest that the solution of the synoptic problem depends upon the acceptance of some form of literary dependence of one or more of the Synoptic Gospels. Subsequent study has now fully confirmed this conclusion.

THEORIES OF DIRECT RELATIONSHIP
OF THE GOSPELS

The hypothesis that the Synoptics are related to one another in some form of literary dependence requires demonstration. Any one of the synoptic writers could have used one or both of the other works with varying degrees of dependency, i.e., Mark could have used Matthew or Luke, or he could have used both of them, etc. Unfortunately, the position of the books in the Bible does not provide a starting point since their position was determined by other considerations. Augustine, noting the place that Matthew occupies and being aware of its widespread use in the church since the second century, thought it was the oldest Gospel and attempted to explain Mark and Luke in terms of their dependence upon Matthew. Most early exploration of the nature of literary dependence accepted the Augustinian perspective as a point of departure. Numerous variations of this hypothesis appeared from time to time, but Professor Karl Lachmann (1835) formulated a thesis that has become the accepted foundation for source analysis of the Synoptic Gospels. He suggested that Mark was the oldest of the Gospels and served as a basic source for Matthew and Luke.[6]

The evidence for Lachmann's thesis has been convincing to the majority of modern scholars, particularly in the form expounded by Professors H. J. Holtzmann (1863) and Bernhard Weiss (1886). According to these scholars, a clear indication of Markan priority appears in the order and

---

[6] Lachmann accepted the theory of a "primitive Gospel." However, he concluded that Mark reproduced the order of this Gospel most accurately. His hypothesis of Markan priority provided the foundation for further research in the literary relationships of the Gospels.

arrangement of the material in the first three Gospels. Not only do they present a common picture of the beginning, progress, and consummation of Jesus' ministry, but this order appears in Mark. Taking Jesus' baptism and temptation as a beginning point, Mark then describes the Galilean ministry with Capernaum as its focus. At the conclusion of this period of Jesus' ministry which appears to have lasted slightly more than a year, Mark has Jesus journey toward the city of Jerusalem where he confronts the religious leaders of the nation. The trial, arrest, crucifixion, and resurrection form the conclusion to the story. Although Matthew and Luke contain insertions of some importance (Matt. 5–7, and other speeches in which he rearranged some Markan material; Luke 6:20–8:3 and 9:51–18:14), their dependence upon Mark is evident from their return to the Markan order after the insertion of independent material. Further confirmation of Lukan and Matthean dependence upon Mark is found in the fact that they present the same order only so long as they follow the Markan order but diverge when they depart from Mark. (Although they both include the story of Jesus' birth, the material seems to have been derived from independent sources.) Additional supporting evidence for the thesis of Markan priority can be found in many places. Almost ninety percent of the Markan material appears in Matthew or Luke. At the same time, there is abundant evidence that both Matthew and Luke undertook to improve some aspects of Mark's grammar. In some cases they correct Mark's scriptural quotations. Finally, Mark seems to preserve a more primitive stage of the tradition than Matthew and Luke. Theological perspectives characteristic of the early stages of the tradition occur in Mark who seems to have felt no sense of the tension between those perspectives and later concepts that appear side by side with them.

71

Matthew and Luke frequently reinterpreted this primitive material in accordance with more developed concepts at the close of the first century. This trend in Matthew and Luke toward a more sophisticated viewpoint is most evident in the area of Christology.

The compelling evidence for Matthean and Lukan literary dependence upon Mark[7] establishes a foundation for further analysis of the nature and structure of synoptic sources. This analysis reveals that almost one third of Matthew and approximately one fourth of Luke contain common material that is absent from Mark. As with other synoptic material, similarities and dissimilarities exist. In some instances the content is closely related, but there are signs of rearrangement and revision. In other cases the kinship extends even

[7] This position has been challenged. Professor William R. Farmer argues for Matthean priority. According to Farmer, the author of Luke's Gospel made direct use of Matthew's Gospel, and Mark, the latest of the Gospels, is dependent upon both Matthew and Luke. Cf. William R. Farmer, *The Synoptic Problem* (New York: The Macmillan Company, 1964). Abbott B. C. Butler had earlier argued for Matthean priority, denying the validity of the Q hypothesis. Cf. B. C. Butler, *The Originality of St. Matthew, A Critique of the Two-Document Hypothesis* (Cambridge: Cambridge University Press, 1951). For a brief but incisive evaluation of Butler's and Farmer's claims, see William A. Beardslee, *Literary Criticism of the New Testament*, New Testament Series (Philadelphia: Fortress Press, 1970), pp. 64-72. Even more recently, Dr. R. L. Lindsey has suggested a different solution of the synoptic problem. According to Lindsey, Luke represents the earliest Gospel. Later, the writer of Mark's Gospel combined Luke with other traditions of the early Christian community. Finally, the author of Matthew's Gospel combined still other strata of early Christian tradition with Mark's Gospel. Cf. R. L. Lindsey, "A New Approach to the Synoptic Gospels," *Christian News from Israel*, ed. Dr. Jona Malachy (Jerusalem: Gal-Or Press, Vol. XXII, no. 2[6], 1971), pp. 56-63. Also, R. L. Lindsey, *A Hebrew Translation of the Gospel of Mark* (Jerusalem: Dugith Press, 1969). Two difficulties are immediately evident in Lindsey's proposal. First, he assumes the existence of a very early Hebrew story of Jesus' life. Second, Lindsey seems to be committed to apologetic defense of the historical accuracy of the synoptic accounts as the prerequisite for synoptic investigation.

to vocabulary, syntax, style, word order, and sentence structure. Since evidently neither Matthew nor Luke used the other, the conclusion is justified that they used an additional, independent source besides Mark. This second source is commonly designated by the letter Q, an abbreviation of the German word *Quelle,* meaning source. Thus, Matthew and Luke were dependent upon these two independent documents from which they derived the majority of their material. This judgment is called the two-source theory. The following diagram illustrates the basic structure of synoptic literary relationships, according to this theory.

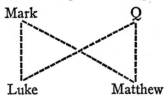

Mark   Q

Luke   Matthew

ADDITIONAL PROBLEMS FOR INVESTIGATION

The two-document theory seems to provide the most tenable explanation of the literary relationships of the Synoptic Gospels. However, general consensus at this point does not mean that all scholars understand the theory in exactly the same way or that they derive identical implications from it. Some reference to these differences of opinion may supply clues to the nature of the hypothesis itself.

Additional Sources of the Gospels: M and L

The material in Mark and the alleged contents of Q do not comprise the total material in Matthew and Luke, i.e., Mark plus Q leaves significant sections of Matthew and Luke unexplained. Various explanations of the nature and origin of this material are possible.

Since the time of B. H. Streeter the material peculiar to Matthew's Gospel (absent from Mark and Q) has been designated by the symbol M. Likewise, material peculiar to Luke (absent from Mark and Q) has been designated L. While M and L provide convenient symbols for referring to these segments of material, they provide no answers regarding the origin of earlier structures of these strata of tradition. Although Streeter avoided any explicit claims regarding the documentary character of this material (M and L), his so-called "four-document hypothesis" (Mark, Q, M, L) seems to suggest the possibility.[8]

The *documentary* character of M and L has not been demonstrated, even though various attempts have been made to define this material more precisely.[9] It now appears that M and L reflect the selective activity of the authors who exercised freedom and creativity in choosing their material from the total oral tradition of the early Christian community. It seems likely that some segments included under the symbols M and L are to be attributed to the authors themselves.

The Structure and Nature of Q

According to definition, Q refers to material that appears in Matthew and Luke but is absent from Mark. It is important to remember that we do not possess this material in its earlier documentary form. Rather, its contents must be defined by a process of critical comparative analysis of the Synoptic Gospels. While the evidence in the Gospels clearly

[8] B. H. Streeter, *The Four Gospels* (London: Macmillan and Company, 5th impression, 1936).

[9] Frederick C. Grant, *The Gospels* (New York: Harper & Brothers, 1957), p. 51.

suggests the existence of a well-defined body of tradition, questions remain concerning the exact limits of this tradition, the form in which it was accessible to the authors of Matthew and Luke, etc.

Q material is composed primarily of speeches and sayings attributed to Jesus with occasional references to John the Baptist.[10] The perspective reflected in much of this material may point to the Jewish-Christian community as the place of its origin, perhaps Jerusalem or Antioch in Syria.

The writers of the Gospels placed Q material in different contexts in their works in accordance with their purposes in writing and their methods of appropriating their sources. Generally speaking, the material in Luke most clearly reflects the earlier form of Q material. In the Gospel of Matthew it occurs primarily in those sections where the author develops his major themes, namely, in the speeches (chapters 5–7; 10; 13; 18; 23; 24–25). In Luke's Gospel, Q material comprises major segments of the Lukan insertions where the author departs from Mark's outline (6:20–8:3; 9:51–18:14).

Questions concerning the date of Q must be answered in the light of the hypothetical nature of its documentary form. Those who have defended the documentary thesis have suggested dates ranging from A.D. 50-70. The primitive form of the sayings and the undeveloped nature of the Christology seem to point to the earlier date. Its reappearance in Matthew and Luke suggests that it can hardly be dated later than A.D. 70.

Attempts to identify the author seem destined to fail because of the absence of the usual signs of editorial activity, such as deliberate reformulation and interpretation, the pres-

---

[10] *Ibid.,* pp. 59-62.

ence of a unifying theological perspective, etc. Efforts have been made to identify Q with the document to which Papias referred, the so-called "sayings" or logia.[11] Although the evidence is not decisive, Papias' reference makes no positive contribution to understanding the material.

The character and context of Q are likewise difficult to determine. Although it would appear that Q material was originally composed in Aramaic, it was apparently known to Matthew and Luke in its Greek form, since some parallels extend to style, vocabulary, and syntax. As has been indicated, Q material focuses upon Jesus as teacher. There is evident emphasis upon Jesus' announcement of the imminence of the kingdom. Christological titles (Son of Man, Messiah, Son of God) are largely missing. Even though Jesus' passion occupied a central place of concern in the earliest Christian community, Q material contains no reference to it.

It is impossible to demonstrate the documentary character of Q, even though the nature of some parallels has been used as evidence for such claims.[12] At the same time, these parallels do show that the tradition was well defined even if it existed in oral form. Variations between Matthew and Luke have convinced some scholars that the authors of these Gospels used different texts. Evidence for these suggestions, together with the claim that Mark reflects some knowledge of Q material, is indecisive.

The Original Structure of Mark's Gospel (Urmarkus)

A casual acquaintance with the general outlines of the two-source theory might suggest that it solves more prob-

---

[11] Eusebius, *The Ecclesiastical History*, III, 39:16.
[12] B. H. Streeter, *The Four Gospels*, Chap. X.

lems than is actually the case. The respective authors of the Gospels exercised a degree of freedom in their use of sources which makes the reconstruction of the exact form of their sources difficult. Some of these problems are so complex that it has been suggested that Matthew and Luke must have used an earlier form of Mark's Gospel ("Urmarkus"). Several observations give support to this proposal: (1) Numerous sections of Mark's Gospel reappear in only one of the Synoptics. For example, Mark 6:17-29 is parallel to Matt. 14:3-12 but is absent from Luke; Mark 1:21-28 occurs in a parallel section in Luke 4:31-37 but is absent from Matthew. (2) In some passages where there is general agreement among the Synoptics, arising most probably through a common use of Mark, Matthew and Luke contain common distinctive disagreements against Mark (Mark 1:9-11; Matt. 3:13-17; Luke 3:21-22, the accounts of Jesus' baptism). (3) Markan material is occasionally absent from Matthew and Luke where it would seem to be relevant. Adequate explanation cannot be given for its omission if it occurred in the form of Mark which Matthew and Luke used. It has even been suggested that Matthew and Luke used different copies of Mark. According to these theories, the present form of Mark represents the conclusion of an extended literary process in which alteration and correction often took place.

The proponents of the Urmarkus theory have rightly called attention to the developmental process of early Christian tradition. Nevertheless, the theory represents a tentative solution at best. In the first place, there is no trace of any copy of the so-called Urmarkus. It must be supposed that every copy at every stage of the process has disappeared. Secondly, critical analysis (form criticism) has failed to discover significant structures in Matthew and Luke which can be attributed to Urmarkus. Renewed consideration is given to the theory from time to time, but the evidence it produces is ambiguous, if not dubious.

The Original Structure of Luke's Gospel (Proto-Luke)

One further effort to clarify the complicated problems connected with synoptic sources perhaps merits discussion here. The essential outlines of the "Proto-Luke" hypothesis were suggested by B. H. Streeter. Streeter pointed to two major sections in Luke's Gospel where the author departs significantly from Mark's outline (6:20–8:3; 9:51–18:14). Also, Luke 3:1–4:30; 9:1-27, and 22:14–24:53 have a loose and somewhat ambiguous relation to Mark which may suggest that Luke is not directly dependent on Mark.

According to Streeter, Luke, the companion of Paul, wrote a Gospel at an early date, perhaps as early as the Gospel of Mark. This Gospel (Proto-Luke) represents a combination of Luke's private sources (L) with Q. Later, Luke allegedly revised his own work in the light of Mark's Gospel. Streeter claimed that Luke frequently preferred his own work over Mark's Gospel. Indeed, according to Streeter, Proto-Luke represents a source for the life of Jesus that is independent from Mark and, in some instances, superior to Mark.

New Testament interpreters have responded to Streeter's proposal with varying degrees of enthusiasm. Like the Urmarkus hypothesis, it attempts to solve problems raised by variations in synoptic material that evidences a degree of kinship. It must be remembered that both proposals represent conjectural constructions for which other explanations are possible.

CONCLUSION

The past century of research has clarified many aspects of the synoptic problem. The results are important for the total scope of biblical interpretation as well as for history and theology. It is clear that the task is not completed. Questions still remain concerning the sources and the exact contribution that the authors made to the present forms of the Gospels. Critical opinion is not unanimous at important points. Nevertheless, some facts of great importance are now clearly evident, e.g., that the authors of the Gospels used both oral and written sources (Mark appears to be an exception as regards the written source) whose general character can be defined with reasonable certainty. This is a permanent contribution of the work of source criticism. Any further interpretation of the nature, character, and message of the Synoptic Gospels must proceed upon this assumption.

It is significant that Matthew and Luke used a written Gospel as one of their sources. This recourse to secondary material eliminates the possibility that their works are factual eyewitness accounts whose authority can be based on a direct relationship with the original events. Direct witnesses would hardly have appealed to secondary sources at such crucial points as the passion week, crucifixion, and resurrection. Secondly, the Gospels clearly did not intend to preserve exact records; how else is it possible to explain the liberty with which they report the deeds and sayings of Jesus during the last week? This fact is clear when Matthew and Luke are compared with Mark. Although written sources for Mark do not exist, there is no evidence that he used his sources in a different manner than Matthew and Luke. Since the authors of the Gospels subordinated their sources to their own purposes and theological viewpoints, the nature of their

79

authority must be understood from this standpoint. If they are interpreted in accordance with the authors' intentions, historical facts do not represent the ultimate goal of interpretation. The authors of the Gospels proclaimed a gospel message of vital importance for their readers. This preaching (kerygmatic) dimension of the Gospels has important implications for understanding the proper function of the material.

Books for Additional Reading

1. F. C. Grant, *The Gospels: Their Origin and Growth* (New York: Harper & Brothers, 1957).
2. H. A. Guy, *A Critical Introduction to the Gospels* (London: Macmillan and Company, 1955), pp. 1-68.
3. T. W. Manson, *The Sayings of Jesus* (London: SCM Press, 1949).
4. Robert M. Montgomery, *The Two-Source Theory and the Synoptic Gospels* (Nashville: Abingdon Press, 1970).
5. B. H. Throckmorton, Jr., ed., *Gospel Parallels* (New York: Thomas Nelson & Sons, 2nd ed., 1957).

Excursus: The Practice of Source Criticism

As has been indicated, the "two-source" hypothesis has come to represent the prevailing answer for the question of interrelationships among the Synoptic Gospels. This hypothesis can appeal to various types of evidence, including the content and arrangement of the Gospels, the form and style of the writings, and the theological perspective of the authors. Any attempt to encompass the total scope of this evidence in summary manner clearly runs the risk of hopeless oversimplification of the issues. However, lest the treatment of sources become an abstraction, some effort must be made to relate alleged principles to concrete segments of scripture. The following abbreviated exercises represent an attempt to illustrate some basic clues which have been discovered in actual comparative analysis of specific segments of scripture.

The following discussion is based upon the arrangement of material provided by *Gospel Parallels*. Although the work of analysis is done best by reference to the Greek text, the accompanying English translation can serve the basic purposes of this study.

1. The Baptism of Jesus (*Gospel Parallels*, p. 10, par. 6).

Matt. 3:13-17	Mark 1:9-11	Luke 3:21-22
13 Then Jesus came from Galilee to the Jordan to John, to be baptized by him. 14 *John would have prevented him, saying, "I need to be baptized by you, and do you come to me?"* 15 *But Jesus answered him, "Let it be so now; for thus it is fitting for us to fulfil all righteousness." Then he consented.*	9 In those days Jesus came from Nazareth of Galilee	21 *Now when all the people were baptized*
16 AND WHEN JESUS WAS BAPTIZED, he went up immediately from the water, and behold, THE HEAVENS WERE OPENED[*] and he SAW THE SPIRIT OF GOD DESCENDING LIKE A DOVE and alighting ON HIM; 17 and lo, A VOICE FROM HEAVEN, saying, "*This* is MY BELOVED SON,[*] WITH WHOM I AM WELL PLEASED."	AND WAS BAPTIZED by John in the Jordan. 10 And when he came up out of the water, immediately he saw THE HEAVENS OPENED AND THE SPIRIT DESCENDING UPON HIM LIKE A DOVE; 11 AND A VOICE CAME FROM HEAVEN, "Thou art MY BELOVED SON;[*] WITH thee I AM WELL PLEASED."	AND WHEN JESUS ALSO HAD BEEN BAPTIZED and *was praying*, THE HEAVEN WAS OPENED, 22 AND THE *Holy* SPIRIT DESCENDED UPON HIM *in bodily form*, AS A DOVE, AND A VOICE CAME FROM HEAVEN, "Thou art MY BELOVED SON;[*] with thee I AM WELL PLEASED."[b]

Small capital and *italic* lines indicate certain kinds of agreements among the Synoptics. (Small capital lines point to common agreement among all three works. *Italic* lines call attention to material in either Matthew or Luke that diverges from Mark. [These *italic* lines do not suggest that Matthew and Luke agree, but only that they differ from Mark. The question of Matthean-Lukan agreement in non-Markan material raises the issue of "Q".])

Cursory analysis of the three accounts of Jesus' baptism reveals broad areas of agreement which suggests some direct contact among the writings: Jesus is baptized, the heavens (Luke, heaven) are opened, the Spirit (Matt., Spirit of God; Luke, Holy Spirit) descends like a dove (Luke, in bodily form) upon Jesus, and the voice from heaven attests Jesus' sonship and the Father's good pleasure.

While these accounts obviously agree, both in general and in some specific details, they also contain various kinds of

82

disagreements. For example, Matthew refers to Galilee rather than Nazareth (Mark) as the point of origin of Jesus' journey, Luke has no specific indication of the geographical location of Jesus' baptism and gives no hint that John baptized Jesus. (According to the order of Luke's Gospel, John was imprisoned prior to the time of Jesus' baptism. Cf. Luke 3:19-20.) Furthermore, Matthew describes John's reticence to baptize Jesus together with Jesus' justifying rationale for the action. Luke's emphasis upon Jesus' prayer following his baptism is peculiar to that Gospel. Finally, only Matthew indicates that the voice spoke to bystanders (*this* is my beloved Son) rather than to Jesus directly (*you* are my beloved Son), as Mark and Luke report.

Some reference to the function of these likenesses and differences in the work of source criticism may be appropriate here. First, it is evident that the areas of common agreement among all synoptic accounts provide no assistance in determining the dependence of one work upon another, i.e., so long as all three Gospels contain identical reports any author could have copied from either of the remaining two accounts. Second, therefore, the areas of disagreement become important for the work of source analysis, since they alone provide an opportunity to investigate the priority of one source over another.

This brief study of a limited segment of material provides examples of issues encountered in the study of the gospel tradition in its entirety. First, the presence of likenesses *and* differences in the same material represents the fundamental riddle in synoptic research. The ability to explain their simultaneous appearance in all strata of synoptic tradition constitutes the acid test for any theory of synoptic interrelationships. Second, in these accounts *where Matthew or Luke diverge from Mark they also diverge from each other.*

83

(For example, Matthew reports John's hesitation to baptize Jesus, but Luke does not follow; Luke adds the reference concerning Jesus' prayer, but Matthew does not follow.) This tendency suggests that neither Matthew nor Luke copied the other and points to the possibility that the Matthean-Lukan agreements originated in their common reliance upon Mark. Third, a survey of the Gospels of Matthew and Luke suggests that these departures from Mark reflect individual interests and perspectives. These purposeful deviations constitute the point of departure for understanding the writers' theological orientation (redaction criticism).

2. John's Messianic Preaching (*Gospel Parallels,* p. 9, par. 4).

Matt. 3:11-12	Mark 1:7-8	Luke 3:15-18
		15 As the people were in expectation, and all men questioned in their hearts concerning John, whether perhaps he were the Christ, 16 John answered them all,
11 "I baptize you with water for repentance, but he who is coming after me is mightier than I, whose sandals I am not worthy to carry;	7 And he preached, saying, "After me comes he who is mightier than I, the thong of whose sandals I am not worthy to stoop down and untie. 8 I have baptized you with water; but he will baptize you with the Holy Spirit."	"I baptize you with water; but he who is mightier than I is coming, the thong of whose sandals I am not worthy to untie;
he will baptize you with the Holy Spirit and with fire. 12 His winnowing fork is in his hand, and he will clear his threshing floor and gather his wheat into the granary, but the chaff he will burn with unquenchable fire."		he will baptize you with the Holy Spirit and with fire. 17 His winnowing fork is in his hand, to clear his threshing floor, and to gather the wheat into his granary; but the chaff he will burn with unquenchable fire." 18 So, with many other exhortations, he preached good news to the people.

Although the tradition concerning John's messianic preaching appears in all three Gospels, there is evidence that Matthew and Luke appropriated material from a document other than the second Gospel. The nature of this evidence will become apparent in the course of the discussion.

In the previous exercise, when Matthew and Luke depart from Mark they also diverge from each other. The material under consideration here provides an interesting example of how *Matthew and Luke may differ from Mark but agree with each other.* (In some instances both writers add material that does not appear in Mark. [Cf. Matt. 3:7-10; Luke 3:7-9; *Gospel Parallels,* p. 9, par. 2.] In other cases, as in this instance, there is a common tradition but Matthew and Luke seem to preserve a variant form.) The evidence for this fact can be seen in the following forms. First, Matthew and Luke preserve the material in different order, i.e., each begins with a saying about baptism with water (Matt. 3:11; Luke 3:16) and follows this statement with the prophecy concerning the "mightier" one who is to come. Mark preserves this tradition in reverse order. Luke provides an introduction to the scene (Luke 3:15), but Matthew appends this pericope directly to his account of John's preaching on repentance (Matt. 3:7-10). Second, Matthew and Luke further depart from Mark in that they contain a common additional saying (Matt. 3:12; Luke 3:17) in which there is detailed agreement in word order and vocabulary. Finally, even though Matthew and Luke preserve Mark's reference to the Holy Spirit, they both add, "and with fire."

Even though the passage under consideration is brief and the divergences raise no major theological problems, it would seem that these Matthean-Lukan agreements against Mark—both in order and content—can hardly be accidental. In both Matthew and Luke this tradition is a component part of larger segments of these Gospels (Matt. 3:7-12; Luke 3:7-18), while Mark contains only two verses which relate to this tradition (Mark 1:7-8). Accordingly, this segment illustrates an additional important principle; namely, when *Matthew and Luke differ from Mark but agree with each other, this agreement arises out of their common dependence upon an additional source* (Q).

The evidence obtained from this brief study of two passages seems to lend support to some elements of the two-document hypothesis. However, it should be emphasized that not all variations among the Synoptic Gospels lend themselves to such easy explanations! In many cases, both variations and parallels are less pronounced and exact. Furthermore, in addition to this kind of evidence, the testimony of style, form, and structure of the entire Gospels must also be considered. Hence, evidence from isolated passages must be evaluated in the light of the larger problem confronted in the total material.

4

The Problem of Oral Tradition:
Form Criticism

Literary criticism has shown that the Christian tradition
concerning Jesus was preserved in oral form prior to the
time of the appearance of Mark's Gospel (approximately A.D.
70). Form criticism is the branch of New Testament research
which is concerned with the isolation, analysis, and inter-

pretation of that oral tradition. Its conclusions have an important bearing upon the study of the early history of the church, the interpretation of New Testament literature, and the understanding of the nature of the Christian gospel.

The methods of research which are used in form criticism were first developed in the study of early oriental and Greek literature. They were later applied to the study of biblical literature. Professor Hermann Gunkel (1861-1932) used them effectively for the interpretation of the Old Testament, particularly for the analysis of the traditions in Genesis and in the Psalms. During the first quarter of this century German New Testament scholars applied these methods to the study of the Synoptic Gospels. The ideas of Professors Karl Ludwig Schmidt,[1] Martin Dibelius,[2] and Rudolf Bultmann[3] attracted widespread attention in Germany, Great Britain,[4] and the United States.[5] Form criticism has come to be accepted as an indispensable foundation for New Testament study. Although it was initially used for the analysis of the oral sources of the Synoptic Gospels, it has also contributed to a clearer understanding of the sources used by Paul and the remaining authors of New Testament books. The English name of the discipline, form criticism, carries unfortunate overtones which do not apply to the original German term *Formgeschichte* (history of form).

The use of form criticism was enhanced by developments in biblical theology at the beginning of the twentieth century.

[1] Karl Ludwig Schmidt, *Der Rahmen der Geschichte Jesu* (Darmstadt: Wissenschaftliche Buchgesellschaft, zweite Auflage; 1964).
[2] Martin Dibelius, *From Tradition to Gospel,* trans. and rev. Bertram Lee Wolf (New York: Charles Scribner's Sons, 1935).
[3] Rudolf Bultmann, *The History of the Synoptic Tradition,* trans. John Marsh (New York: Harper & Row, 1963).
[4] Vincent Taylor, *The Formation of the Gospel Tradition.*
[5] Rudolf Bultmann and Karl Kundsin, *Form Criticism.*

Professor Martin Kähler's essay, published in 1896, contained an insight that has created new dimensions in New Testament research in this century. He first pointed out that Christian faith focuses upon the exalted Lord; i.e., the confession of Jesus Christ as Lord points toward the reigning Lord who rules at the right hand of the Father.[6] Nineteenth-century research had failed to see that references to Jesus, the Palestinian Jew, and references to Jesus Christ, the exalted Lord, do not express identical viewpoints. To be sure, Christian confession pointed to Jesus as the one who had been exalted by the resurrection from the dead; nevertheless, faith focused upon him in terms of his status as Lord. Kähler's essay was followed five years later by a work written by William Wrede. Wrede suggested that the notion of messianic secrecy which appears most prominently in Mark's Gospel does not describe Jesus' actual intention, but rather that it expresses an idea created by the author of Mark's Gospel.[7] In order to test Kähler's and Wrede's theses it was necessary to define the sources that the Gospel writers used. The analysis of those sources raised the problem of oral tradition, the specific concern of form criticism.

The results of literary criticism in the nineteenth century also contributed to the rise of form-critical research. Source criticism had shown that Mark served as a common source for Matthew and Luke. However, it was clear that a great deal of Lukan and Matthean material had not been derived from their Markan source. Regardless of the conclusions which were accepted concerning the nature of Q, it became clear that Mark's sources were largely, if not totally, oral.

[6] Martin Kähler, *The So-Called Historical Jesus and the Historic, Biblical Christ,* ed. and trans. Carl E. Braaten (Philadelphia: Fortress Press, 1964).

[7] William Wrede, *The Messianic Secret,* trans. J. C. G. Greig (Cambridge: James Clark and Greenwood, S.C.: Attic Press, 1971).

Thus, better analysis was required for the Markan sources, for M, L, and Q. (Cf. Chapter 3.)

It is probable that some lingering hopes for the success of nineteenth-century historical research in the Gospels also contributed to the extended use of form-critical study. Although Kähler's and Wrede's proposals had undermined those expectations, almost three decades had to pass before that fact became abundantly clear. We should remember, however, that the originators of form-critical study for the New Testament were motivated by other purposes.

THE FOUNDATIONS OF FORM-CRITICAL RESEARCH

The work of form criticism is based upon the assumption that the structure and language of oral tradition reflect the environment in which the tradition arose. Ancient tribes and cultures developed forms of ritual and types of language which exhibit certain common characteristics. These similarities are most evident in the ritual patterns which arose in connection with crucial events in human experience such as birth, dedication, marriage, entrance into battle, and death. Psychological and sociological factors doubtless played an important part in the process of development. Those influences were especially powerful in the rise of religious ritual patterns. Repetition of these rites tended to create a common form and to give them the stamp of authority for later generations. (Illustrations of these principles can be seen in modern times. For example, it is possible to anticipate the form and the language which will be used at the dedication of a memorial, at a ceremony marking the opening of a new public facility, at the launching of a ship, or at a memorial funeral service.) This tendency of ritual and language to absorb, express, and propagate dimensions of the life situations in which they are used preserves important clues to the historical and religious contexts in which they arose. Subsequent altered circumstances created the necessity for adaptation, but evidence of earlier form and usage remains. Form criticism assumes that the forms appearing in the Gospels reflect both the original situation in which they arose and the circumstances in which Christians first adapted them for specific Christian usage. The Gospel writers placed them in still another setting which can be distinguished from the earlier ones.

Specific objections have been raised against the use of form criticism for the interpretation of the Gospels. Opponents have pointed out that the conclusions to which form criticism points are often tentative and reflect the fact that the interpreter's subjective viewpoint exercises an unwarranted influence, making agreement among interpreters impossible. The discipline has sometimes been branded as "the cult of subjectivity." To be sure, the interpreter does exercise his own subjective judgment in important respects. The differing results at which scholars often arrive are an indication of this fact: unanimous agreement is difficult, if not impossible, to achieve. At the same time, we must remember that there is a degree of contingency present in all interpretation, particularly in those areas in which historical judgment is involved. The demand that subjectivity be eliminated as the prior condition for valid research is rooted in the insistence that all research must conform to the pattern developed in the exact sciences. The unjustifiable nature of this demand will be treated later (Chapter 7). The validity of form criticism cannot be subject to this kind of assessment. Rather, its value must be measured by its ability to provide access to the specific era in Christian history represented by the period of oral tradition. Since the products of this period were later incorporated into the written Gospels, it is necessary to interpret the forces and influences which operated in those earlier stages of the tradition.

Attempts have been made to circumscribe the work of form criticism by limiting its function to the analysis of forms. The discipline is said to forsake its legitimate function when it passes judgment upon the historical character of certain segments of the Synoptic Gospels. The objectors maintain that the name of the discipline itself implies this limitation. While it is true that form-critical research assumes the right to express historical judgment, the discipline cannot be said to proceed contrary to the direction indicated by its name *Formgeschichte*. Such an objection assumes that it is possible to isolate the work of analysis and interpretation from the necessary task of describing the circumstances that influenced the rise of the forms. Quite to the contrary, when the form critic engages in historical research he is performing one dimension of his task. If the objector should follow the implications of his demand, it would become necessary for the form critic to deliver the results of his investigation to the historian for evaluation. This procedure would require that the historian and form critic simply exchange roles.

ASSUMPTIONS OF FORM CRITICISM

Form-critical investigation attempts to discover the original (earlier) forms of the material used by the authors of the Gospels. This task actually involves the reconstruction of the history of the tradition that the authors used. Assuming that the basic principles that operate in the formation of oral tradition in general operated also in the development of the Gospel tradition, form criticism seeks to reconstruct the process by which Christian tradition assumed its synoptic structures. Obviously, it is related to source criticism (Chapter 3) and to redaction criticism (Chapter 5), but it is distinct from them because its area of concern is limited to oral tradition. The following discussion indicates some assumptions upon which its work is based.

Form criticism assumes that Christian tradition circulated in the form of isolated units of material (pericopae) during the oral period. The structure of this material varied according to its contents, such as isolated sayings, parables, prophetic announcements, miracle stories, and legends. With varying degrees of success, these forms can be traced to the ministry of Jesus, but it is certain that they were influenced by the needs and problems which existed in the church. This important fact is often overlooked in the interpretation of the Gospels. The appearance of Mark's Gospel represented the first concrete evidence of a concern to preserve the tradition in unified literary form. In Mark, this interest can be safely attributed to the author of the Gospel. Prior to that time, the Christian community seems to have remained content to preserve its recollections of Jesus in the form of isolated stories that circulated independently.

Form criticism assumes that the original units of material can be classified according to general categories or forms that developed according to the principles already described. They reflect the nature of the situation in which they arose. In general, oral tradition can be divided into two groups, namely, sayings and narratives. It is sometimes difficult to determine the exact limits of particular forms since they were frequently altered in the process of preservation. Nevertheless, careful observation enables the student to discern the presence of distinctive patterns in the Gospel accounts.

Form criticism further assumes that the forms within the Gospels were influenced by the life and needs of the early church, i.e., the intentions and problems of the church contributed to the type of material which it created and preserved. It has been suggested that this material points toward preaching as the primary concern of the early church.[8] Although Dibelius' suggestion probably oversimplifies the actual circumstances, it is clear that proclamation was a primary concern of the early church. Worship was the core from which additional demands were made upon the church, such as apologetic teaching, ethical instruction, etc. It is accurate to say that the interests and needs of the church provided the context in which oral tradition assumed its earliest forms.

Finally, form criticism assumes that the biographical, geographical, and chronological patterns that appear in the Gospels reflect the creative activity of the authors. The foundations for this assumption are created in the work of source criticism (cf. Chapter 3), but they are confirmed further in the actual work of form criticism. A comparative study of Matthew, Luke, and Mark reveals that Matthew and Luke did not reproduce the Markan structure. Quite to the contrary, they frequently deliberately altered it. There is no reason to suppose that Mark used his oral sources in a different manner. This significant fact enables the interpreter to identify editorial material and to gain direct access to the earlier strata of the tradition.

FORMS OF ORAL TRADITION

Form-critical research is able to identify two basic types of material in the Synoptic Gospels; they are the earlier forms and the editorial additions contributed by the authors of the

[8] Martin Dibelius, *From Tradition to Gospel.*

Gospels. The oral tradition that appears in the Gospels is classified according to two general categories; namely, the words of Jesus and the narrative material that interprets his ministry. Each group can be further defined according to its content.

The Words of Jesus

A glance at the Synoptic Gospels shows that the words of Jesus occupy a special place of importance in them. Extended sections are devoted to his teaching and preaching. In giving this material a place of primary importance the writers were doubtless influenced by an attitude which existed among Christian disciples from the beginning. It is obvious that Jesus' proclamation—his teaching and preaching—contained a decisive challenge for his hearers. The commitment of his earliest followers to the rigorous life of discipleship seems to have expressed their response to the challenge of his message. However, it is amazing to discover that the preaching of the earliest Christian community did not appeal to Jesus, the teacher and preacher, as its source of authority. Rather, it pointed to the crucified-resurrected Son of Man as its only foundation. Paul's letters, all of which appeared before any other book in the New Testament was written, are explicit at this point (cf. Rom. 1:4; I Cor. 15:3-4). Thus, even though the early Christians maintained continuing interest in the words of Jesus, they did not remember him primarily as a prophet, nor did they refer to his words as the heart of their message. This fact of the greatest importance for the interpretation of the Gospels is frequently overlooked. Two of its more obvious implications deserve emphasis: (1) The words which the early Christians attributed to Jesus were understood from the perspective of his exalted status, i.e.,

95

their authority was based upon his crucifixion and subsequent resurrection. These Christians did not intend to preserve the words of their earthly master in isolation from their heavenly Lord. (2) The Christian consciousness of the presence of the Holy Spirit (occasionally called the Spirit of Jesus, Acts 16:7) created a bond of unity between Jesus of Nazareth and their reigning Lord. What the Christians discerned the Spirit to be saying was understood to be essentially what Jesus had said during his sojourn among them. No absolute distinction was maintained between the actual words of the historical Jesus and the words of the Holy Spirit.

One group of sayings attributed to Jesus casts him in the role of a prophet. The position occupied by the prophet in Israel's history doubtless contributed to this understanding of Jesus. These prophetic announcements call attention to the nearness of God's judgment and deliverance (Mark 1:15a), announce the arrival of the messianic era (Matt. 11:5), promise rewards for self-denial (Mark 10:29-30), condemn those who reject Jesus (Matt. 11:21-24), and warn against indifference (Luke 17:23-24). Jesus, as prophet, is also said to have referred to the future—he pointed out the uncertainty of the time for the coming of the Son of Man (Mark 13:32), predicted the destruction of Jerusalem (Luke 19:42-44), and warned of God's judgment upon the church (Matt. 25:41-46). Read in isolation, the scope and number of these prophetic utterances could suggest that the church understood Jesus primarily as a prophet. These prophetic forms represent the structure which the confession of the exalted Lord normally assumed in a Jewish-Christian community that had been conditioned by its previous Jewish religious history. Such forms preserve evidence of the continuity of the church within a Jewish context.

Since the teacher of wisdom and the prophet performed

such divergent functions in the life of Israel, the use of the prophet motif might be expected to have excluded that of the teacher of wisdom. However, these motifs appear side by side in the Synoptics, a fact that reflects the manifold character of early Christian tradition. In some cases Jesus is pictured as teacher of timeless religious truths (Matt. 5:14b; 12:34b; Luke 6:43 ff.). He is also described as a man of practical wisdom who invited men to apply his insights to the performance of their daily religious duties (Mark 3:27; Matt. 12:35). Obviously the motif of a teacher of wisdom was of limited use in the Christian community, but the presence of this motif in the Synoptic Gospels testifies to the vitality of forms which had existed in some segments of early Christianity.

Many of the synoptic sayings of Jesus describe him as a man of conflict. In most cases his opponents are Jewish religious leaders (Mark 11:15-19), but in one instance the controversy concerns a political ruler (Luke 13:31-32). The subject matter of these controversies varies widely: a question concerning the proper observance of the Law (Mark 3:1-6), an issue relating to the nature of Jesus' authority (Mark 3:20-30), or even logical dilemmas presented by Jesus' opponents (Mark 12:18-27). The subjects suggest that these forms arose within the Jewish community, but it must be remembered that the Jewish regulations concerning ritual purity later became a burning issue in the Gentile church.

It is possible to multiply the classification of the types of sayings (sometimes called pronouncement sayings or *apothegms*) which appear in the Gospels. In all cases they emphasize the importance of Jesus' words. A statement made by Jesus may contain the essential point of an extended narrative in which it is embedded. Consequently, recognition of

97

the nature of the form enables the interpreter to understand the original function of the material.

On the basis of form, no clear distinction can be made between the authentic words of Jesus and those which were attributed to him by the early Christian community. The purpose of the analysis of forms is related directly to the discovery of the contexts in which the various forms arose. Thus, form criticism reveals more information about the life of the early Christian church than about the historical circumstances of Jesus' life. At the same time, evidence for the origin of certain material within the life of the church is also proof that it cannot be traced to the historical circumstances of Jesus' life.

Narrative Material

Narrative material (form) in the Gospels is distinguished from the sayings by its form and purpose. The difference emerged out of the function which it performed. The sayings emphasized the importance of Jesus' words as teacher, prophet, etc. Narrative material emphasized other dimensions of the church's remembrance of Jesus, such as his exorcistic (casting out of demonic spirits) work, his activity as a miracle worker, his zeal for God's will to be done, and his concern for the poor and downtrodden people. The narrative or story form is better adapted to preserve these impressions than a single, pointed statement. Since both these forms were preserved in the tradition of the church, it is not surprising that they often exerted mutual influence upon each other. For example, a saying, expanded into a controversy story (Mark 2:6-10), is sometimes incorporated into the larger complex of a miracle story (Mark 2:1-12).

The editorial process tended to place both sayings and narrative material in the context of certain typical situations, such as those related to the crowds, to Jesus' disciples or opponents, to the seashore, or to the mountain. This process of collection did not, however, lead directly to the unifying theological concerns which caused Mark to write his Gospel in the form of a life of Jesus.

Parables constitute a primary form of narrative material in the synoptic tradition. According to the Synoptic Gospels, Jesus used the parable as his basic mode of discourse. Indeed, Mark goes so far as to claim that Jesus spoke exclusively in parables (Mark 4:34. Cf. also Matt. 13:34). The synoptic parables do not rigidly conform to a single pattern, standing somewhere between the proverb on one hand and the allegorical story on the other. Likewise, the content of these parables encompasses the total scope of Jesus' message. Because Jesus' parables seem to have resisted revision and alteration of structure more than other forms of the tradition, it has been claimed that they provide direct historical access to Jesus' thought. However, from the beginning interpreters have been aware of problems concerning their meaning, as the witness of the synoptic writers indicates (Mark 4:11-12; Matt. 13:51; Luke 8:9-10). Even though the structure of the parables can be discerned with reasonable certainty, problems regarding the original context in which they were spoken continue to raise perplexing questions. Current investigation of the relation of content and literary form in biblical literature has provided new avenues for understanding the parables.[9]

Miracle stories comprise a significant element in each of the Gospels, particularly in Mark, which indicates that they

[9] Cf. Joachim Jeremias, *Rediscovering the Parables,* trans. S. H. Hooke (New York: Charles Scribner's Sons, 1966) ; Dan Otto Via, Jr., *The Parables* (Philadelphia: Fortress Press, 1967) ; Amos N. Wilder, *The Language of the Gospel* (New York: Harper & Row, 1964), Chaps. IV-V.

occupied a place of importance in the life of the earliest church. Both Jewish and Hellenistic (first-century thought under strong Greek influence) literature preserve abundant evidence of miracle stories. Although it is impossible to determine the exact environment in which the miracle stories arose, they conform more closely to the types which appear in Hellenistic literature. Professor Bultmann has described the basic form of these stories: The exorcist (priest or religious person) confronts the demon-possessed man, the demon acknowledges the superior power and authority of the exorcist, the act of exorcism takes place, and objective evidence of the success of the exorcism is produced.[10] The miracle stories in the Gospels conform to this same general type or pattern (cf. Mark 2:1-12; 5:1-20). The stories of physical healing (Mark 1:29-31) and nature miracles (Mark 6:45-52) exhibit the same pattern with minor variations.

The narrative material in the Gospels also contains legendary material. It preserves specific traditional aspects that relate to Jesus' attitudes and purposes. Obviously, these dimensions of Jesus' life were less adaptable to expression through the concrete form of deeds or sayings. Consequently, stories were created which served to express the church's remembrance of him in these matters. Since these stories do not contradict the historical picture of Jesus which other forms preserve, it is difficult to distinguish between factual and legendary material. Some references that seem to contain legendary interpretations of Jesus' attitudes and purposes appear in Luke 22:51b which emphasizes Jesus' compassion; Matt. 19:13 ff. which portrays his concern for outcasts and children; Mark 1:12-13 which describes his victory over demonic powers (like the exorcism of the miracle story).

[10] Rudolf Bultmann, *The History of the Synoptic Tradition*, p. 210.

Occasionally questions are raised concerning the presence of legendary material in the Gospels. An understanding of the nature and purpose of the Gospels provides some answers to these questions. In the first place, ancient writers did not evaluate material according to the historical standards of the modern era. The legendary nature of a story did not invalidate the lesson it was designed to teach. Secondly, the authors of the Gospels used the tradition as it existed in their day. There is no evidence that they acted as historical critics in the attempt to distinguish between historical and legendary material. Thirdly, the early church in creating the tradition was not primarily concerned to produce a historical facsimile of Jesus. Rather, his life was interpreted from the standpoint of his exalted status as resurrected Lord. This perspective permeated the tradition concerning his life. Finally, the tradition functioned to proclaim the meaning of Jesus' lordship for the hearers of the tradition. The distinction between history and legend, therefore, was often blurred in the interest of the message it was designed to present. The discussion in Chapter 9 is devoted to a survey of the larger problems of history and historical understanding.

CONCLUSION

Form criticism has contributed significantly to a better understanding of the nature of early Christian life and thought. These insights make it possible to draw specific conclusions and enable the interpreter to apply some general principles that have been substantiated with reasonable certainty.

1. Earliest Christian tradition existed in oral form. Although the appearance of the written Gospels set

tentative limits for this tradition, it continued to represent an important segment of the total Christian tradition until the close of the first century, perhaps even until the last quarter of the second century.

2. Oral tradition existed first in the form of isolated stories or units of material (pericopae). There were certain tendencies toward collection of these units of material, but these units represented the basic form of the tradition until the time of Mark's Gospel.

3. The interest, purposes, and problems of the early Christian community contributed significantly toward the forms which the tradition assumed. To be sure, the church did not create the tradition without regard to the historical life of Jesus, but its life and needs constituted the context in which the tradition assumed its initial form.

4. The Synoptic Gospels represent one of the many stages in the formation of the total Christian tradition. The stage represented by the Gospels in this process of preservation-interpretation-transformation of the tradition exhibits a new concern; namely, a biographical interest in the life of Jesus.

5. The structures of the Gospels—even Mark—are determined by theological-confessional interests. Consequently, they do not provide a basis for reconstruction of a biographical life of Jesus. They are not motivated by chronological or psychological goals.

Books for Additional Reading

1. Rudolf Bultmann and Karl Kundsin, *Form Criticism,* trans. F. C. Grant (New York: Harper Torchbook, 1962).
2. Edgar V. McKnight, *What Is Form Criticism?* New Testament Series (Philadelphia: Fortress Press, 1969).
3. Robert M. Montgomery and W. Richard Stegner, *Forms in the Gospels: I. The Pronouncement Story* (Nashville: Abingdon Press, 1970).
4. Vincent Taylor, *The Formation of the Gospel Tradition* (London: Macmillan and Company, 2nd ed., 1935).

Excursus: The Pronouncement Story and the Miracle Story

Pronouncement stories and miracle stories occur frequently in the Synoptic Gospels. Together they comprise a significant proportion of the total material in these Gospels. Examples one and two illustrate the forms of these stories. Although the distinctive characteristics of these literary forms are clearly identifiable, alterations frequently arose through the processes of preservation and transmission. The third example given below has to do with this process.

1. The Pronouncement Story (Apothegm, Paradigm). Cf. *Gospel Parallels,* p. 64, par. 89.

Matt. 12:46-50	Mark 3:31-35	Luke 8:19-21
46 While he was still speaking to the people, behold, his mother and his brothers stood	(*3:23-30, § 86, pp. 61-62*) 31 And his mother and his brothers came; and standing	(*§ 104, p. 77*) 19 Then his mother and his brothers came to him, but they

outside, asking to speak to him.'	outside they sent to him and called him. [32] And a crowd was sitting about him; and they said to him, "Your mother and your brothers* are outside, asking for you." [33] And he replied,	could not reach him for the crowd. [20] And he was told, "Your mother and your brothers are standing outside, desiring to see you." [21] But he said to them,
[48] But he replied to the man who told him, "Who is my mother, and who are my brothers?" [49] And stretching out his hand toward his disciples, he said, "Here are my mother and my brothers! [50] For whoever does the will of my Father in heaven is my brother, and sister, and mother."	"Who are my mother and my brothers?" [34] And looking around on those who sat about him, he said, "Here are my mother and my brothers! [35] Whoever does the will of God is my brother, and sister, and mother."	"My mother and my brothers are those who hear the word of God and do it."

The pronouncement story focuses attention upon a statement attributed to Jesus. Other elements of the story—details of time, geographical location, other participants in the events, etc.—receive only minimal attention. Redactors were inclined to enrich these limited and generalized references in accordance with the interests of the church during the era in which the redaction occurred. Hence, expanded details represent evidence of redactional activity and may provide historical evidence for evaluating the stage of tradition represented by the form of the story.

The pericope under consideration here conforms to the basic pattern of the pronouncement story: In addition to the absence of details concerning the temporal and geographical setting of the story, even the names of the members of Jesus' own family are omitted. These generalizations and omissions serve to enhance the importance of Jesus' statement: "Whoever does the will of God is my brother, sister, and mother." Such a pronouncement seems to constitute a response to certain restrictive tendencies in early Christianity, perhaps those originating in some segments of the Jewish-Christian community. Although Matthew and Luke contain minor alterations of Mark's report, they retain the basic pattern of the pronouncement story. (For additional examples of the

105

pronouncement pattern, see Mark 9:38-41; Matt. 5:38-42; Luke 5:36-38.)

2. The Miracle Story. Cf. *Gospel Parallels*, pp. 71-72, par. 105.

Matt. 8:18 (§ 49, p. 34)	Mark 4:35-41 (4:33-34, § 99, p. 70)	Luke 8:22-25
Now when Jesus saw great crowds around him, he gave orders to go over to the other side. 8:23-27 (§ 50, p. 34): 23 And when he got into the boat, his disciples followed him. 24 And behold there arose a great storm on the sea, so that the boat was being swamped by the waves; but he was asleep. 25 And they went and woke him, saying, "Save, Lord; we are perishing." 26 And he said to them, "Why are you afraid, O men of little faith?" Then he rose and rebuked the winds and the sea; and there was a great calm.	35 On that day, when evening had come, he said to them, "Let us go across to the other side." 36 And leaving the crowd, they took him with them, just as he was, in the boat. And other boats were with him. 37 And a great storm of wind arose, and the waves beat into the boat, so that the boat was already filling. 38 But he was in the stern, asleep on the cushion; and they woke him and said to him, "Teacher, do you not care if we perish?" 39 And he awoke and rebuked the wind, and said to the sea, "Peace! Be still!" And the wind ceased, and there was a great calm.	22 One day he got into a boat with his disciples, and he said to them, "Let us go across to the other side of the lake." So they set out, 23 and as they sailed he fell asleep. And a storm of wind came down on the lake, and they were filling with water, and were in danger. 24 And they went and woke him, saying, "Master, Master, we are perishing!" And he awoke and rebuked the wind and the raging waves; and they ceased, and there was a calm.
27 And the men marveled, saying, "What sort of man is this, that even winds and sea obey him?"	40 He said to them, "Why are you afraid? Have you no faith?" 41 And they were filled with awe, and said to one another, "Who then is this, that even wind and sea obey him?"	25 He said to them, "Where is your faith?" And they were afraid, and they marveled, saying to one another, "Who then is this, that he commands even wind and water, and they obey him?"

The obvious contrasts between the pronouncement story and the miracle story are rooted in their purposes: The pronouncement story emphasizes Jesus' statement, but the miracle story focuses attention upon the miracle for its own sake. Consequently, details are absent from the pronouncement story, but the miracle story provides lavish description of the circumstances surrounding the miracle. The miracle story contains three essential elements in its structure, namely, the description of the circumstances in which the miracle occurs, the account of the actual miracle, and the description of the effects of the miracle upon the recipient and/or the bystanders.

In this miracle story Mark uses four verses to emphasize the extreme difficulties of the situation (vss. 35-38). Since this miracle involves only the spoken word, it is indicated in vs. 39a. The conclusion of the story (vss. 39b-41) describes the effect of the miracle upon the disciples. In this instance, too, Matthew and Luke have introduced certain changes in Mark's report. At the same time, these alterations in no wise obliterate the basic pattern of the miracle story. (For an additional example of the structure of the miracle story, see Mark 1:40-45; Matt. 8:1-4; Luke 5:12-16. Cf. *Gospel Parallels,* p. 31, par. 45.)

3. Miracle Story combined with Pronouncement Story. Cf. *Gospel Parallels,* pp. 35-36, par. 52.

Matt. 9:1-8	Mark 2:1-12 *(1:40-45, § 45, p. 31f.)*	Luke 5:17-26 *(5:12-16, § 45, p. 31f.)*
1 And getting into a boat he crossed over and came to his own city.	1 And when he returned to Capernaum after some days, it was reported that he was at home. 2 And many were gathered together, so that there was no longer room for them, not even about the door; and he was preaching the word to them.	17 On one of those days, as he was teaching, there were Pharisees and teachers of the law sitting by, who had come from every village of Galilee and Judea and from Jerusalem; and the power of the Lord was with him to heal.[¹]
2 And behold, they brought to him a paralytic, lying on his bed;	3 And they came, bringing to him a paralytic carried by four men.	18 And behold, men were bringing on a bed a man who was paralyzed, and they sought to bring him in and lay him before Jesus;[¹] 19 but finding no way to bring him in, because of the crowd, they went up on the roof and let him down with his bed through the tiles into the midst before Jesus.
4 And when they could not get near him		
and when Jesus saw their faith he said to the paralytic, "Take	because of the crowd, they removed the roof above him; and when they had made an opening, they let down the pallet on which the paralytic lay. 5 And when Jesus saw their faith,	20 And when he saw their faith

heart, my son; your sins are forgiven."

3 And behold, some of the scribes said to themselves, "This man is blaspheming."

4 But Jesus, knowing [m] their thoughts, said, "Why do you think evil in your hearts? 5 For which is easier, to say, 'Your sins are forgiven,'[n] or to say, 'Rise and walk'? 6 But that you may know that the Son of man has authority on earth to forgive sins"—he then said to the paralytic—"Rise, take up your bed and go home." 7 And he rose and went home. 8 When the crowds saw it, they were afraid, and they glorified God, who had given such authority to men.

---

he said to the paralytic, "My son, your sins are forgiven."

6 Now some of the scribes were sitting there, questioning in their hearts, 7 "Why does this man speak thus? It is blasphemy! Who can forgive sins but God alone?"

8 And immediately Jesus, perceiving in his spirit that they thus questioned within themselves, said to them, "Why do you question thus in your hearts? 9 Which is easier, to say to the paralytic, 'Your sins are forgiven,' or to say, 'Rise, take up your pallet and walk'? 10 But that you may know that the Son of man has authority on earth to forgive sins"—he said to the paralytic— 11 "I say to you, rise, take up your pallet and go home." 12 And he rose, and immediately took up the pallet and went out before them all; so that they were all amazed and glorified God, saying, "We never saw anything like this!"

---

he said, "Man, your sins are forgiven you."

21 And the scribes and the Pharisees began to question, saying, "Who is this that speaks blasphemies? Who can forgive sins but God only?"

22 When Jesus perceived their questionings, he answered them, "Why do you question in your hearts? 23 Which is easier, to say, 'Your sins are forgiven you,' or to say, 'Rise and walk'? 24 But that you may know that the Son of man has authority on earth to forgive sins"—he said to the man who was paralyzed—"I say to you, rise, take up your bed and go home." 25 And immediately he rose before them, and took up that on which he lay, and went home, glorifying God. 26 And amazement seized them all, and they glorified God and were filled with awe, saying, "We have seen strange things today."

While Christians utilized contemporary literary forms in formulating and proclaiming their message, they at the same time subordinated these forms to their own purposes. Consequently, the Synoptic Gospels, as well as the New Testament as a whole, contain many examples of altered and mixed literary forms. The scripture given above contains a miracle story that has been incorporated within the larger structure of a pronouncement story in order to serve the purpose of the pronouncement story. Thus, two distinct stories that earlier circulated separately now appear as a single unit.

A cursory study of the Markan account produces interesting results. First, the pericope begins according to the style of the miracle story (Mark 2:1-5a). Second, the second element of the pericope (2:5b-10) interrupts the miracle story with material that conforms to the pattern of the pronouncement story. Furthermore, the content of this material does not relate directly to the miracle but rather to the forgiveness of sins. Third, following the section concerning the forgiveness of sins (a pronouncement story focusing upon the saying, "The Son of Man has authority upon earth to forgive sins"), vss. 11-12 provide the normal conclusion for the miracle story interrupted at 5a. (This fact becomes clear when the story is read by omitting 5b-10.) Thus, two distinct literary types or "forms" appear within a single pericope. What explanation is available for this fact, and what is Mark's intended emphasis?

The answer to these questions may be sought in the history of early Christian tradition, i.e., does this material reflect issues that played a role in the life of the early Christian community? First, there is evidence that certain opponents challenged the church's proclamation of the forgiveness of sins in "Jesus' name" (Matt. 16:19; 18:18 ff.; Mark 2:10). Second, certain segments within the early church—apparently, always a minority—seem to have understood the miracle tradition as *proof* for the Christian message (Matt. 12:39 *versus* Mark 8:11-12; perhaps one source appropriated by the writer of the Fourth Gospel). Consequently, the present structure of Mark's account may represent the attempt to support the church's proclamation of the forgiveness of sins in Jesus' name by appeal to the miracle tradition. If such is the case, Mark understands the total pericope as a pronouncement story (2:5b-10) for which the miracle story (2:1-5a, 11-12) provides the unusual setting and, at the same time, a degree of authentication.

109

5

The Problem of Theology: Redaction Criticism

Form and source criticism have shown that the Gospels are not biographical accounts of Jesus' life and ministry. The presence of three books in the New Testament, each differing from the other in many respects, points toward this conclusion.[1] However, form and source criticism alone can-

[1] B. H. Throckmorton, Jr., ed., *Gospel Parallels*.

not solve all the problems raised by these differences. Many questions remain when the work of analyzing the sources has been completed. The incompleteness of the results of form and source criticism is rooted in the fact that the scope of their investigation is limited to the history of the material before it was incorporated into its present form.

A study of the Gospels reveals that their authors played important roles in creating their present structures. Contrary to earlier opinion, the authors were not mere compilers of existing tradition but acted independently and creatively in interpreting it for their own generation. Thus, they were the last in a long line of agents who created, preserved, and interpreted the developing tradition. The attempt to understand the Gospels involves evaluation of the authors' distinctive contribution to the forms of the tradition which the Gospels present.

Redaction criticism is the youngest member of the family of critical disciplines in New Testament research. In retrospect it is possible to see that the results of earlier investigation pointed toward the necessity of such a method of studying the Gospels. It has attracted serious attention only since the close of the Second World War, therefore some of its conclusions are still tentative and subject to revision. Nevertheless, this method of study has already made valuable contributions toward better understanding of biblical literature. The results of source and form criticism focused attention upon those strata of material in the Synoptic Gospels which must be attributed to the authors, the final redactors (editors and interpreters) of the tradition. The discovery of the authors' important roles in the creation of the Gospels raised the question of their purposes. Redaction criticism investigates the authors' messages and purposes as disclosed in their works and considers their methods of composition. It also

111

analyzes the use of their sources and reconstructs the historical situation in which they wrote.

REDACTION CRITICISM:
ITS ORIGIN AND METHODOLOGY

The Origin of Redaction Criticism

Redaction criticism arose in part as a response to emerging questions concerning the historical character of the Gospels. These questions were raised in the latter half of the nineteenth century, but their importance was first recognized in this century. Both critical and theological issues have contributed to this development, aided in each instance by insights derived from the social sciences.

The first indication of the shape of things to come was given by the discovery that the Gospels differ significantly from one another and from the preaching of the early church. However, historical perspectives in general hindered the proper evaluation of this discovery. According to the generally accepted norms of historical understanding in the nineteenth century, historical literature was interpreted according to the norm of factuality, i.e., its claim to truth was measured by the objective facts which it reported. From this viewpoint, the deviations in the Gospel accounts pointed toward editorial corruptions and errors, either by the authors of the Gospels or by the Christian community that created the earlier oral form of the tradition.

Working on the basis of the historical assumptions of nineteenth-century thought in general, New Testament scholars attempted to recover the original "pure" Gospel in its uncorrupted form. This Gospel was identified with the actual words of Jesus. In case those words were not accessible

112

in their original form, it was assumed that they could be found in the apostolic tradition which was thought to have preserved them without error. Thus, the assumption that the genuine Gospel lay somewhere behind the present forms of the Gospels condemned the Gospels to a place of secondary importance. The contributions of the authors of the Gospels to their individual works were considered to be irrelevant at best and corruptive at worst. In any case, the recovery of the authors' specific contributions to the present forms of the Gospels could only be understood as a peripheral concern for New Testament scholarship. Those who opposed the idea that a distinction could be made between the "pure" Gospel and the Gospel accounts usually attempted to support their arguments by claiming that the Gospels contain eyewitness reports of the events to which they refer. However, investigation showed that the Gospels do not represent eyewitness reports. Progress beyond this stage of discussion was dependent upon correction of the limitation in historical understanding that was common to both these groups. This correction has come slowly and with great difficulty.

The rise of redaction criticism was more directly related to the development of critical methodology than to the change in historical understanding, although neither process could have occurred apart from the other. Form and source criticism paved the way for the emergence of redaction criticism by defining the precise issue. Literary source criticism showed that Matthew and Luke deliberately altered their Markan source. This insight pointed directly toward the necessity of redaction criticism.

In addition to the limitations in historical understanding, emerging theological problems further hindered consideration of the issues related to the work of redaction criticism. The fate of William Wrede's work is an illustration of a fruit-

113

ful insight largely overlooked for half a century. Building upon previous developments, Wrede showed that the secrecy motif in Mark's Gospel does not represent a factual report of Jesus' intention, but that the author of Mark's Gospel created the idea and imposed it upon his material with varying degrees of consistency.[2] This suggestion was lost in the midst of the storm of controversy that arose in response to Albert Schweitzer's suggestion that Jesus expected the catastrophic end of history during his lifetime.[3] Wrede's proposal, together with the earlier suggestion made by Martin Kähler, that the Gospels call for faith in the exalted Lord rather than Jesus of Nazareth,[4] was reviewed from time to time, but the implications of Kähler's and Wrede's suggestions were ignored.

Similarities between method and purpose in form and redaction criticism have led to the suggestion that the task of redaction criticism is actually identical with that of form criticism. In some respects it may be said to represent an extension of form criticism. But there are differences in emphases, goals, and procedures which should not be overlooked. In point of time, form criticism preceded redaction criticism by three decades and provided the foundations for its work. Form criticism is concerned with the interpretation and analysis of the influence of the Christian community upon the structures of oral tradition. Redaction criticism attempts to interpret the author's intention in using both oral and written tradition in the creation of his own work. Mathematically speaking, oral tradition plus literary sources

[2] William Wrede, *The Messianic Secret.*

[3] Albert Schweitzer, *The Quest of the Historical Jesus,* trans. W. Montgomery (London: Adam and Charles Black, 3rd ed., 1963). Schweitzer's work was related to the thought of Johannes Weiss and served to refute nineteenth-century thought concerning eschatology.

[4] Martin Kähler, *The So-Called Historical Jesus and the Historic, Biblical Christ.*

plus redactionary material equal the Gospels. Redaction criticism is concerned specifically with the interpretation of redactionary materials and purposes in the present forms of the canonical Gospels.

Methodology of Redaction Criticism

Redaction criticism assumes that the authors of the Gospels acted purposefully in writing their works. This assumption is supported by evidence at various levels in the Gospels. In some instances the authors added material to that which they found in their sources. In other cases they omitted, reinterpreted, emphasized, or de-emphasized certain elements which appeared in their sources. It is also clear that the authors created temporal, geographical, or even ideal or typical contexts in which they placed their source materials.

The work of defining the authors' specific contributions to the present forms and contents of the Gospels is carried out by the formation of hypotheses that seek to explain the presence of materials and structures foreign to the authors' sources. In this respect redaction criticism is based upon the results of source and form criticism. If a specific hypothesis can be supported by evidence, it then forms the basis for further study and analysis.

The work of redaction criticism requires that a distinction be made between three strata of material and historical contexts in the development of the tradition. They are the original situation, the situation in which the tradition was preserved and developed, and the situation in which the Gospels assumed their present forms. Thus, the work of redaction criticism calls for the reconstruction of the entire history of the tradition, but it is specifically concerned to interpret the final phase of that process. Some specific types of question

115

which redaction criticism seeks to answer appear in connection with the interpretation of Mark 1:1-11 (cf. the Lukan and Matthean parallels).[5]

A certain textual problem related to Mark 1:1 has implications for the work of redaction criticism. The problem has to do with the reading "Son of God" which is preserved in many manuscripts. It is difficult to reach a final conclusion on the basis of manuscript evidence alone. The titles "Son of God," "Son," and "beloved Son" occur in Mark's Gospel in connection with the description of crucial experiences in Jesus' life.[6] Either of two explanations regarding the division in the manuscript evidence seems to be plausible. It is possible that a later scribe added "Son of God" to the text he was copying because he had noted the importance of the title at other places in Mark. On the other hand, "Son of God" could represent the original reading which a Jewish-Christian scribe omitted in his copy because he preferred the title Jesus Christ (Jesus is Messiah). In case "Son of God" represents the original reading, it could provide an important clue to the author's basic message. However, if it represents a scribal addition, it only indicates an understanding of Jesus in some segments of the church at a later date. Even though textual criticism can provide no final answer in this case, the conclusions of redaction criticism are affected by the evidence which textual criticism provides.

The word "gospel" (Greek, *euaggelion,* meaning "good news") in Mark 1:1 raises an additional question. It occurs six times in Mark, without further qualification in each case. Matthew contains the word only four times, and in three instances it is further qualified by "Kingdom" or

[5] B. H. Throckmorton, Jr., ed., *Gospel Parallels,* pp. 8-11.
[6] Mark 1:11, baptism; 3:11; 5:7, the confession of the demoniacs; 9:7, the transfiguration; 15:39, the confession of the soldier at the cross, etc.

"kingdom of heaven." The word does not occur in the Gospel of Luke. Since Matthew and Luke used this material in Mark as their common source, their use of Mark may represent a significant clue to their thought. Mark appears to indicate by his usage of the term that he understood it in a technical sense, i.e., that he understood his entire work as an act of proclamation. In omitting or qualifying the term "gospel," the authors of Matthew and Luke revealed either that they disagreed with the author of Mark or that they misunderstood him. Whichever the case, they wrote their works from different perspectives than the author of Mark. It is the task of redaction criticism to define these differences and delineate their influence upon the messages of the individual Gospels.

The authors of Matthew and Luke created different contexts for their Markan material, with the result that they differ from each other as well as from Mark. Mark's Gospel begins with a report of the ministry of John the Baptist. In both Matthew and Luke, John's ministry is placed after extended narratives related to Jesus' birth and infancy. These different kinds of introduction contain further clues to the messages and intentions of the Gospels.

Each Gospel writer placed his material in a different historical context: Mark evidenced little concern for historical accuracy, Matthew related his description of Jesus' infancy to the land of Galilee, and Luke appended precise references to Jewish and Roman history. In each case, the authors' historical viewpoint points to an important element in his purpose and message.

The authors of both Matthew and Luke made important alterations in the baptismal accounts that they found in Mark. Mark's account is characterized by the simplicity with which he tells the story of Jesus' baptism by John.

117

Matthew added a section that describes John's protest that he was unworthy (Matt. 3:14), a statement which seems to reflect a later controversy between the disciples of John and the Christians. Furthermore, according to Matthew, Jesus justified his baptism by a reference to the Law (Matt. 3:15; it is necessary to fulfill all righteousness). Luke added a reference about the Spirit descending in a "bodily" form.

Indications of editorial procedures can be multiplied through a study of the larger contexts of the individual Gospels. The references above are related to the use of written sources, but there is no reason to suppose that the authors of the Gospels used their oral sources in a different manner. Redaction criticism seeks to discover clues in isolated instances which may reveal elements of a pattern of thought expressing the author's central message.

THE RESULTS OF REDACTION CRITICISM: THE THEOLOGY OF THE GOSPELS

The rise of redaction criticism has stimulated new interest in the purpose and message of the Gospels. The discussion that has ensued has contributed to the clarification of many aspects of each author's thought and purpose. A survey of major proposals suggested as clues to the messages of the Gospels will help to understand some aspects from which each Gospel is currently interpreted.

The Theology of Mark's Gospel

The work of redaction criticism in Mark's Gospel is complicated by the absence of literary sources for the present form of the Gospel. Consequently, inner criteria must serve to distinguish between the sources and redactionary material.

118

William Wrede first called attention to the significance of the secrecy motif in Mark's Gospel.[7] He suggested that this motif, the so-called "messianic secret," expresses a theological concept which originated after the resurrection. According to Wrede, Jesus' post-resurrection appearances provided the basis for the disciples' confession of his messiahship. Therefore, the concept of secrecy represents a by-product of the early Christian community's continuing interest in the earthly life of Jesus, interpreted from the standpoint of his resurrection. Wrede's designation of the motif of secrecy in Mark's Gospel as the "messianic secret" limits the idea too narrowly (the secrecy motif is related to Jesus as Son of God [3:11-12], Son of Man [8:30], and Son of David [10:47 ff.]). Nevertheless, Wrede's basic contention has been confirmed: The concept of secrecy in Mark's Gospel represents a theological idea rather than a historical account of Jesus' actual intention. This theological idea doubtless arose in Christian tradition prior to the time of Mark's Gospel. The author of Mark's Gospel applied the concept to the total life of Jesus. It represents an important element in the thought of Mark's Gospel.

The geographical term "Galilee" is important in the Gospel of Mark. Did he use it to designate something more than a geographical section in Palestine? The geographical structure in the Gospel must be attributed to the author, since oral tradition did not contain it. According to Mark, Galilee represented the focal point of reference for Jesus' ministry: Jesus came from Galilee to be baptized (1:9), he returned there to initiate his ministry (1:14), his public ministry of teaching and healing was carried on there (1:14–9:50), he left Galilee only to go to Jerusalem at the close of his ministry (10:1 ff.), and he promised to meet the dis-

[7] William Wrede, *The Messianic Secret.*

ciples there after the resurrection (16:7). Interpreters have given different answers to the significance of Mark's emphasis upon Galilee. Ernst Lohmeyer suggested that the Gospel was written in Galilee where a church had existed from the beginning. He concluded that the Galilean church preserved a different Christology and a different form of celebration for the Lord's Supper.[8] It has not been shown that Lohmeyer's alleged church in Galilee actually existed. However, his suggestion called attention to the fact that the place in which a book is composed may influence its theological perspective in significant ways. Willi Marxsen has made an alternative proposal. Marxsen suggested that Mark's Gospel was written in Galilee immediately preceding the fall of Jerusalem (A.D. 70). The events connected with the destruction of the city are said to have convinced the author of Mark that the return of Christ was imminent. Therefore, he exhorted Christians in Jerusalem to flee to Galilee where Christ would appear (13:14 ff.; 16:7).[9] Marxsen's interpretation depends upon the prior acceptance of Galilee as the place where Mark was written. This assumption has not been proved and therefore weakens his suggestion. Neither Lohmeyer's nor Marxsen's proposal seems capable of proof. However, they have raised the probability that Galilee does not represent a simple geographical designation in Mark's Gospel. Could it be that the term Galilee symbolically stands for Gentile Christianity as a whole, including Rome, i.e., does it serve to support Gentile Christianity in the face of Jewish-Christian objections?

James M. Robinson has suggested that Mark's under-

[8] Ernst Lohmeyer, *Galiläa und Jerusalem* (Göttingen: Vandenhoeck & Ruprecht, 1936).

[9] Willi Marxsen, *Mark the Evangelist,* trans. Roy A. Harrisville (Nashville: Abingdon Press, 1969).

standing of history, i.e., Jesus' history, provides the key for interpreting his message. According to Robinson, the author wrote about actual history but interpreted it as the realm where transcendent powers were in conflict.[10] Jesus' baptism is said to have initiated God's challenge to demonic authority. Mark describes the continuation of this conflict in the ministry of Jesus and points to the cross as its culmination, Robinson suggests. Further, the history of the church is said to represent an extension of this conflict which is to be consummated by the return of Christ. It is difficult to discover evidence for Mark's concern with the problem of history this side of the Cross, particularly if that concern is understood to relate to the history of the church and the delay of the return of Christ. Robinson's suggestion presupposes a development of a theological perspective which is hardly present in Mark's account.

Philipp Vielhauer has pointed to Christology as the focus of Mark's concern. He believes that the Gospel is based upon the structure of the drama of ancient Egyptian rites of installation for the king.[11] This pattern is reflected in other sections of New Testament literature (I Tim. 3:16; Heb. 1:5-13; Rev. 5). The drama includes three acts: The king receives the divine gift of the Spirit from the Father (God) and is adopted; he is then presented to the pantheon of the gods; and finally, he is proclaimed as the ruler of the world. Vielhauer identifies Jesus' baptism (Mark 1:11) with the adoption; the transfiguration (9:7) with the presentation; and the crucifixion (15:39) with the acclamation of divine lordship over the world. If one is inclined to doubt the use

[10] James M. Robinson, *The Problem of History in Mark,* Studies in Biblical Theology No. 21 (Naperville, Ill.: Alec R. Allenson, 1957).

[11] Philipp Vielhauer, "Erwägungen zur Christologie des Markusevangeliums," *Aufsätze zum Neuen Testament* (München: Chr. Kaiser Verlag, 1965).

121

of Egyptian drama to speak about Jesus Christ, he should remember the nature of the Christian confession: It also speaks of divine lordship and exaltation. The value of Vielhauer's suggestion is limited because it refers to limited areas of Mark's Gospel without explaining how other christological motifs relate to the ritual pattern which he proposes. For example, how is the christological emphasis related to the concept of secrecy, to Galilee, etc.? Also, what can be said of the place of origin of Mark's Gospel?

Hans Conzelmann attempts to integrate major motifs of the book under a single theme. He describes the Gospel as a post-Easter commentary upon the church's message of the crucified-resurrected Lord which is focused upon the idea of revelation.[12] According to Conzelmann, Mark's concern is directed to the period between baptism and crucifixion. Galilee is important as a place of manifestation: Jesus preached there and will return there. Jerusalem represents the divinely determined destiny of Jesus as the crucified One. The motif of secrecy suggests that the proclamation can be understood only from the standpoint of resurrection. Conzelmann's proposal represents an attempt to correlate the results of previous research into a unified description of Mark's message. In this respect he has achieved a maturity sometimes absent in less comprehensive proposals.

The Theology of Matthew's Gospel

The author of Matthew's Gospel indicates his basic concerns by pointed and direct arguments. These polemical statements appear in every major section of the book. The question that the interpreter must solve relates to the author's consistency in perspective. Certain rigid and exclusive statements

[12] Hans Conzelmann, *An Outline of the Theology of the New Testament,* trans. John Bowden (New York: Harper & Row, 1969), pp. 140-44.

seem to point clearly to the author's purpose and message, if they are understood in isolation from the remainder of the work, while other equally definite assertions seem to suggest a different viewpoint. Thus, the task of the interpreter is to discover a single inclusive perspective which explains the message and purpose of the entire book without overlooking or denying the antitheses that are clearly present.

There can be no doubt that the meaning and function of the Law for the Christian community constituted a primary problem for the author of Matthew's Gospel. This concern distinguishes Matthew from Mark and Luke. According to Matthew, Jesus came to fulfill rather than to annul the Law (5:17). He was baptized for this purpose (3:15), he patterned his teaching according to the structure and themes of the Law (5–7), and he even commanded his disciples to observe its regulations (23:3). Christian discipleship implies that the disciple understand the meaning of the Law (13:11). Further, God's judgment is to be based upon the disciple's performance of its requirements (7:24-27). Membership in the church, a mixture of faithful and unfaithful disciples, does not alleviate standing under the judgment of God who will separate true and false disciples on the basis of their actions (13:24-30). Such pronouncements could suggest that Matthew's Gospel expresses the viewpoint of a segment of Christianity which had become a sect of Judaism.

Other strains of thought in Matthew seem to indicate a different perspective. There is no reference to the necessity of circumcision, there is no claim made for the importance of ritual purity, and there is no emphasis upon ceremonial Law as a whole. These demands constituted the basic foundations for the observance of the Law. The Pharisees, the interpreters of the Law, are severely condemned (Matt. 23). The strict demands for fulfillment of the Law are ameliorated by love for God and neighbor (5:43-48; 19:17-19) which is defined as the fulfillment of the Law. Discipleship consists in following the pattern set by the lowly, suffering Jesus. Even though Jesus limited the mission of his disciples to the Jewish nation (10:5-6), his final command as the resurrected Lord encompassed the entire world (28:16-20). How are these inclusive and exclusive viewpoints related to each other?

The scope of the author's concern was not limited to the question of the Law. The continuing validity of the Law expressed one dimension of the problem of understanding the continuity of God's purposes and promises. What did the existence of the church as God's agent for the redemption of the world imply concerning the present status of Israel, the earlier instrument for that mission? According to Matthew, the church, the true Israel, has supplanted the Israel of old (28:16-20), since Israel had forfeited its status by the rejection of Jesus. However, according to Matthew, the church as the true Israel does not limit Christianity to Judaism, nor does the church's existence imply that Jesus is to be understood as a Jewish national Messiah. Rather, the church which was then persecuted by Judaism was to realize its existence by following the pattern set by the lowly suffering servant as exemplified in the ministry of Jesus. Its future was still to lead through the refining fire of God's judgment who alone can separate the wheat from the chaff.

In the light of these antithetical viewpoints, it is difficult to determine the central purpose and focus of Matthew's message. Does it lie in the acceptance of one emphasis to the exclusion of the other, or is it possible to discover an inclusive perspective which unites or transcends both of them? The

124

question of the historical context in which the book was written is important for the answer to these questions.

Professors Günther Bornkamm and Gerhard Barth have identified the author of Matthew with a segment of Christianity closely related to Jewish thought, perhaps even to the synagogue.[13] The author is said to have done battle with two opponents at the same time: He affirmed the validity of the Law in opposition to a libertine group which rejected the idea of continuity with Israel, and he refuted a legalistic point of view which would have made Christianity merely an extension of Judaism. By pointing to love as the fulfillment of the Law, he assumed a mediating position between these two groups.

Wolfgang Trilling thinks that the key to Matthew's message is to be found in 28:16-20.[14] According to his viewpoint, the author represented a group within Christianity which had already broken with Judaism. The tension evident between the two strata of material in the book resulted from the author's failure to sublimate his sources to the purposes of his own message.

Reinhart Hummel chooses another alternative for understanding Matthew and takes his point of departure from the stratum that indicates a closer identification with Jewish thought.[15] In his judgment, Matthew represented a segment of the church which had maintained its Jewish sympathies, but which had rejected the Pharisaic expression of Judaism as it emerged after the destruction of Jerusalem in A.D. 70.

Georg Strecker has suggested that the Gospel of Matthew

[13] Günther Bornkamm, Gerhard Barth, and Heinz Joachim Held, *Tradition and Interpretation in Matthew*, trans. Percy Scott (Philadelphia: Westminster Press, 1963).

[14] Wolfgang Trilling, *Das wahre Israel* (Leipzig: St. Benno Verlag, 1959).

[15] Reinhart Hummel, *Die Auseinandersetzung zwischen Kirche und Judentum im Matthäusevangelium* (München: Chr. Kaiser Verlag, 1963).

represents a theological interpretation of the author's historical perspective.[16] Strecker thinks that the author of the Gospel, a Gentile Christian, was primarily concerned with the Christian's existence in continuing human history understood from the standpoint of Christology. Matthew interprets Jesus as the proclaimer of God's ethical demand. This demand, announced earlier by the prophets but rejected by the Jews, now forms the essential content of the church's message. The title of Strecker's work, *Der Weg der Gerechtigkeit* (The Way of Righteousness), reflects his evaluation of Matthew's emphasis upon the individual Christian's heightened ethical responsibility.

Finally, Hans Conzelmann has pointed to a complex of ideas which he thinks express the central message of the book. According to Conzelmann, this context is defined by the concepts of Law, Israel, Christology, and eschatology.[17] Matthew treated these subjects in view of this question: What is the relation of Christianity to earlier and current forms of Judaism if the church is to continue its historical existence?

Obviously, it is not possible to reconcile in detail all the proposals which have been discussed. One function of redaction criticism is to focus upon the emphases existing in the various Gospels. The results of previous study in Matthew's Gospel seem to indicate some general conclusions which may be drawn with reasonable certainty. In the first place, some strata of Matthean sources can certainly be traced to the early Jewish church of which the church in

[16] Georg Strecker, *Der Weg der Gerechtigkeit* (Göttingen: Vandenhoeck & Ruprecht, 1962). Cf. also, Georg Strecker, "The Concept of History in Matthew," *Journal of the American Academy of Religion,* XXXV, no. 3, 219-30.

[17] Hans Conzelmann, *An Outline of the Theology of the New Testament,* pp. 144-49.

Jerusalem was the chief representative. The author may have shared certain elements of this early Jewish-Christian perspective. If he did, serious research must try to distinguish between the sources which the author used and his own contribution to them. Secondly, other strata in the Gospel of Matthew stand in tension with strict Judaism. It seems reasonable to attribute this material to the author of Matthew, since he is responsible for the present form of the book. Third, the Gospel of Matthew was written in a historical situation where the questions of past and future had become burning issues. These issues may have been brought into focus by questions related to the nature and mission of the church. Finally, Matthew's eschatological orientation provides a clue to the nature of his thought. Perhaps his Gospel is an attempt to deal with problems arising out of his "halfway" stance between Mark and Luke.

The Theology of Luke

It has long been evident to New Testament scholars that the subject of history represented a basic concern of the author of Luke-Acts. However, the delineation of the author's specific historical perspective has proved to be one of the most complicated tasks in New Testament interpretation. Early students of the problem naturally approached the issue from the standpoint of historical understanding in their own era. Later developments have shown that their viewpoints were both inadequate and misleading. They assumed that the author of Luke-Acts understood history in the same way as nineteenth-century historians! Their investigation was confined to the recovery of the objective form of the tradition available to Luke. The text of Acts was analyzed with reference to Luke's alleged sources, a procedure which resulted in attributing different

127

sources to segments of single verses. In this way the author was understood as a literary mechanic who occupied himself with the task of combining and compiling fragments of diverse historical traditions. Meanwhile, the possibility that the author could have contributed creative theological insights of his own was consistently overlooked.

More than anyone elsc, Martin Dibelius pointed the way out of the stalemate in Lukan investigation. Utilizing the techniques of form criticism which he had helped to develop in synoptic research, he investigated another aspect of Lukan thought by comparing the author's method with that of other ancient historians. Dibelius pointed to the speeches in Acts (2:14 ff.; 3:12 ff.; 4:8 ff.; etc.) as the decisive material for understanding the author's method and thought.[18] He suggested that the speeches are primarily Lukan creations which reflect his distinctive emphasis. In this way Dibelius diverted attention away from the meticulous analysis of sources to the consideration of the author's message. Although some attention had been given earlier to Luke's distinctive purpose, i.e., to his "tendency" in writing, the search for a fuller understanding of Lukan theology was largely stimulated by Dibelius' insights.

Philipp Vielhauer advanced beyond the structure of Dibelius' work. He investigated the contrasts between Luke's presentation of Pauline thought in Acts and Paul's own thought in his epistles.[19] His basic contribution to further progress consisted in clarifying Luke's viewpoint. Vielhauer called attention to the fact that Luke wrote as a

[18] Martin Dibelius, "The Speeches in Acts and Ancient Historiography," *Studies in the Acts of the Apostles,* ed. Heinrich Greeven; trans. Mary Ling (London: SCM Press, 1956), pp. 138-85.

[19] Philipp Vielhauer, "On the 'Paulinism' of Acts," *Studies in Luke-Acts,* ed. Leander E. Keck and J. Louis Martyn (Nashville: Abingdon Press, 1966), pp. 33-50.

representative of the church at the close of the first century. This church had developed a historical consciousness which enabled it to make a distinction between itself and the earliest church in terms of their historical dimensions.

The work of Hans Conzelmann attracted great attention and served to clarify further some of the basic elements in Luke's thought. His insistence upon the necessity of redaction criticism as a tool for study not only stimulated its use in Luke-Acts but also in Matthew and Mark. Conzelmann suggested that Luke's work represented a serious attempt to deal with the problem of history at a time when it had become clear that Christians no longer confronted either the situation of the original disciples or that of the earliest church.[20] His interpretation of Lukan thought can be summarized from two standpoints. First, Luke attempted to solve the historical problems posed by the passing of time in terms of discontinuity and continuity. Insofar as discontinuity is concerned, Luke described God's plan of salvation (salvation history) as encompassing three distinct periods or phases: the period of the prophets who promised salvation, the period of Jesus who fulfilled the prophetic promise, and the period of the church (the age of the Spirit) which looks forward to its ultimate victory at the parousia (the return of Christ). With respect to continuity, Luke understood each period as the extension of the previous one which had been fulfilled. The parousia was to mark the consummation of the present era, the age of the church. Thus, Luke-Acts represents an

[20] Hans Conzelmann, *The Theology of Saint Luke,* trans. Geoffrey Buswell (New York: Harper & Row, 1961). The German title of the work, *Die Mitte der Zeit* (the center of the time), indicates the nature of the author's thesis. Jesus lived in the middle period of the history of salvation, i.e., between the Law and the Prophets and the present post-resurrection period of the church. Conzelmann's most recent work, *An Outline of the Theology of the New Testament,* incorporates the results of discussion stimulated by the earlier work.

integrated interpretation of the past, and at the same time it illuminates the nature and mission of the church in its experience in continuing world history. Second, Conzelmann pointed to the centrality of eschatology in Luke's thought. Writing at a time when the expectation of the parousia could no longer be fulfilled in its original form (the early Christians had expected it to occur in their lifetime), Luke set about to reinterpret it in a form that would be meaningful for his own day. He did not eliminate it, but it no longer represented his focal point of concern (Acts 1:7 ff.). The church as a Spirit-created fellowship which functions to proclaim the universal gospel supplanted such an expectation as the key to its self-understanding.

The present stage of the discussion of Lukan theology is determined largely by the perspectives outlined in the preceding summary. According to Professor Ulrich Wilckens, contemporary discussion must focus upon the problem of "how Luke understands the structure of the history of salvation." Wilckens protests that redaction criticism has not distinguished sharply enough between the author's personal contribution and that which he inherited from earlier tradition, particularly with respect to the tradition as it relates to Jesus. Wilckens maintains that the problem of the delayed parousia had been solved in principle by focusing attention upon the person of Jesus. He goes on to suggest that some contemporary evaluations of Luke are based too narrowly upon an understanding of Paul in current thought which is rooted in existentialism.[21] Wilckens' rejoinder is a response to certain modern tendencies to devaluate Luke as a writer who departed from earlier Christian perspectives, as for instance in his emphasis in Acts upon tradition, which Käsemann

[21] Ulrich Wilckens, "Interpreting Luke-Acts in a Period of Existentialist Theology," *Studies in Luke-Acts,* p. 65.

thinks created a powerful stimulus toward the acceptance of the authority of apostolic tradition in the second-century church.[22]

The foregoing survey provides conclusive proof that the discussion of Lukan thought has not been concluded. Rather, the survey calls attention to decisive questions for New Testament interpreters. In the case of Luke-Acts, the problems of history, eschatology, and tradition continue to pose basic challenges for understanding the thought world of early Christianity.

CONCLUSION

A brief discussion of the results of redaction criticism does not provide an adequate basis for final conclusions regarding the teaching of the Synoptic Gospels. It serves rather to emphasize the complicated issues which are involved in making such judgments. At the same time, a survey may also point out some aspects of the foundation upon which the work of interpretation must proceed. Within these limitations, it may be helpful to indicate some results of the preceding discussion.

1. The creation of the Synoptic Gospels represented a development of crucial significance in the history of early Christianity. Prior to the composition of Mark's Gospel, the Christian message was proclaimed for almost four decades without an apparent sense of the need for a comprehensive interpretation of the meaning of Jesus' life and ministry. The importance of the factors that created the awareness of such a need can hardly be overestimated.

[22] Ernst Käsemann, "Paulus und der Früh-Katholizismus," *Exegetische Versuche und Besinnungen* (Göttingen: Vandenhoeck & Ruprecht, 1964), II, 239-52.

2. The Gospels are to be understood as the work of individual authors who interpreted the meaning of Jesus with deliberate intention. Although they appropriated earlier fragmentary traditions, they structured and interpreted these traditions according to their own theological purposes.

3. Christian tradition concerning Jesus did not assume a unified or authoritative form until after the composition of the Synoptic Gospels.

4. As in the case of earlier oral tradition, the needs and the problems of the church influenced the form of the Synoptic Gospels.

Books for Additional Reading

1. Reginald H. Fuller, *A Critical Introduction to the New Testament* (London: Gerald Duckworth and Co., 1966), pp. 81-122.
2. Norman Perrin, *What Is Redaction Criticism?* New Testament Series (Philadelphia: Fortress Press, 1969).
3. Joachim Rohde, *Rediscovering the Teaching of the Evangelists,* trans. Dorothea M. Barton (Philadelphia: The Westminster Press, 1968).

Excursus: The Practice of Redaction Criticism

A single pericope may express an idea that is basic to the thought of an entire Gospel. However, the *evidence* for this fact must be gleaned from the total work, since clues to the author's message and intention are never confined to a single segment of his work. This process of clarification and correlation of evidence encompasses every dimension of the composition, including the author's techniques (use of sources, creation of new material, employment of literary forms, etc.).

The scope of this discussion precludes detailed examination of the theology of a Synoptic Gospel. The general results of this research can be found in publications that have appeared during the preceding two decades. On the basis of these

133

results, the intention here is to illustrate the perspective and elementary principles employed in redaction criticism by reference to a limited section of the Gospel of Matthew.

MATTHEW 11:2-6 (LUKE 7:18-23). JOHN'S QUESTION CONCERNING JESUS

This interesting passage has been interpreted in many ways, depending in large measure upon assumptions concerning the nature of the synoptic writings. Two widely accepted results of modern study constitute the basis for this discussion. First, the central concern of this pericope focuses upon the subject of Christology: "Are you the promised Messiah (the coming One), or shall we await another (Matt. 11:3; Luke 7:19b)? Second, this passage, like other biblical material concerned with John's relation to Jesus, reflects issues that arose in the early Christian community, presumably within Jewish-Christian circles (Matt. 11:2-6 and Luke 7:18-23 are derived from the common Q source). Clues to the nature of these issues appear in fragments of Christian apologetic in many places in the New Testament (Matt. 3:14-15; Mark 1:7; Luke 7:28; John 1:19-34; Acts 19:1-3, etc.). Consequently, the material under consideration here does not constitute an authentic biographical report of the Baptist's deteriorating relationship with Jesus. Rather, it reflects the church's interpretation of John's role in Jesus' ministry, a matter that transcends their actual historical relationship.

Matthew discloses his concern in the introductory setting which he creates for the story. According to Matthew, when John, the prisoner, heard of the *works* of the Messiah he dispatched disciples to inquire concerning the meaning of

Jesus' ministry (Matt. 11:2). What is the meaning of *works* in this context? This question indicates our central concern in this discussion.

The larger context of Matthew's work may provide a preliminary basis for identifying Matthew's thought. Although it might be assumed that Matt. 11:2 represents a continuation of the thought of chapter 10, it is difficult to discover the relation of *works* to the content of that chapter. (Following the report of Jesus' commission to the Twelve, the remainder of the chapter sets forth instructions for Christian discipleship, perhaps with primary reference to the contemporary situation.) Hence, Matt. 10:1–11:1 seems to be an insertion that interrupts the stream of thought from 9:34–11:2. (This insertion, introduced by vss. 35-38, treats the issue of authority as it concerns Christian disciples. The question of authority is implicitly involved in Matt. 5:1–9:34, but it is explicitly raised in 11:2 in terms of John's relation to Jesus.) If 10:1–11:1 represents an explanatory diversion from the writer's central line of thought, the reference to the *works* of the Messiah in 11:2 can be understood quite naturally to refer to the miracle stories in 8:1–9:34. However, this interpretation of the miracles as the *works* of the Messiah seems to conflict with the writer's perspective elsewhere.

Matthew's concept of miracle can also be determined by reference to his use of Markan material. As is well known, the miracle tradition plays an important role in the second Gospel. (Following the report of the call of the first disciples, Mark has a lengthy description of Jesus' activity as exorcist and miracle worker [1:21-34]. This account intends to describe the character of Jesus' ministry as a whole, i.e., the miracles authenticate Jesus whom the church now proclaims as its Lord.) Comparison of Matthew and Mark

135

shows that Matthew has deliberately revised Mark's structure. First, Matthew has omitted Mark's miracle collection (1:21-34) and has reduced this section to three summary verses (Matt. 4:23-25) which call attention to the miracles as acts of healing. Second, Matthew has inserted the lengthy Sermon on the Mount (Matt. 5–7) which depicts Jesus as authoritative teacher (Matt. 7:28-29). Finally, following the Sermon on the Mount, Matthew belatedly appends his own collection of miracle stories. Thus, although Matthew retains the miracle tradition which he found in the Markan source, the Messiah of the "word" takes precedence over the Messiah of the "deed" as the basic christological motif. How does this subordination of miracle to teaching in Matt. 4:23–9:34 relate to the emphasis upon miracle in 11:2?

One distinctive characteristic of Matthew's Gospel has to do with the recurrence of certain expressions at important junctures in the book (7:28; 11:1; 13:53; 19:1; 26:2). These summary expressions seem to perform a cohesive function in the book. In each instance mentioned above, the general expression begins with the formula, *"kai hote etelesen ho Iēsous . . ."* ("and when Jesus completed . . ."). This formula seems to indicate the conclusion of one stage in the writer's thought. At the same time, it can be expanded into a transitional introduction to subsequent material. Thus, Matt. 7:28 provides the conclusion for the important christological discourse—the Sermon on the Mount—for which 4:23-25 supplies the introduction. However, 9:35 simply repeats 4:23, a fact which seems contrary to the writer's general practice. Nevertheless, this secondary-type conclusion may provide a clue to the author's thought concerning the relation of the teaching and miracle traditions which circulated in Christian circles. Further, it also suggests that the writer intends that 4:23–9:35 is to be understood as a unity. This evidence

136

supports the conclusions reached above, i.e., Matthew deliberately retains Mark's miracle tradition but revises the *order of priority* between miracle and word which he found in Mark (Mark 1:39).

A final question remains concerning Matthew's positive understanding of the miracle tradition. We have noted Matthew's emphasis upon the miracle as acts of healing (4:23). Although the following verse retains Mark's reference to the demonic, it concludes with the assertion, "he healed them." As has been indicated, Matt. 9:35 merely repeats 4:23. However, Matt. 9:36 refers to Jesus' "compassion" for the distraught and dispersed crowds. This understanding of the miracles as acts of mercy and compassion seems to be characteristic of Matthew's work as a whole. It is consonant with other references to Jesus as the meek and humble Messiah whose miracles mediate mercy and compassion (9:13; 14:14; 15:32; 20:34). Therefore, Matthew's revision of his Markan source seems to be grounded in a different understanding of the function of miracle as a christological motif.

In summary, what can be said regarding Matthew's understanding of *works* in 11:2? First, it seems that Matthew interprets miracles as the *works* of the Messiah. Second, Matthew understands the miracles primarily as acts of healing arising out of mercy and compassion. As deeds of mercy, they are secondary to the *word* as the basic christological motif. Third, Matthew's concept of miracle is consistent with the Q tradition preserved in Matt. 11:2-6 and Luke 7:18-19, 22-23. Fourth, Matthew deliberately retains the two christological motifs current in early Christian tradition (teaching and miracle). In this context, miracle, rooted in the Hellenistic mentality, is expressed most forcefully in Mark, while teaching, animated initially by the Jewish mentality, dominates the Matthean perspective.

6

Pauline Literature

Paul's letters comprise a significant segment of the New Testament canon. These letters, together with the Gospels, have been accepted as definitive expressions of the Christian faith since the second century. However, this fact—that they *together* have been understood in this way—raises important questions. These questions relate to the differences between Paul's letters and the Gospels.

Perhaps the most obvious difference between Pauline literature and the Gospels has to do with literary form, i.e., the Pauline letter/epistle[1] and the historical narrative of the

[1] The literary character of a work represents an important consideration in interpretation. For example, a letter is directed to a local situation, but an epistle is concerned with general conditions that do not involve specific local issues (Adolf Deissmann was the first to make this distinction in his *Bible Studies*). Paul's writings are best understood as letters although he did not adhere rigidly to the form of the letter. Cf. Willi Marxsen, *Introduction to the New Testament,* trans. G. Buswell (Philadelphia: Fortress Press, 1968), p. 23; Amos N. Wilder, *The Language of the Gospel* (New York: Harper & Row, 1964); William A. Beardslee, *Literary Criticism of the New Testament* (Philadelphia: Fortress Press, 1970).

Gospels. These differing literary forms reflect the purposes and viewpoints of their authors. Hence, they raise questions concerning the use of a single methodology for interpreting both types of material. For example, the disciplines of source, form, and redaction criticism arose in connection with problems encountered in the Synoptic Gospels. Can these tools be used to interpret Paul's letters? In other words, is it necessary to develop a special "Pauline" methodology in order to understand the Apostle's thought?

Even though the Gospels do not reflect significant elements of Paul's theology,[2] both Paul and the Synoptics are related to earlier Christian tradition which they incorporate and interpret. Consequently, critical tools which serve to set forth the content and structure of prior Christian tradition—source and form criticism—can function both in Pauline and synoptic interpretation, even though the specific content of Paul's sources differs from that of the Synoptics' sources. Similarly, the techniques employed in redaction criticism are also fruitful for determining the character of Paul's sources.[3] Obviously, the work of textual criticism is continuous in the entire New Testament since it serves to reconstruct the original texts.

Paul's major importance in early Christian history arises out of his theological contribution. His letters contain his distinctive interpretation of earlier Christian tradition. It is

[2] One unexpected result of historical research has to do with the extent of Paul's isolation from the larger Christian community. The Gospels seem to have arisen in relative isolation from the Pauline tradition, even though Paul's latest letter (Romans) appeared more than a decade earlier than the earliest Gospel (Mark). Also, Paul's letters seem to have exerted only negligible influence upon other New Testament material which appeared before A.D. 95.

[3] Paul's theological viewpoint can be seen most clearly in his use of early Christian confessional formulas (Rom. 1:3 ff.; Phil. 2:5-11; I Cor. 11:23-25, etc.).

139

not surprising that this interpretation often transcends and partially transforms that tradition.

The apostle Paul had contact with two distinct and important cultures, the Jewish and the Hellenistic (Greek). He has sometimes been described as the mediator of the Christian message between these cultures. It is difficult to determine the precise degree of influence which Jewish and Hellenistic modes of thought exerted upon Paul's Christian perspective. This historical question is important since it influences the approach used to interpret Paul's thought. This problem in methodology will be discussed in connection with the history of New Testament scholarship.

PAUL THE APOSTLE

The Apostle Paul and Early Christian History

The New Testament seems to portray Paul the Apostle as the most prominent figure in early Christian history besides Jesus. New Testament research has generally proceeded upon this assumption. F. C. Baur, who first applied historical-critical principles to the task of reconstructing a comprehensive history of the early Christian movement, attributed a pivotal role to the apostle Paul. Since Baur's time the issues in Pauline research have influenced the course of New Testament investigation as a whole. Certainly, any serious attempt to interpret the development of early Christian life and thought must include a consistent explanation of the role of Paul the Apostle.

In spite of general agreement regarding Paul's pivotal importance in Christian history, a century of critical investigation has not led to corresponding agreement concerning the precise character of the Apostle's contribution. At the

140

present time vigorous debate continues regarding important aspects of Paul's position in the early church.

A wide variety of models and motifs have been used to explain Paul's role in early Christianity (the Jewish or Hellenistic rabbi, the Greek innovator, the mystic, the eschatological prophet, etc.). These models reflect important methodological presuppositions. It may be that the periodic uncertainty regarding Paul's relevance/irrelevance for modern man has arisen in part out of an underlying uncertainty concerning appropriate procedures in methodology.

Paul and the New Testament

This discussion does not require detailed treatment of questions that normally occur in introductions to the New Testament, such as the chronology of Paul's life, the date, purpose, place of origin, destination, authenticity, etc., of Paul's letters.[4] However, decisions regarding these issues provide the basis for further theological discussion. For example, Paul's theology is understood by reference to the letters that are attributed to him. Hence, it is necessary to indicate the basic assumptions which constitute the foundation for subsequent discussion.

Thirteen New Testament letters lay direct claim to Pauline authorship. Although Hebrews makes no such claim, this work, too, was attributed to Paul before the close of the second century. Furthermore, Paul occupies a prominent place in the book of Acts which also purports to preserve an abundance of Pauline material. When we remember that

[4] Cf. Willi Marxsen, *Introduction to the New Testament*, pp. 17-109; Paul Feine, Johannes Behm, and Werner Georg Kümmel, *Introduction to the New Testament*, trans. A. J. Mattill, Jr. (Nashville: Abingdon Press, 1966), pp. 176 ff.

we do not possess a single work written by Jesus or one of the Twelve, this alleged Pauline material is indeed impressive. What is the validity of these claims for Paul?

Historical-critical research has led to a sharp revision of the material ascribed to Paul. The claim for Pauline authorship of Hebrews is no longer seriously considered. The Pastoral Epistles (I and II Tim. and Titus) are generally interpreted as the work of a second-century student of Paul's thought. There is impressive evidence that Colossians and Ephesians were composed by a Pauline disciple during the closing decades of the first century. It is possible that II Thessalonians also belongs to the list of pseudonymous Pauline works (written by another person and ascribed to Paul).[5] Thus, Romans, I and II Corinthians, Galatians, Philippians, I Thessalonians, and Philemon represent the undisputed sources for Paul's thought. Due to the nature of the sources and the author's purpose, material in Acts can be accepted as decisive evidence for Paul's thought only when genuine support for it can be found in authentic Pauline writings.

Paul's Status in the Early Church

Paul has sometimes been described as the "hero" of the early Christian movement who dominated the entire Chris-

[5] These judgments are based upon various kinds of evidence. First, the language, style, and vocabulary of the disputed letters differ noticeably from the undisputed Pauline writings. Second, the disputed letters seem to be directed to a historical situation which differs from that of Paul's lifetime. Third, and most important, the disputed letters reflect a divergent theological perspective from that evidenced in Paul's undisputed works. This fact is most evident where Paul's language is used with a different connotation. Also, Paul customarily confronted erroneous teachings by reference to basic theological implications of the Christian confession (the meaning of the cross in I Cor. [cf. I Cor. 1:18–4:21] and the meaning of faith in Rom. [cf. Rom. 1:16–3:20]). On the contrary, the disputed letters often appeal to the authority of a developed tradition that is attributed to the apostle Paul (II Tim. 2:2; Eph. 2:20, etc.).

tian pattern of life during the early decades of its existence. Accordingly, Paul is frequently given credit for defining the essential limits of missionary expansion. If such were the case, a biography of Paul—based upon thirteen letters and the book of Acts—would constitute a reliable history of Christianity to the time of the Apostle's death (*ca.* A.D. 60 or, according to some calculations, A.D. 64). This traditional picture of Paul requires critical reassessment.

A reliable picture of the Apostle's role in the early church must be based on the following considerations. First, primary source material is to be restricted to the undisputed Pauline letters. Second, Paul's image as the undisputed leader in all Christian circles must be revised by reference to his opponents. Even such notable leaders as Peter and Barnabas are occasionally reckoned in this group (Gal. 15:36ff.; Acts 10:39). Furthermore, Paul's letters indicate widespread opposition to his leadership, not only in Galatia and Corinth but also in Philippi and Rome. Third, consideration must be given to the Apostle's dependence upon the earliest Christian community (Rom. 16:7). The heart of Paul's message often reflects his indebtedness to those who were Christians "before" him (I Cor. 11:23-25; 15:3-5).[6] Even when no explicit acknowledgment appears, Paul's writings frequently contain earlier liturgical and confessional formulas (Rom. 1:3-5; I Thess. 1:3; Phil. 2:5-11).[7] Fourth, it should also

---

[6] A. M. Hunter, *Paul and His Predecessors* (London: SCM Press, 1940, rev. ed., 1961). It should be noted, however, that Paul did not mechanically take over previous confessions but used them for his own theological purposes.

[7] The precise limits of this pre-Pauline material must be determined by critical reconstruction. The following summary represents widely accepted conclusions concerning these three passages. Romans 1:3 preserves a christological formula relating to Jesus' Davidic descent that arose very early in Jewish-Christian circles. It does not occur elsewhere in Paul's writings. Romans 1:4 contains a christological confession

143

be remembered that Paul neither initiated nor defined the limits of the Christian missionary movement. Acts contains numerous indirect references to unnamed disciples whose efforts resulted in establishment of such significant churches as those at Antioch, Damascus, Alexandria, and Rome. Finally, it is striking that Paul seems to have exerted such limited influence upon the total church during the decades following his death. To be sure, historical information for this era is exceedingly limited, but available evidence suggests that Paul's influence was restricted largely to the churches he established. New Testament works composed before A.D. 95 contain hardly a trace of Pauline thought.[8]

The suggested revised portrait of the apostle Paul does not, of itself, represent depreciation of his importance or denial of his evident theological genius. Rather, properly understood, it sheds light upon the nature of his incisive contribution. The permanent significance of Paul's contribution to the Christian faith is to be seen in the locus and quality of his theological stimulation. Paul, the theologian, represents an appropriate designation for the devoted disciple of Jesus Christ. Indeed, the Apostle effectively set the

---

oriented to the motif of resurrection-exaltation. This twofold confession had been combined prior to Paul's use of it. In the introduction to the book of Romans Paul relates the confession to the exercise of his ministry as a "called" apostle of the gospel. I Thessalonians 1:3 contains the early Christian triad of faith, hope, and love that appears in many places in the New Testament. It is interesting to compare its form here with I Cor. 13, a more extensive early Christian hymn which Paul appropriated. Philippians 2:5-11 incorporates an early Christian hymn (vss. 6-11) of two stanzas (6-8 and 9-11) that describes the descent and ascent of the pre-existent Son of God. This pattern of thought appears in numerous other places in the New Testament with minor variations (cf. Heb. 1:1-3; I Tim. 3:16, etc.). Paul uses the hymn as the basis for his exhortation to humility.

[8] If Colossians and Ephesians appeared during the period 75-90, they represent an exception. It seems preferable, however, to date these works near or after A.D. 90.

feet of the infant Christian movement in the path of theological reflection. His teaching on justification by faith has repeatedly kindled new fires on the hearth of the church. In fact, this courageous champion of Christian theology seems always to respond anew to the church's call for renewed stimulation and insight.

HISTORY OF PAULINE RESEARCH

The historical issue constitutes the underlying problem in Pauline research as well as in the whole field of biblical interpretation. Although the problem of history emerged as early as the sixteenth century, theologians at that time did not recognize its importance for their work.

Ferdinand Christian Baur

F. C. Baur raised historical questions that have troubled theologians until the present time.[9] In some respects he awakened theologians to the larger scope of their task. Although Baur did not disparage the importance of historical *data,* he focused attention upon the work of *interpretation.* Baur called for an interpretation of Christianity that recognizes it as a *historical phenomenon.* Hence, his comprehensive *historical* explanation of the origin and development of the Christian movement represents a turning point in theological scholarship. This fact calls for recognition even though Baur's dependence upon Hegel's philosophy limited the permanent value of his work.

Baur departed from the prevailing practice in his time by using Paul, rather than the Synoptics or the Fourth Gospel, as his point of departure. He thought that the conflict be-

---

[9] Cf. pp. 229 ff.

tween the Jewish and Gentile segments of early Christianity[10] provides the clue to the development of the movement.
Baur found support for his viewpoint in the letters to the
Corinthians, specifically in such references as I Cor. 1:12.
Applying Hegel's dialectical principle (thesis, antithesis, synthesis), Baur reconstructed Christian history until the middle
of the second century. According to this pattern, Jewish
Christianity (the thesis) evoked Gentile Christianity (the
antithesis) which in turn resulted in the catholic church
of the second century (the synthesis).

Baur's scheme of history involved judgments concerning
biblical literature, including Paul's letters. Only those writings which reflect the Jewish-Gentile conflict are to be accepted as authentic Pauline material (Rom., I and II Cor.,
and Gal.). Other alleged Pauline letters, plus the book of
Acts, are said to express the viewpoint of their second-century authors who sought to justify the solution of this conflict which had already been reached in the early second-
century church. Baur's thought on these matters influenced
New Testament research for the remainder of the century.

As could have been anticipated, Baur's proposal evoked
widespread repercussions. However, the scope of his hypothesis was such that it was difficult to deal with isolated
elements of his thought. As opponents of his viewpoint soon
discovered, any real discussion of the issues leads to a critical
assessment of Baur's philosophical assumptions. In retrospect, it is now possible to point out some basic errors in the
scheme. First, Baur misunderstood Paul's relationship with
Jewish Christianity. By identifying the Apostle with Gentile

[10] This conflict arose over the meaning of the Law for Christians.
Some Jewish Christians insisted upon the binding authority of the Law,
even for Gentile Christians. Other Jewish Christians (Hellenistic), together with Gentile Christians, rejected this claim.

146

Christianity exclusively, Baur obscured significant Jewish elements in Paul's thought; namely, his doctrine of creation, his teaching on justification by faith, his concept of the Law, and his anthropology (concept of man). Second, Baur's scheme of history hopelessly isolated Paul from his predecessors and successors in the faith.[11] Baur's errors at this level may be traced to an oversimplification of the pattern of early Christian history. The correction of these errors involves a critique of his Hegelian hypothesis, plus more adequate historical data.

In spite of Baur's limitations, his emphasis upon the historical nature of Christianity has permanently enriched the discipline of theological research. The primacy of the historical question in contemporary biblical discussion is evidence for the incisive nature of his thought. For example, what is the relation of history and faith? How can faith depend upon facts of the past, since these facts about the past can be determined only with a relative degree of certainty? On the other hand, is it appropriate to think about the past in any other way? Albert Schweitzer paid tribute to Baur's profound insight when he complained that those who followed Baur failed to meet the full measure of Baur's challenge.[12] W. G. Kümmel has reiterated Schweitzer's judgment: "Since Baur's time, scientific work on the New Testa-

---

[11] According to the basic tenets of Hegel's scheme which Baur accepted, the thesis evokes the antithesis, both of which are incorporated and transcended in the synthesis. If this pattern had been operative in early Christian history as Baur asserted, catholic Christianity in the second century would have preserved basic elements of Pauline and early Jewish-Christian theology. However, this is not the case. Furthermore, Baur could not explain the rise of Paul's alleged Gentile perspective out of original Jewish Christianity. In other words, Baur's proposal represents a philosophical rather than a historical endeavor in which the issue of historical continuity is of primary importance.

[12] Albert Schweitzer, *Paul and His Interpreters,* trans. W. Montgomery (London: Adam and Charles Black, 1948), p. VIII.

147

ment has been possible only when the fundamental methodological principles he indicated have been followed and his overall historical view has been superseded or improved."[13]

Pauline Research Subsequent to Baur

Baur's structure of thought largely determined the context of biblical interpretation during the era subsequent to his death. The work of supplementing and correcting his ideas assumed two general patterns. On one hand, scholars undertook the task of research in various unexplored areas of Christian origins and early Christian history. Even at the present time, these data provide important foundations for further research. On the other hand, theologians faced the challenge of correcting Baur's historical assumptions and his resultant scheme of Christian history. This work was complicated by the appearance of two new options in the realm of scientific thought; namely, positivism in the social sciences and evolution in the natural sciences. Since adherents of the scientific method—developed in the field of the so-called exact sciences—claimed universal validity for their principles, it is not surprising that they developed "historical" interpretations of Christianity. At any rate, in this crucible, biblical scholarship learned the necessity of dealing with the issues involved in a Christian understanding of history.

Historical Research

New Testament literature, especially Pauline literature, reflects Christianity's Jewish heritage. This evidence is so

[13] W. G. Kümmel, *The New Testament: The History of the Investigation of Its Problems,* trans. S. MacLean Gilmour and Howard C. Kee (Nashville: Abingdon Press, 1972), p. 143.

clear that Christian scholars traditionally answered the question of Christian origins by almost exclusive reference to Jewish sources. However, this scholarship, prior to the era of Strauss and Baur, had operated with a severely restricted understanding of Jewish religion. According to this understanding, first-century Jewish religion (Judaism) consisted of an outdated system of legalistic codes. One important consequence of nineteenth-century historical research relates to the correction of this misunderstanding. In the place of the alleged static system embodied in ancient cultic molds, first-century Judaism appears as one stage of a dynamic process. Although Judaism maintains a kind of historical continuity with the "religion of the fathers," it is important to relate it to the turning point involved in the events surrounding the Babylonian captivity (587/86 B.C.). Furthermore, it is clear that decisive new elements entered the movement from time to time, especially during the era that followed 198 B.C.[14] Accordingly, the vast body of Jewish noncanonical religious literature—the so-called Apocrypha and Pseudepigrapha[15]—contains important sources for illuminating the character of Paul's Jewish background. Continuing investigation has shown a hitherto unrecognized variety in first-century Judaism, even including Hellenistic elements. Moreover, this variety permeated the entire scope of Jewish religious understanding, including such central concepts as anthropology, eschatology, and messiahship. Recent discoveries have further documented this portrait of Judaism.

---

[14] Emil Schürer, *A History of the Jewish People in the Times of Jesus Christ,* trans. John McPherson, *et al.* (Edinburg: T and T Clark, 1901), 5 vols. For a recent condensed work of this type, see Werner Foerster, *From the Exile to Christ,* trans. Gordon E. Harris (Philadelphia: Fortress Press, 1964).

[15] R. H. Charles, ed., *The Apocrypha and Pseudepigrapha of the Old Testament* (Oxford: At the Clarendon Press, 1913), 2 vols.

The Dead Sea Scrolls not only represent a type of sectarian Judaism, but they also contain striking parallels with Christian writings, particularly with some passages in Paul's letters.[16]

Prior to the middle of the last century, biblical scholars ordinarily relegated Hellenistic thought and culture to a place of secondary importance. Paul's letters were frequently expounded with little reference to their Hellenistic heritage. However, here, too, historians and archaeologists have inaugurated a new era in Pauline interpretation by providing more intimate glimpses into Hellenistic thought and culture. Studies in comparative grammar have created better foundations for understanding the biblical languages. Papyrus manuscripts have proved that the Greek of the New Testament represents the language of ordinary conversation and communication during the first century.[17] Extensive research in oriental,[18] Greek,[19] and Egyptian[20] religious systems has provided modern man with expanded sources of information. Gnostic[21] and Stoic[22] thought can now be determined with greater precision. The recovery of this information[23] brought

[16] Cf. A. Dupont-Sommer, *The Essene Writings from Qumran*, trans. G. Vermes (New York: The World Publishing Company, 1962). Also, A. R. C. Leaney, *The Rule of Qumran and Its Meaning* (Philadelphia: Fortress Press, 1966).

[17] Adolf Deissmann, *Light from the Ancient East*, trans. Lionel R. M. Strachan (London: Hodder & Stoughton, 4th ed., 1927).

[18] Franz Cumont, *Oriental Religions in Roman Paganism*, authorized translation (New York: Dover Publications, 1956).

[19] Erwin Rohde, *Psyche*, trans. W. B. Hillis (New York: Harcourt, Brace, and Company, 1925).

[20] Richard Reitzenstein, *Die hellenistischen Mysterienreligionen* (Stuttgart: B. G. Teubner, reprint of 3rd ed. [1927], 1956).

[21] W. Bousset, *Hauptprobleme der Gnosis* (Göttingen: Vandenhoeck & Ruprecht, 1907).

[22] P. Wendland, *Die hellenistische-römische Kultur in ihren Beziehungen zu Judentum und Christentum* (Tübingen: J. C. B. Mohr, 1907).

[23] Like Judaism, Hellenism is a complex phenomenon. Because of its

about a crisis in biblical scholarship by demonstrating striking parallels between the terminology of oriental-Hellenistic religions and New Testament literature. In the case of Paul's writings, these parallels relate to such basic ideas as death, resurrection, spirit, baptism, and the Lord's Supper.

The tireless labor of historical scholars during the past century created a fund of historical data that is of permanent value. To be sure, the recovery of historical facts cannot be equated with the total work of interpretation, since these facts call for interpretation. Nevertheless, experience has shown that such data are indispensable. The findings of theologians and historians are related to available data.

The History-of-Religions School

The history-of-religions school *(die religionsgeschichtliche Schule)* is the name that is given to a movement that applies the principles of historical interpretation to religion. This effort may concern either religion as a general phenomenon of human experience or the form and thought of a single religious system. The history-of-religions approach was first applied to biblical interpretation during the latter half of the nineteenth century. As the original name shows, the movement arose in Germany, but proponents of this approach soon made their influence felt elsewhere, particularly in France and Great Britain.

Numerous factors created the occasion for the rise of the history-of-religions movement. First, the deepening awareness of the meaning of history that marked the general intellectual climate of the nineteenth century provided the

---

syncretistic nature, it is important to distinguish its thought patterns from those of classical Greek thought. For the nature of this syncretism, see Hans Jonas, *The Gnostic Religion* (Boston: Beacon Press, 1958), pp. 3-47.

broad foundation for the movement. Second, disillusionment with philosophy as a metaphysical discipline (Hegel, 1790-1831, represented the last great attempt) opened the door for other approaches to the issue of unity and meaning in human existence. Third, scientific research in all fields, including history, created an incomparable body of factual, but isolated, data. This fragmentation of knowledge could not permanently endure. In this context, the history-of-religions movement proposed the principle of historical development—itself a hypothesis—as the clue to understanding religion, both in its universal and in its specific expression. Thus, the acceptance of the history-of-religions approach also involved a decision regarding methodology.

Following Baur, biblical scholars, particularly in Germany, often divided into groups or schools of thought based on their response to Baur's ideas. The history-of-religions movement was attractive to some members of various groups in that it offered a new option. In the first place, this movement offered an alternative to positivism[24] which defined biblical research in terms of the recovery of historical facts understood according to the norms of the exact sciences. Although this stance sought to adhere to the strict demands of scientific methodology, it could only do so by the sacrifice of theology. Second, the history-of-religions movement also provided an alternative to Hegel's philosophy as a principle of historical explanation. Even before Baur's death, the limitations of his scheme were becoming evident. At the same time, Baur's proposal had shown the necessity for a comprehensive historical principle of explanation. Third, the history-of-religions method contained an answer to the

[24] Auguste Comte (1798-1857) is called the father of the movement in the social sciences known as "positivism." Comte attempted to develop the social sciences according to the principles of the exact sciences.

152

problem of fragmentation of knowledge, even in comparative religion. For example, how does Christianity relate to other religious systems? An answer for this question was urgently needed in the light of expanding historical and archaeological discoveries. The history-of-religions movement provided an answer by assigning each religion a place in the ascending scale of religious development. Christianity was said to represent the goal toward which this development pointed. The consequences of this assumption soon began to appear.

Pauline literature proved to be a rich field of research for disciples of the history-of-religions movement. Both Jewish and Hellenistic sources were investigated with vigor and thoroughness. This work created data for two very different portraits of the Apostle. For members of the "Hellenistic" school of thought, Paul is an example of the Hellenistic ec-static who proclaimed a mystical doctrine of salvation. This mentality appears in the oriental-Hellenistic mystery reli-gions.[25] On the contrary, representatives of the "Jewish" school of thought described the Apostle as a loyal adherent to his Jewish heritage, either the rabbinical[26] or the apocalyp-tic[27] strain. As could be expected, a mediating position at-tempted to reconcile these extremes by arguing that Paul's thought—indeed, Christian thought in general—represents the end-product of syncretism.[28]

The history-of-religions movement has expanded and en-

[25] Cf. Richard Reitzenstein, *Die hellenistischen Mysterienreligionen.*
[26] W. D. Davies, *Paul and Rabbinic Judaism* (London: S.P.C.K., 2nd ed., 1955), represents a recent example of this viewpoint.
[27] Albert Schweitzer, *The Mysticism of Paul the Apostle,* trans. W. Montgomery (London: Adam and Charles Black, 1931).
[28] Otto Pfleiderer, *The Development of Christianity,* trans. Daniel A. Huebsch (New York: B. W. Huebsch, 1910). Pfleiderer has been called the father of the *religionsgeschichtliche Schule.* Cf. *idem, The Influence of the Apostle Paul on the Development of Christianity,* trans. J. Fred-erick Smith (New York: Charles Scribner's Sons, 1885).

riched our historical understanding of Christianity. Clearly, Christian concepts, terminology, and practice are embedded in, and indebted to, the syncretistic religious and cultural life of its time. For example, Jesus is best understood as a part of, rather than apart from, first-century Judaism. Likewise, Paul freely appropriated basic elements of Jewish and Hellenistic thought in proclaiming his gospel. As a result of better sources of information, it is no longer possible to identify the truth of the Christian message with the claim to originality. The discovery of the historical relatedness of Christianity to its own environment represents a permanent gain in theological understanding.

As is frequently the case, to identify the strength of the history-of-religions movement is also to point to its weakness. As has been indicated, the history-of-religions viewpoint has to do with methodology. It intended originally to perform a twofold service for biblical scholarship. First, it provided biblical scholarship with an additional alternative to Baur's Hegelianism on one hand and to positivism on the other. Second, the history-of-religions movement also attempted to provide a principle of interpretation for Christianity that takes due recognition of the data created by expanded scientific research. However, this movement, too, based its proposal upon a hypothesis. This hypothesis assumed that Darwin's principle of evolution—developed in the field of biology—can be applied to historical interpretation. Herein lay a fatal flaw for the work of the history-of-religions movement. During the nineteenth century, proponents of this method customarily interpreted likenesses in religious systems as a sign of dependence. Hence, superficial parallels between Christianity and non-Christian religions were accepted as evidence for Christian dependence upon these religious systems. Also, religion was investigated as an isolated phenomenon, rather than as an expression of man's total self-understanding which arises out of his historical heritage and experience. Consequently, history of-religions scholarship overlooked the fact that mystery terminology in Paul's letters does not in itself prove that Paul used such language in the same way as the Greek priests at Eleusis. For example, it cannot be shown that Paul's understanding of baptism and the Lord's Supper corresponds with the mentality of the sources from which he apparently inherited the terminology.[29] Similar judgments were frequently rendered concerning other focal Pauline doctrines, such as resurrection, spirit, atonement, and anthropology. This tendency dominated the work of the history-of-religions movement—particularly with reference to its work in Hellenism—to such an extent that it had been widely discredited by the close of the First World War. More recently, efforts have been made to preserve the legitimate insights of this approach without limiting the methodology to the evolutionary hypothesis.[30]

THE CRISIS: JESUS *OR* PAUL?

Since the problem of history constituted the underlying issue in theological discussion during the nineteenth century, it is not surprising that Pauline research led to a crisis involving a historical problem. The issue crystallized in the

[29] W. Heitmüller, *Taufe und Abendmahl im Urchristentum* (Tübingen: J. C. B. Mohr [Paul Siebeck], 1911). Cf. also W. Bousset, *Kyrios Christos,* trans. John E. Steely (Nashville: Abingdon Press, 1970). According to this viewpoint, baptism and the Lord's Supper are mystical sacraments that impart immortality.

[30] Rudolf Bultmann, *Primitive Christianity in Its Contemporary Setting,* trans. R. H. Fuller (London: Thames and Hudson, 1956).

form of a question: Jesus *or* Paul, i.e., is Jesus *or* Paul the responsible founder of the stream of Christianity which created New Testament literature? The critical foundation for this issue consisted of the discovery that Jesus' preaching of the Kingdom of God (Mark 1:14) expresses a focus different from that of Paul's sophisticated Christology (Rom. 1:4; 10:9; Phil. 2:5-11; etc.). Scholars were able to construct impressive arguments for either Jesus *or* Paul.[31] However, at the turn of the present century it was difficult for theologians to provide a historical interpretation of the early Christian movement in which there was evident continuity between Jesus and Paul.

The theological and historical undertaking which Strauss and Baur initiated with such enthusiasm seemed to be floundering in confusion at the close of the nineteenth century. Biblical interpretation had developed into such a fragmented discipline that agreement concerning the important problems was difficult. Synoptic research (the Jesus of history *or* the Christ of faith?)[32] and Pauline scholarship (Jesus *or* Paul?) shared a common frustration. Further progress awaited the rise of clearer perspective regarding the meaning of historicity, the development of greater sensitivity to the theological character of biblical literature, and the creation of more precise critical tools for determining theological issues. Although there was evidence of progress in these areas at the turn of the century, the decisive developments were postponed for more than two decades.

[31] William Wrede, "Paulus," *Das Paulusbild in der neueren deutschen Forschung*, K. H. Rengstorf, ed. (Darmstadt: Wissenschaftliche Buchgesellschaft, 1964), pp. 1-94. Wrede argued that "he [Paul] became the first Christian theologian and through his theology decisively transformed the nascent religion" (p. 94).

[32] Cf. Chap. 9.

HISTORY AND THEOLOGY:
THE QUEST FOR SYNTHESIS

Karl Barth's commentary on Romans[33] marks a turning point in twentieth-century theological discussion: it also represents a call for revolution in methodology. Barth was thoroughly grounded in nineteenth-century critical procedures. However, in his commentary on Romans he formulated an incisive critique of the role of critical methodology in biblical interpretation. In Barth's opinion, proponents of historical-critical methodology had substituted historical answers—what did the text intend to say to the original recipients, or what are the sources of biblical concepts and symbols?—for theological answers—what does the text now say to modern man? Like Kähler two decades earlier, Barth did not totally repudiate the work of historical-critical investigation. Rather, he accepted this work as a necessary preliminary stage in biblical interpretation. At the same time, the work of interpretation is only accomplished when "I [the interpreter] am driven on until I stand with nothing before me but the enigma of the matter; till the document seems hardly to exist as a document; till I have already forgotten that I am not its author; till I know the author so well that I allow him to speak in my name and am even able to speak in his name myself." [34] Barth thereby raised the question of hermeneutics, an issue that had lain dormant during most of the modern period.

Barth possessed a kind of theological instinct that frequently made him sensitive to theological limitations in generally accepted conclusions. His critique of critical procedures

[33] Karl Barth, *The Epistle to the Romans,* trans. Edwyn C. Hoskyns (London: Oxford University Press, 4th impression of 1933 ed., 1957).
[34] *Ibid.,* p. 8.

in his day witnesses to this fact. Unfortunately, however, theological instinct alone cannot serve as substitute for methodology, particularly when the crucial questions of faith and history are at stake. Barth not only relegated critical methodology to a preliminary role in biblical interpretation, but often his pronouncements also reflected lack of consideration for generally accepted conclusions of critical scholarship. This seems to represent a basic limitation of Barth's work. To be sure, critical reconstruction must not be equated with the work of interpretation. At the same time, interpretation is to proceed along the path marked out by responsible critical procedures. If the historical dimensions of Christianity have any significance for understanding the Christian message in modern times, critical methodology represents a necessary part of the theologian's equipment.

Rudolf Bultmann, a focal figure in twentieth-century New Testament scholarship, initially applauded Barth's call for theological advance. Bultmann, too, sensed the sterility of biblical research focused solely upon the past. However, Barth, the systematic theologian, and Bultmann, the biblical theologian, viewed the issue through different lenses. In contrast with Barth, Bultmann adhered strictly to historical-critical exegetical practices. In his judgment, Barth oversimplified the issue in his attempt to "let Paul speak for himself in this generation." Rather, according to Bultmann, biblical literature is *theological* literature, i.e., it expresses the writer's thoughts which arose out of his stance in faith. However, the writer's thoughts—singly or collectively—do not exhaust the ground of his faith (God, who confronts man in the preaching of the crucified-resurrected Jesus Christ).[35] Furthermore, the biblical writers' thoughts are

[35] Rudolf Bultmann, *Theology of the New Testament,* II, 237-40.

158

not only incomplete, they are also only relatively appropriate,[36] i.e., human language and concepts refer to God in
anthropological terms. Hence, for Bultmann, the scriptures
document a movement of faith which interpretation seeks to
extend. In this perspective, interpretation—involving historical-critical procedures—is the process through which the
scriptures speak to the present time. Such an understanding
of scripture involves a comprehensive theory of hermeneutics. Barth and Bultmann's disagreement arose at this point.

Salvation-history *(Heilsgeschichte)* designates a theological point of view that has been espoused spo-
radically throughout Christian history, beginning as early
as Irenaeus *(ca.* A.D. 175). Johann Christian Konrad von
Hofmann was the most influential exponent of this view in
the nineteenth century, and Oscar Cullmann has become the
best-known exponent of the position in this century.[37] According to this conception, God's action-in-history for man's
salvation can be seen as a series of events which occurred in
accordance with a predetermined plan. Creation marked the
initiation of the program which is to be consummated with
the final judgment and the renewal (restoration) of all
things. Proponents of the history-of-salvation scheme point
to biblical references (history of Israel, Christ as the fulfillment of prophecy, the expectation of Christ's return, etc.)
in support of their claims. This scheme contains attractive
features, including an alleged continuity. However, serious
objections can be raised against this viewpoint. First, it is
based upon a limited understanding of the nature of the scrip-

---

[36] *Ibid.,* pp. 160-64.

[37] Oscar Cullmann, *Christ and Time,* trans. Floyd V. Filson (Phila-
delphia: The Westminster Press, 1964); *idem, The Christology of the
New Testament,* trans. Shirley C. Guthrie and Charles A. M. Hall
(Philadelphia: The Westminster Press, 1959), pp. 145-46.

tures. Although the salvation-history pattern does occur in the scriptures, this pattern is itself the product of faith in retrospect or prospect. The continuity contained is a product of faith and cannot be transferred to historical structures, either in the past or future. Second, and related to the first objection, salvation-history understands God's acts as analogous to human acts. To be sure, the scriptures refer to God's acts in history, but they do not understand such acts historically, i.e., subject to historical investigation. This tendency to objectify God's action is characteristic of the salvation-history perspective. Third, salvation-history fails to do justice to the biblical concept of eschatology. Granted that patterns of eschatology do occur in the scriptures—in Paul, for example—such works as Colossians or the Fourth Gospel cannot be pressed into the scheme. Furthermore, is it justifiable to impose the linear concept of time upon the "course" of divine actions? In Pauline research, proponents of salvation-history have most often based their arguments on Romans 9–11.[38]

THE CENTER OF PAUL'S THEOLOGY

Martin Luther's audacious claim that Paul's teaching on justification by faith constitutes the center or norm for interpreting the Apostle's entire thought—indeed, the thought of the entire New Testament—contained implications that even Luther could not anticipate. This principle of content-criticism *(Sachkritik)* is based upon the insight that biblical writings contain the authors' reflections upon contemporary situations from the perspective of faith in Jesus Christ. In

[38] Oscar Cullmann, *Salvation in History*, trans. Sidney B. Sowers (New York: Harper & Row, 1967), pp. 248-68.

other words, the scriptures are understood as theological material. Accordingly, they reflect varying degrees of insight at various levels of maturity. Consequently, the content of total scripture—its witness to Jesus Christ—provides the norm for interpreting individual passages. For example, Luther described the book of James as an "epistle of straw" because of the absence of basic reference to Christ.

It seems fitting, then, to call attention to three important areas of Paul's thought that have been taken as the center of his theology, namely, justification by faith, anthropology, and eschatology.

Justification by Faith

It may be argued that Protestants have understood the teaching on justification by faith as the center of Paul's thought, but there have also been notable exceptions to this viewpoint. For example, Baur argued that Paul's thought focuses upon the doctrine of reconciliation, i.e., overcoming the conflict between "flesh" and "spirit." Later, the history-of-religions movement located the center of Paul's thought either in a sacramental idea of salvation (baptism and the Lord's Supper)[39] or in mystical identification with Christ ("being in Christ").[40] At the turn of the century, William Wrede rightly rejected these nontheological approaches to Pauline thought, contending rather that Paul's "theology is his religion."[41] At the same time, Wrede interpreted Pauline thought without reference to justification by faith. In Wrede's opinion, this teaching is only a weapon (*Kamp-*

[39] Cf. p. 155, n. 29.
[40] Albert Schweitzer, *The Mysticism of Paul the Apostle*, p. 3.
[41] William Wrede, "Paulus," *Das Paulusbild in der neueren deutschen Forschung*, p. 42.

feslehre, "fighting doctrine") which the Apostle used on the occasion of conflict with Jewish opponents.[42] Hence, even though justification by faith has served as a kind of motto for Protestants, Protestant theologians have sometimes paid little attention to the meaning of the motto. Günther Bornkamm and Ernst Käsemann have recently complained that contemporary Protestant thought either misunderstands and neglects[43] or outrightly repudiates[44] the traditional Protestant viewpoint.

The criteria for evaluating the function of Paul's doctrine of justification by faith are ultimately theological in nature. At the same time, theological judgment is related to exegetical methodology. Hence, it is not surprising that the current discussion involves both exegetical and theological issues.[45]

Professor Käsemann is largely responsible for the present structure of the debate on the meaning and function of Paul's teaching on justification by faith. Bultmann's emphasis upon anthropology[46] his stimulated Käsemann's work. However,

[42] *Ibid.,* p. 67.

[43] Günther Bornkamm, *Paul,* trans. D. M. G. Stalker (New York: Harper & Row, 1971), p. 135.

[44] Ernst Käsemann, "Justification and Salvation History in the Epistle to the Romans," *Perspectives on Paul,* trans. Margaret Kohl (Philadelphia: Fortress Press, 1971), pp. 60-78.

[45] The following works comprise only a skeleton selection from current literature: Ernst Käsemann, "The Righteousness of God in Paul," *New Testament Questions of Today,* trans. W. J. Montague (Philadelphia: Fortress Press, 1969), pp. 168-82; Rudolf Bultmann, "δικαιοσύνη θεοῦ," *Journal of Biblical Literature,* LXXXIII (1964), 12 ff.; *idem, Theology of the New Testament,* I, 270-85; Hans Conzelmann, *An Outline of the Theology of the New Testament,* trans. John Bowden (New York: Harper & Row, 1969), pp. 214-20; *idem,* "Current Problems in Pauline Research," *Interpretation,* XXII (April, 1968), 175-82; John Knox, *Chapters in a Life of Paul* (Nashville: Abingdon-Cokesbury Press, 1950), pp. 146-55.

[46] Ernst Käsemann, "On Paul's Anthropology," *Perspectives on Paul,* p. 2.

Käsemann's arguments encompass the larger theological concerns of Protestant thought during the past century. He defines the problem by a twofold question: "First, is it, as a fighting doctrine, so conditioned by its time that we must call it obsolete today? Secondly, does it, as Protestants generally suppose, primarily take its bearings from the individual, so that it has to be supplemented or even replaced by a standpoint based on salvation history?" [47] Käsemann's negative answers to these questions are contained in numerous articles.[48] While acknowledging the function of the teaching on justification as *Kampfeslehre*, Käsemann denies that this judgment can be restricted to this teaching alone. Rather, the entire corpus of Paul's letters is said to serve as an instrument of conflict. Furthermore, Käsemann denies that Paul's teaching is primarily oriented toward the individual. On the contrary, Paul's doctrine of justification refers to God's revelation—in Jesus Christ—of his sovereignty over his creation. Consequently, the traditional emphasis upon the "gift" character of God's righteousness (justification) obscures God's call for total obedience, according to Käsemann.[49] As could be expected, these arguments have elicited a wide variety of responses. Käsemann's anticipated commentary on Romans will doubtless expand the debate by fully disclosing the broad exegetical and theological foundations of his argument.

The preceding summary indicates that renewed consideration of Paul's doctrine of justification by faith has not led to unanimity of opinion in matters of detail, even in Protes-

[47] Ernst Käsemann, "Justification and Salvation History in the Epistle to the Romans," *Perspectives on Paul*, p. 71.

[48] Cf. p. 162, n. 45.

[49] Ernst Käsemann, "The Righteousness of God in Paul," *New Testament Questions of Today*, p. 180.

tant circles. The details of these disagreements cannot be sketched here. However, these reflections have also enhanced the possibility of expanded consensus in important areas. First, impressive exegetical and theological evidence can be adduced to support the claim that the doctrine of justification by faith constitutes the theological center of Paul's thought. Second, the general contours of this doctrine can be defined by reference to certain basic ideas: (a) The doctrine is eschatological in character, i.e., God confronts man in the proclamation of the crucified-resurrected Christ. (b) The doctrine asserts that God the Creator confronts man the creature as sovereign. (c) This confrontation radically alters man's situation, i.e., it mediates God's grace (his gracious gift of acceptance) and demand (call for faith as man's continuing response). To the degree that such consensus exists, it can provide a basis for further discussion and clarification.

Anthropology

Paul's letters contain numerous terms that can be classified under the category of anthropology (teaching about man). Among these terms (body, soul, heart, mind, etc.), "flesh" (sarx) and "spirit" (pneuma) occur at important junctures in the Apostle's writings. Hence, it is plausible that they have been understood to provide a clue to the center of Paul's theology.

Professor Hermann Lüdemann initiated the modern discussion of Pauline anthropology.[50] According to Lüdemann, Paul's letters reflect two distinct anthropological perspectives,

---

[50] Hermann Lüdemann, *Die Anthropologie des Apostels Paulus und ihre Stellung innerhalb seiner Heilslehre* (Kiel: Universitäts-Buchhandlung P. Toeche, 1872).

namely, Jewish and Hellenistic. In the (earlier) Jewish concept, "flesh" refers to man's creaturely status. In the (later) Hellenistic sense, "flesh" represents the material stuff of man's body which is at the same time the root or source of sin. Based on these assumptions. Lüdemann claimed that Paul's writings also reflect a twofold doctrine of salvation corresponding to his twofold idea of anthropology. On one hand, Paul's doctrine of justification arises from his Jewish understanding of man as "flesh." On the other hand, Paul's writings are also said to contain the idea of salvation by which the "spirit" overcomes or nullifies the "flesh." This concept is traced to Paul's Hellenistic heritage and is expressed most clearly in his doctrine of baptism. Lüdemann thought that these Jewish and Hellenistic ideas reflected stages in Paul's theological development. Various other attempts were made later to explain the relationship of these divergent concepts. In any case, Lüdemann's ideas provided the structure for interpreting Paul's thought until near the close of the nineteenth century.

The discussion of Paul's theology has focused again in this century upon the subject of anthropology. Two developments have been influential in creating the context for the current debate: (1) The correction of Lüdemann's basic thesis through better understanding of the nature of first-century thought. (2) Rudolf Bultmann's incisive reference to the biblical understanding of anthropology. Bultmann's thesis, steadfastly defended throughout his lengthy career, can be best understood by reference to his own words: "For Paul, *God* is not a metaphysical being and thus is not an object of speculation, but rather is the God whose action does not take place primarily in cosmic occurrences, but in relation to man in history. On the other hand, he does not understand *man* as an isolated being within the world, but rather always

165

sees him in his relation to God. Therefore, it follows that what God and man mean for Paul can only be understood together as a unity and that his 'theology' can be presented as anthropology." [51] "It [Paul's theology] does not deal with the world and man as they are in themselves, but constantly sees the world and man in their relation to God. Every assertion about God is simultaneously an assertion about man and vice versa. For this reason, and in this sense Paul's theology is, at the same time, anthropology." [52] Accordingly, Bultmann treats Pauline theology under the categories "Man Prior to Faith" and "Man Under Faith." [53] Even a casual acquaintance with Bultmann's writings teaches one the necessity of giving careful attention to his language. His statements reflect carefully defined usage of such words as God, world, man, revelation, and history.[54] Bultmann does not claim that Paul develops an explicit doctrine of man. What he does claim is that Paul understands man's situation "under faith" in correlation with God's self-disclosure and that Paul's attempt to speak about God or man involves the man-God correlation. In other words, Paul does not "describe" either man or God in isolation.

Bultmann's bold thesis has been challenged at various points. W. D. Stacey concludes that, "The Apostle was not primarily interested in anthropology, or, to be more definite and yet still exact, he was not interested in anthropology at all." [55] Hans Conzelmann thinks that Paul uses anthropological terms in a neutral sense, i.e., faith does not alter the

---

[51] Rudolf Bultmann, *Existence and Faith,* trans. and ed. Schubert M. Ogden (New York: Meridian Books, 1960), pp. 127-28.

[52] Rudolf Bultmann, *Theology of the New Testament,* I, 191.

[53] *Ibid.,* pp. 190-352.

[54] Cf. Rudolf Bultmann, *Existence and Faith.*

[55] W. David Stacey, *The Pauline View of Man* (London: MacMillan and Company, 1956), p. 238.

structures of human existence.[56] Ernst Käsemann has challenged Bultmann's use of anthropology as the key to Paul's thought. Käsemann denies that Paul describes man as an individual who has his destiny "in his own hands," as Bultmann's interpretation of faith may suggest. Rather, man's individuality arises out of certain "givens" which determine his situation, i.e., the world and the cosmic powers which contend with God for lordship over man.[57] Indeed, Paul's emphasis upon "decision" refers only to the believer, according to Käsemann.[58]

In spite of the energy with which the investigation has been pursued, modern debate over Paul's doctrine of man has not led to unity of opinion regarding the role of this doctrine in the Apostle's total thought. Indeed, opposing judgments are sometimes expressed in such rigid terms that it is difficult to discover common grounds for further discussion as, for example, the statements of Bultmann and Stacey illustrate. Nevertheless, it is possible to point to positive gains that have accrued from the debate, particularly with reference to the context in which the issue is now defined. Some of these gains can be indicated here.

In the first place, it is clear that Paul's doctrine of man occupies an important place in his thought. The Apostle's extensive use of a wide variety of anthropological terms—body, spirit, soul, flesh, mind, heart, etc.—reflects his concern with the subject. Hence, an adequate account of Pauline theology must deal with the content and function of the Apostle's doctrine of man. Second, Paul does not develop his doctrine of man for its own sake. He does not provide an

[56] Hans Conzelmann, *An Outline of the Theology of the New Testament*, p. 174.

[57] Ernst Käsemann, "On Paul's Anthropology," *Perspectives on Paul*, p. 29.

[58] *Ibid.*, p. 31.

abstract philosophy of human existence, nor does he undertake a scientific analysis of the structures of human nature. For example, Paul uses anthropological terms—body, flesh, spirit, soul, etc.—to refer to the whole man. Third, Paul develops his doctrine of man in correlation with his total Christian perspective. Therefore, anthropology represents a point of reference for interpreting the meaning of the gospel, with particular reference to Christology. Anthropology explicates the "way things are" in the light of God's self-disclosure in Jesus Christ. Finally, the claim that Paul's anthropology *is* theology (Bultmann) focuses attention upon the structure of the Apostle's thought at the expense of the dynamic character of that structure. On the other hand, the assertion that Paul is not interested in anthropology at all (Stacey) fails to give proper attention to the actual content of the Apostle's thought.

Eschatology

Eschatology emerged as a subject of primary concern in theological discussion near the close of the past century. Prior to that time, biblical theology focused attention upon Jesus, the ethical teacher, whose central concern is expressed in the Sermon on the Mount. Within this pattern eschatology was equated with the dogma of "inevitable progress" which served as the watchword of nineteenth-century thought. Near the close of the century two exciting works by Richard Kabisch[59] and Johannes Weiss[60] opened the door to a new

[59] Richard Kabisch, *Die Eschatologie des Apostels Paulus in ihren Zusammenhängen mit dem Gesamtbegriff des Paulinismus* (Göttingen: Vandenhoeck & Ruprecht, 1893).

[60] Johannes Weiss, *Jesus' Proclamation of the Kingdom of God,* trans., ed., and introduction by Richard Hyde Hiers and David Larrimore Holland (Philadelphia: Fortress Press, 1971).

era in biblical interpretation. Numerous factors paved the way for this development including expanded historical research in Jewish literature, the rise of the history-of-religions school of thought, and the creation of better critical tools for understanding the New Testament.

Albert Schweitzer's spectacular work soon overshadowed those of Kabisch and Weiss. Schweitzer described Jesus[61] as an apocalyptic[62] preacher who expected the sudden eruption of God's kingdom to put an end to human history. Schweitzer claimed that this apocalyptic perspective also provides the essential clue to Paul's thought.[63] According to Schweitzer, Paul combined two ideas to form the basis for his theology, namely, the Jewish apocalyptic concept of history and the Christian confession of Jesus as the Messiah who had *already* appeared. However, the course of human history continued after Jesus' resurrection, in spite of the fact that the appearance of the Messiah had been understood as the realization of God's purposes in history. Schweitzer argued that Paul's doctrine of the return of Christ *(parousia)* represented his solution to this problem. But even the expectation of the *parousia* did not materialize as Paul had anticipated. Accordingly, Paul met this second failure in expectation by his mystical concept of salvation (man in Christ).[64] Obviously, Schweitzer's interpretation of Paul's theology raises serious questions. First of all, if Paul's theology can be explained by reference to apocalyptic pat-

---

[61] Albert Schweitzer, *The Quest of the Historical Jesus,* trans. W. Montgomery (London: Adam and Charles Black, reprint of 2nd ed. [1911], 1945).

[62] According to the apocalyptic viewpoint, God will put an end to world history by cataclysmic intervention. This judgment will mean deliverance for the faithful and destruction for God's enemies.

[63] Albert Schweitzer, *Paul and His Interpreters.*

[64] Albert Schweitzer, *The Mysticism of Paul the Apostle.*

terns solely, how can the Apostle speak to twentieth-century man who no longer thinks in these terms? Further, if Paul's doctrine of salvation arose out of his effort to adjust to the errors of his own thought, a shadow has been cast upon the validity of the Apostle's total message. Schweitzer's error lay in that fact that he misread Paul's theology by locating its focus in the doctrine of the *parousia*. At the same time, his proposal thrust the doctrine of eschatology into the mainstream of twentieth-century theological discussion.

Apocalyptic eschatology, involving an orientation toward the future, stands in sharp contrast with eschatology rooted in the doctrine of inevitable progress in history. Thus, it is not surprising that attempts have been made to correct or supplant Schweitzer's apocalyptic portrait of Jesus and Paul. It has even been argued that Paul's thought is oriented exclusively toward the present. Two movements whose diversity is well known have called attention to Paul's understanding of the present. These movements have been led by two notable scholars of this century, C. H. Dodd (realized eschatology) and Rudolf Bultmann (existentialist theology). According to Dodd, "It is in the epistles of Paul therefore, that full justice is done for the first time to the principle of 'realized eschatology' which is vital to the whole *kerygma*. That supernatural order of life which the apocalyptists had predicted in terms of pure fantasy is now described as an actual fact of experience." [65] For quite different reasons, Bultmann contends that Paul's message focuses upon the present. In Bultmann's opinion, the nature of the kerygma requires emphasis upon the present moment of decision. The kerygma—the proclamation of the crucified-resurrected One —confronts man with God's demand for faith (decision).

[65] C. H. Dodd, *The Apostolic Preaching and Its Developments* (New York: Harper & Brothers, 1962), p. 65.

Since faith actually inaugurates God's action of salvation, i.e., it appropriates God's offered salvation, it is the eschatological event. According to Bultmann, eschatology is thereby rescued from the structure of a future speculative event and identified with present reality. In his words, "The salvation-occurrence is the *eschatological occurrence* which puts to end the old aeon." [66]

Ernst Käsemann has reopened the case for apocalyptic eschatology in Paul's thought, but with important modifications. Käsemann thinks that apocalyptic structures of thought provided Paul with a weapon against the errors of Hellenistic mentality which claimed to have fully appropriated salvation. (The church at Corinth was troubled by some members who claimed that baptism represented an experience of union with the Spirit of the exalted Lord. The believer—the baptized person—was said to be subsequently exempt from the conditions of earthly existence. Therefore, they rejected the model of the crucified Jesus, the claims for ethical responsibility, etc., on the grounds that they had already transcended the realm of mundane existence.) Hence, Paul is said to have carried on his conflict with these opponents "under the sign of apocalyptic." [67] According to Käsemann, the Christ-event is decisive for Paul in that it serves to inaugurate the present age in which God contends with antagonistic cosmic powers for ultimate lordship over his own creation. Hence, apocalyptic provides the "eschatological reservation" in the conflict against the present eschatology of the Hellenistic enthusiasts. [68]

Attempts have been made to deal with the evident tensions between present and future in Paul's writings. On one hand,

[66] Rudolf Bultmann, *Theology of the New Testament*, I, 306.
[67] Ernst Käsemann, *New Testament Questions of Today*, p. 132.
[68] *Ibid.*, p. 136.

171

it is claimed that apocalyptists, including Paul, use language symbolically.[69] Other interpreters have sought to show a development within Paul's thought, i.e., in the beginning Paul expected an early *parousia,* but he gradually shifted his emphasis to the present experience of salvation.[70] These latter efforts are handicapped by the fact that Paul's letters do not support such a development.

No other segment of Paul's thought has attracted greater attention in this century than his eschatology. Yet, three-quarters of a century of discussion seems to have further emphasized the riddle. Neither the "present" nor the "future" school of thought has been able to win a majority consensus. The prospect of new evidence to support either position does not seem promising. Past attempts to mediate between the extremes have been unsuccessful. In spite of the fact that eschatology involves significant segments of Paul's thought, the future course of the debate is not now evident. It may be that the present impasse results in part from an overemphasis upon "present" and "future" as basic categories for understanding Paul's thought. If eschatology represents the Apostle's attempt to "tell it like it is" from his particular stance, categories not strictly oriented to time may provide better access to Paul's essential message. In any case, while few interpreters deny the importance of Paul's eschatological language, the claim is now rarely made that eschatology represents the center of Paul's theology.

CONCLUSION

We have surveyed limited aspects of the extended journey of historical-critical scholarship in its attempts to under-

[69] W. D. Davies, *Paul and Rabbinic Judaism,* p. 320.
[70] A. M. Hunter, *Paul and His Predecessors,* p. 98.

stand Paul's message in modern times. This pilgrimage has been marked by exciting discovery, temporary detours, and even dead-end streets. As has been true in biblical scholarship as a whole, these "exercises in probability" have laid some issues to rest. At the same time, others have emerged in their place. Obviously, the journey has not resulted in unity of viewpoint regarding many issues. The necessity for further effort scarcely needs to be indicated. Indeed, it is clear that the answer to the question, "What does Paul say to *us*?" must be sought afresh in each generation. One thing has, however, become progressively clear: The prospects for relevant answers to this question are brightest in those quarters that are aware of the successes *and* failures of previous attempts.

Books for Additional Reading

1. Günther Bornkamm, *Paul,* trans. D. M. G. Stalker (New York: Harper & Row, 1971).
2. Archibald M. Hunter, *The Gospel According to St. Paul* (Philadelphia: The Westminster Press, 1966).
3. Wayne A. Meeks, ed., *The Writings of St. Paul* (New York: W. W. Norton & Company, 1972).

7

Johannine Literature

The Fourth Gospel and the three Epistles attributed to "John" have characteristics in common which separate them from other New Testament literature. The church's use of this material has been marked by numerous uncertainties, including initial hesitation concerning the canonical status of II and III John. In spite of extensive modern investigation, Johannine literature confronts contemporary scholarship with puzzling riddles. Indeed, no other section of New Testament material has challenged the basic assumptions of historical-critical research more persistently or yielded to its structures of investigation more reluctantly.

The current dilemma in Johannine research is rooted in the basic assumptions of historical-critical methodology. For, as Professor Kümmel has recently said, "The scientific concern with the understanding of the New Testament must, precisely when it is pursued in the context of the church and from the presupposition of faith, take account of the fact that we also *can* come to a believing hearing of the message of the New Testament only in *one* way: namely, by seeking to make the utterances of the ancient authors of the New Testament understandable, just as their contemporary readers or hearers could and had to understand them. Hence there is no other access to the understanding of the New Testament writings than the method of historical research, which is valid for *all* writings of antiquity." [1] Although Kümmel has voiced the claims of historical interpretation in exclusive terms, he has at the same time accurately expressed the fundamental assumptions of contemporary biblical scholarship. However, this hypothesis confronts Johannine scholarship with an embarrassing situation. For, as Ernst Käsemann has indicated, "All of us are more or less groping in darkness when we are asked to give information about the historical background of this Gospel [John], information which would determine our understanding of the whole book and not merely of individual details. Nowhere else in the New Testament do we find ourselves in a greater dilemma than in John." [2] Although some interpreters may render a more optimistic appraisal of the present state of affairs in

[1] W. G. Kümmel, *The Theology of the New Testament*, trans. John E. Steely (Nashville: Abingdon Press, 1973), p. 16.

[2] Ernst Käsemann, *The Testament of Jesus,* trans. Gerhard Krodel (Philadelphia: Fortress Press, 1968), p. 1.

Johannine studies,[3] it must be conceded that only tentative answers can be given for every major question related to the specific historical background of the Fourth Gospel. In the light of the exclusive claims that have been put forth for historical-critical methodology, what does this disparity between goals and achievements in John's Gospel imply? Two dimensions of the issue are evident. On one hand, the validity of the critical approach to the interpretation of scripture may be involved. Does the attempt to understand the scriptures historically reach an impasse in the Fourth Gospel, i.e., are the structures of historical investigation valid for some forms of scripture—for example, the Synoptics and Acts—but inappropriate for others—for example, John and I Corinthians 13? On the other hand, in case the claims of critical methodology can be sustained, must the church reckon with the possibility that a significant segment of its scriptures is not understood, or even misunderstood? Study of John's Gospel provides one occasion for consideration of these questions.

Even though detailed information is not available at many points (date, author, destination, place of origin, particular occasion, history of earlier stages of the tradition, etc.), historical research has at the same time made valuable contributions to our understanding of John's Gospel by clarifying issues concerning the larger context in which the Gospel appeared. In the first place, the date of the Fourth Gospel has been defined with reasonable certainty. To be sure, it is not possible to give a specific date for the book (for example, A.D. 90 as opposed to A.D. 85 or 100), but it is clear that John's Gospel is not to be understood as a product of the conflict with Gnosticism in the middle of the second century.

[3] James M. Robinson, "The Johannine Trajectory," *Trajectories Through Early Christianity,* James M. Robinson and Helmut Koester (Philadelphia: Fortress Press, 1971), pp. 232-68.

The discovery of a papyrus fragment (P^{52} dated as early as A.D. 115 but no later than A.D. 125) containing parts of John 18:33-35, 37-38 points toward the year A.D. 100 as the latest feasible date for John's Gospel. Second, it is generally acknowledged that the earlier assumption concerning the apostolic character of John's Gospel is invalid. Apart from the evidence in the nature of the material itself, neither internal evidence nor early Christian tradition establishes the claim for apostolic authorship. (It should be noted that some early Christian tradition supports the claim for apostolic authorship, but investigation has shown that this tradition is historically unreliable. Rather, it represents an apologetic attempt to validate Christian material according to the norm of apostolic testimony.) Third, it has been possible to define the relation of John's Gospel to other New Testament writings with greater accuracy. Johannine dependence upon Paul and the Synoptics no longer represents an assured point of departure. Furthermore, the Johannine Epistles and the book of Revelation cannot be used as an aid to understanding the thought of the Fourth Gospel. Fourth, it follows from what has been said that it is no longer viable to follow Schleiermacher's example in using John's Gospel as the basis for the life and thought of Jesus. Regardless of the problems connected with the synoptic accounts, they still constitute the point of departure for discussion of the life of Jesus.

Although general information regarding the larger context in which John's Gospel arose cannot serve as substitute for specific data concerning the historical circumstances in which the writer composed his work, such information does enable interpreters to advance beyond the questions raised in precritical investigation. The following discussion indicates some areas in which this advance has taken place.

THE JOHANNINE CORPUS

The superscription to the Fourth Gospel ascribes the work to "John" *(kata Iōannēn)* without further identification. As many as four additional New Testament books have been attributed to this same author, namely, I, II, III John, and Revelation.

Prior to the modern era, "John" was generally identified as John the Apostle, the son of Zebedee. However, none of the above-mentioned writings makes this explicit claim. Such claims arose out of early Christians efforts to establish the authority of certain works by appeal to their apostolic origin (the first Gospel was attributed to Matthew, the Gospel of Mark was said to contain Peter's testimony, and the Pastoral Epistles were written in the name of Paul). These claims arose primarily out of apologetic rather than historical concerns. The great majority of modern interpreters agree that none of the four books attributed to "John" can be traced to John the Apostle. In fact, it now seems clear that no book in the New Testament canon represents the work of one of the original twelve disciples. At the same time, interpreters have pursued a related question, namely: Is the writer of the Fourth Gospel also the author of the book of Revelation or one (or more) of the Epistles?

The book of Revelation identifies its author as "John" (1:1, 4, 9; 22:8). Although claims for common authorship of the Fourth Gospel and Revelation were made as early as the second century, this claim never won universal acceptance. Dionysius of Alexandria (A.D. 190/195-264/265) argued against common authorship.[4] Nevertheless, identity of authorship of the Fourth Gospel and Revelation was

---

[4] Eusebius, *Ecclesiastical History,* VII:25:1-27.

widely accepted until modern times. However, critical scholarship has shown that these works differ radically at two important points, namely, language and thought (eschatology, in particular). The evidence against common authorship for John's Gospel and Revelation is conclusive.

It is impossible to determine the exact relation of the Epistles to the Fourth Gospel. The Gospel and the First Epistle are frequently ascribed to the same author. However, theological differences between the two works seem to support a different conclusion. The Epistles most probably represent the work of a later writer—perhaps even a school of writers—who depended heavily upon the thought of the Fourth Gospel. At any rate, the Epistles—particularly II and III John—do not make an independent theological contribution to the thought of the Johannine corpus. Detailed treatment of these complex issues appear in available literature on the subject.[5] In this discussion, "John" and "Johannine" refer to the Fourth Gospel, unless otherwise indicated. The author of this work seems to have been an unknown Christian who wrote near the close of the first Christian century.

HISTORICAL TRADITION IN THE FOURTH GOSPEL

As was the case with the first three Gospels, problems involving the historical character of the Fourth Gospel have been seriously investigated only since the beginning of the

---

[5] Paul Feine, Johannes Behm, and Werner Georg Kümmel, *Introduction to the New Testament,* trans. A. J. Mattill, Jr. (Nashville: Abingdon Press, 1966); Willi Marxsen, *Introduction to the New Testament,* trans. G. Buswell (Philadelphia: Fortress Press, 1968); R. C. Briggs, "Contemporary Study of the Johannine Epistles," *Review and Expositor,* vol. 68, no. 4 (Autumn 1970), pp. 411-22.

nineteenth century. Prior to that time, the concerns of systematic theology had largely determined the context of biblical interpretation, i.e., biblical texts served as evidence or "proof texts" for theological discussion. Within this frame of reference the distinctive elements of the various Gospel traditions, including their historical character, were largely overlooked.

F. D. E. Schleiermacher's acceptance of the Gospel of John as the basis for the life of Jesus (1819) called attention to the question of history in the Johannine tradition. Although D. F. Strauss rejected Schleiermacher's position at this point, Strauss's understanding of the mythical character of biblical literature also served to sublimate the question of history to other issues. Nevertheless, Strauss contended that the Synoptics stand in closer historical proximity to the actual events of Jesus' life. His comparison of the synoptic and Johannine accounts convinced him that a choice must be made—either John *or* the Synoptics but not a combination of the two—for the life of Jesus. According to Strauss, the Gospel of John represents a later stage of the synoptic tradition when the mythological mentality had come to play a more dominant role (this idea has been shown to be untenable[6]). Although neither Schleiermacher nor Strauss was able to *define* the historical issue in the Fourth Gospel, together they focused attention upon the problem in a manner that could not be forgotten.

F. C. Baur's insights on Paul [7] are more forcefully remembered than his work on the Gospels.[8] However, two aspects of Baur's thought on the Gospels deserve mention. First, he

[6] Cf. pp. 228-29.
[7] Cf. pp. 145-48.
[8] F. C. Baur, *Kritische Untersuchungen über die kanonischen Evangelien, ihr Verhältnis zu einander, ihr Charakter und Ursprung* (Tübingen: L. F. Fues, 1847).

provided substantial support for the superiority of the synoptic tradition. Second, Baur claimed that the writer of the Fourth Gospel was motivated *primarily* by the desire to glorify Jesus, i.e., he did not intend to create a historical account. Baur's recognition of the theological motivation involved in the creation of the Gospels marked a permanent advance in understanding them, even though the implications of this insight have been only recently pursued.

Investigation of the Fourth Gospel during the latter half of the nineteenth century continued largely along the lines laid down by Strauss and Baur. Without recounting the details of the intricate process, it can be said that tentative consensus had been achieved at two points at the close of the century. First, the synoptic tradition—rather than the Fourth Gospel—represents the primary witness to the life of Jesus. Second, the basic interest of the Fourth Gospel focuses upon theology rather than history. H. J. Holtzmann expressed the majority opinion of his time with his claim that the Fourth Gospel is more concerned to teach about history than to serve as a historical document.[9] To be sure, Holtzmann's viewpoint was not universally accepted even in Germany. As late as 1934, F. Büchsel continued to argue for the historical reliability of John's Gospel.[10] From the beginning, the continental viewpoint has found only limited acceptance in Great Britain.[11]

[9] H. J. Holtzmann, *Evangelium des Johannes*, Handkommentar zum Neuen Testament, dritte neubearbeitete Auflage, W. Bauer, ed. (Tübingen: Verlag von J. C. B. Mohr [Paul Siebeck], 1908), p. 2.

[10] F. Büchsel, *Das Evangelium des Johannes*, Das Neue Testament Deutsch IV (Göttingen: Vandenhoeck & Ruprecht, 1934). Büchsel makes the unlikely suggestion that the Apostle's later reflections make the Fourth Gospel superior to the Synoptics which depended on secondary sources.

[11] W. Sanday, *The Criticism of the Fourth Gospel* (New York: Charles Scribner's Sons, 1905).

In spite of the advance indicated in the preceding discussion, twentieth-century scholarship has not entirely abandoned the question of history in the Fourth Gospel. However, advances in critical methodology, coupled with accompanying changes in the general theological climate, have rendered the issue less volatile. Some indication of the nature of these changes may be appropriate here.

First, the attempt to write a life of Jesus—in the sense of a biography—has now been generally abandoned even on the basis of the synoptic tradition.[12] Hence, the earlier alleged historical tension between the synoptic and Johannine traditions has lost much of its importance.

Second, the earlier appraisal of the Synoptic Gospels as nontheological works has been thoroughly revised through the work of redaction criticism.[13]

Third, it follows that the tradition about Jesus did not first assume its theological character at a late stage of its development. Rather, as analysis of the earliest strata of the tradition indicates,[14] theological perspectives played a role in the development of Christian tradition from the beginning. It may even be true that the appearance of Mark's Gospel represents an early attempt to anchor developing theological traditions in history. At any rate, chronological proximity to the earliest events in Christian history—the so-called apostolic period—does not guarantee historical accuracy.

Fourth, progress in critical analysis has focused attention upon the strata of material preserved in the individual Gospels. Consequently, the issue is not so much, "How does John's Gospel as a whole compare with the Synoptics as a source for the life of Jesus?" but rather, "How does John's

[12] Cf. Chapter 9.
[13] Cf. Chapter 5.
[14] Cf. Chapters 3-4.

description of specific events or epochs in Jesus' life—the cleansing of the temple, for example—compare with synoptic reports?" [15]

Fifth, in the light of the foregoing discussion, John's secondary concern with historical facts no longer represents the basis for deprecatory assessment of his work. Recognition of the theological character of all biblical material has opened the way for an appropriate hearing of the Johannine witness!

JOHANNINE SOURCES

As in other biblical material, the question of sources plays an important role in the interpretation of the Gospel of John. If these sources can be defined with a reasonable degree of certainty, they provide a point of departure for discerning the author's theological intention.

Interpreters have encountered continuing problems in their search for the specific sources behind the Fourth Gospel. As has been indicated, the concrete historical occasion for the work cannot be determined. Second, the author has so thoroughly assimilated his sources into his own work that it is extremely difficult to reconstruct their earlier form. Accordingly, the principles of form criticism developed in relation to synoptic research have borne only limited fruit in the Fourth Gospel, i.e., research in John's Gospel does not reveal the "forms" of the earlier tradition as is the case in the Synoptics. Furthermore, there are no written sources available as is the case with Matthew and Luke.

It may be fruitful to indicate some basic issues in Johan-

[15] C. H. Dodd, *Historical Tradition in the Fourth Gospel* (Cambridge: At the University Press, 1963).

nine research in the form of certain questions. Did the Johannine mode of thought arise first in the creation of the Gospel, or can the major Johannine motifs be traced to an earlier epoch in Christian history? In case the latter possibility is true, what can be said regarding the geographical locale in which these motifs arose? Did the Johannine perspective arise in Christian or non-Christian (Hellenistic or Gnostic) circles? Does John's theology reflect a distinctive stance of Christian tradition that developed in relative isolation from other streams of New Testament thought? Partial answers to some of these questions can be sought by reference to the major strata of New Testament thought, particularly those reflected in the Synoptic Gospels and in the letters of the apostle Paul.

The Fourth Gospel and the Synoptics

Parallels between John and the first three Gospels have been used as evidence to support the claim that the Fourth Gospel is directly dependent upon one or more of the Synoptics. This hypothesis must be tested by investigation of the nature and extent of the agreements and disagreements between the respective writings.

The most striking areas of correspondence between the Fourth Gospel and the Synoptics appear in the passion narratives (John 18–19; Mark 14–15; Matt. 26–27; Luke 22–23). Agreements in these accounts suggest a common ancestry. However, this fact does not prove John's literary dependence on the Synoptics. In fact, John's treatment of the material seems to point to another conclusion. To be sure, John does follow an established tradition that doubtless stems from the earliest Christian era. It has been generally assumed

184

that he even possessed a written source.[16] However, John's treatment of the passion material suggests that he depends on a source other than one of the Synoptics. Since the differences between John and the Synoptics do not seem to reflect the distinctive viewpoint of the writer of the Fourth Gospel,[17] it appears that they belong to the tradition which John utilized.[18]

Besides the passion narratives, John and the Synoptics preserve common material at numerous points. Examples of this common material can be seen in the account of healing of the Roman officer's son (John 4:46-54; Matt. 8:51; Luke 7:1-10), the feeding of the five thousand and the subsequent journey across the Sea of Galilee (John 6:1-21; Mark 6:30-52; Luke 9:10-17; Matt. 14:13-33), etc. Some Johannine passages seem to reflect knowledge of events reported in the first three Gospels. For example, John 1:32-33 may indicate acquaintance with the tradition in Mark 1:16-20. Finally, it is significant that John used the form of historical narrative which appeared first in Mark's Gospel. Since John's witness would not have required such a literary form, it seems likely that this choice reflects knowledge of one or more of the Synoptics.

However convincingly the similarities between John and the Synoptics may seem to argue for direct Johannine dependence, this evidence must be evaluated in the light of striking differences. First, contradictions occur between John and the Synoptics which cannot be reconciled historically. The Synoptics locate Jesus' ministry almost exclusively in

---

[16] Rudolf Bultmann, *The Gospel of John,* trans. G. R. Beasley-Murray, General Editor (Philadelphia: The Westminster Press, 1971), p. 637.

[17] *Ibid.,* pp. 642-43.

[18] For a different interpretation of this issue, see C. K. Barrett, *The Gospel According to St. John* (London: S.P.C.K., 1955), p. 431, where the author argues that John is dependent on the Gospel of Mark.

the land of Galilee, but the Fourth Gospel focuses upon Judea. Further, the Fourth Gospel locates the cleansing of the Temple at the beginning of Jesus' ministry—as a kind of prologue—while the Synoptics describe this event as the climax of Jesus' extended conflict with Jewish religious leaders over the Law, a subject to which John makes no allusion. Also, according to the Synoptics, Jesus' last meal with the disciples—a Passover meal—provided the occasion for the institution of the Lord's Supper. In contrast, John makes no mention of the institution of the Supper but describes the last meal as an occasion for Jesus' instruction in humility. (John indicates the date for the last meal *before* the Passover [13:1]. Hence, according to the Fourth Gospel, the last meal was an ordinary meal rather than a Passover meal.) Second, the central subject matter of the Johannine and synoptic traditions differs. The Synoptics describe Jesus' ministry within the structure of baptism, temptation, exorcism, transfiguration, and passion. The Fourth Gospel focuses upon Jesus' extensive christological discourses—in contrast with the synoptic picture of Jesus as a teacher who used the parabolic form of discourse almost exclusively (Mark 4:34)—upon the theme of his mission as Revealer. The first three Gospels do not use the motif of Revealer. The differences between the two traditions are so basic and extensive that a historical comparison between the two traditions is impossible.

Professor Hans Conzelmann has drawn the logical conclusion regarding John's relation to the Synoptics: "No compelling proof has been advanced of literary dependence of John on one of the synoptic gospels." [19] Arguments that John was at least acquainted with one or more of the Synop-

[19] Hans Conzelmann, *An Outline of the Theology of the New Testament,* trans. John Bowden (New York: Harper & Row, 1969), p. 324.

tics do not advance the discussion, since the alleged acquaintance exercised no discernible influence upon the actual composition of John's Gospel, either positively or negatively.[20]

If the Synoptics do not represent literary sources of John's Gospel, the common elements in the two traditions must be explained as the result of contact during the period of oral tradition. Unfortunately, the circumstances under which this contact occurred cannot be determined. It is probable that the distinctive differences which separate Mark from John already existed in their respective sources, since the major motifs of the Fourth Gospel are not to be attributed to the author. This fact suggests that the Johannine perspective and mode of thought arose early in Christian history, possibly even in Palestine.

The Gospel of John and Paul

The effort to define John's relation to Paul raises a different set of questions from those encountered in the first three Gospels. Paul expresses his thought in the literary form of the letter, but John, like the Synoptics, relies upon the historical narrative. While John evidences some concern for the pattern of Jesus' life, Paul makes only scant reference to the events of Jesus' life. Hence, little formal comparison between the material is possible.

The lack of kinship between John and Paul is further confirmed by study of their respective vocabularies. Paul's basic vocabulary is largely missing from the Fourth Gospel, and characteristic Johannine expressions do not appear in Paul's letters. Furthermore, even those terms which occur

[20] It has been suggested that the Fourth Gospel is related to one or more of the Synoptics, either in dependence upon them or as an attempt to correct them. The case has not been proved for either claim.

with some degree of frequency in both John and Paul often connote different theological concepts.

Not only are there differences in vocabulary, but Paul and John also use different categories of thought. The Apostle's emphasis upon the themes of justification, faith, the cross as atoning event, the future dimension of salvation, the function of the Law, and the role of Israel in Christian understanding of history does not occur in John. In contrast, the central Johannine concerns relate to Jesus' mission as Revealer, the crucial importance of faith in appropriating the revelation—Paul understands faith in dialectic tension with works—the present character of judgment and eternal life, and love as the definitive mark of the Christian community. John's identification of the Jews with the unbelieving world hardly leaves room for Paul's treatment of Israel in "salvation-history" (Rom. 9–11). The evidence leads to a firm conclusion: John does not depend upon Paul as a direct source for his Gospel. Furthermore, it can also be said that no other segment of New Testament material represents such a source. Thus, the Fourth Gospel stands alone in the New Testament, i.e., there is no direct dependence upon a single work in the canon.

Development of the Johannine Tradition

In the absence of definable sources of the Fourth Gospel, it is difficult to determine the historical development of the tradition. It once seemed possible to understand John as the culminating point of a process that encompassed total early Christian thought: John allegedly represents the synthesis of the major streams of Christian ideas, particularly the thought of Paul and the Synoptics. Does Professor Kümmel's recent suggestion represent a variation of this idea?

According to Kümmel, Johannine theology stands at the end of a process which incorporates three strata of Christian tradition, namely, the preaching of Jesus, the thought of Paul, and the theology of the Synoptics. To be sure, Kümmel acknowledges that the Fourth Gospel neither reflects the structure of Jesus' preaching nor represents the extension of Paul's theology.[21] Nevertheless, Kümmel defends the claims for "unity in diversity" in the New Testament, claims which he relates to the existence of the canon.[22] However, there are problems which stand in the way of accepting this judgment. First, Kümmel raises the issue of unity in relation to the canon. Quite apart from the external character of this problem, it has not been shown that the idea of unity played any significant role in the rise of the New Testament canon. Second, if the alleged synthesis of the synoptic and Pauline traditions had actually occurred, the final product of the development (John's Gospel) could be expected to preserve formal elements of the Pauline and synoptic traditions. As has been shown, this is not the case.

John's apparent literary independence of other New Testament writings does not imply total lack of contact with these traditions at every stage of their development. Obviously, the Fourth Gospel shares the common Christian confession of Jesus Christ, crucified and exalted. There is even evidence of John's kinship with some elements within the synoptic and Pauline traditions: John preserves limited segments of material that also appear in the Synoptics, and both John and Paul appropriate Hellenistic (Gnostic) motifs. However, this kinship can be explained best by reference to the

[21] W. G. Kümmel, *The Theology of the New Testament*, p. 334.

[22] *Ibid.*, pp. 327-28. Kümmel concludes his discussion of the Synoptics, Paul, and John under the title, "Jesus—Paul—John: The Heart of the New Testament" (p. 327).

189

preliterary stage of the tradition, i.e., prior to the time of Paul's writings or of the creation of the Synoptics.

THE LITERARY STRUCTURE OF THE FOURTH GOSPEL

Failure to recover concrete external sources of the Fourth Gospel has led to the search for internal clues to the author's message and purpose. Because of differences between the literary character of John and the Synoptics,[23] form and source criticism have rendered only limited service in this search. In this respect, Johannine research has often appeared to be a pioneer undertaking. Literary analysis has played an important role in Johannine research, particularly since the close of the First World War.[24]

Rudolf Bultmann contends that understanding John's Gospel depends upon understanding its literary character. He thinks that this understanding depends upon the answer to two primary questions: (1) What is the original form of the Fourth Gospel, i.e., in what order did the responsible author arrange his work? (2) What is the author's relation to his tradition, i.e., to what extent does the Fourth Gospel represent the author's own creation, and to what degree did the writer rework traditional material? [25] Bultmann's precise formulation should not divert attention from the complexity of the problem. A major part of Johannine research in this century has been devoted to these questions.

[23] Cf. pp. 184-87.

[24] Siegfried Schulz, *Untersuchungen zur Menschensohn-Christologie im Johannesevangelium* (Göttingen: Vandenhoeck & Ruprecht, 1957). Schulz lists thirteen methodological approaches to the Fourth Gospel and proposes an additional one! Pp. 81 ff., 94 ff.

[25] Rudolf Bultmann, "Johannesevangelium," *Die Religion in Geschichte und Gegenwart*, 3rd ed., 3. Band (Tübingen: J. C. B. Mohr [Paul Siebeck], 1959), pp. 840 ff.

There is evidence to support the claim that the present literary structure of the Fourth Gospel is secondary, i.e., it represents the work of a later writer who revised the original work. This judgment is based on the fact that numerous sections of the book do not fit readily into a logical or sequential pattern. For example, chapter 21 seems to have been appended to an earlier work which concluded with the author's statement of purpose at 20:31.[26] The unity of the book is further disturbed at numerous other places, including 6:1 which may follow 4:54 instead of chapter 5; 14:51 which seems to point to 18:1 rather than to chapters 15–17, etc. It has been argued that the theory of redaction gives too large an opportunity for the exercise of the interpreter's subjective fancy. While this objection cannot be objectively refuted, it is difficult to overlook the problems raised by discontinuities throughout the book. If the present order of the Fourth Gospel is original, it is difficult to understand the writer's logic. If, on the other hand, the theory of the alleged disruptions can be sustained, the first step in interpretation concerns the reconstruction of the limits of the original work.[27]

Two types of explanations have been offered for the disruptions in the Fourth Gospel. On one hand, it is claimed that the present order of the book arose accidentally, either through displacement of certain leaves at a very early date[28] or by interruption of the author's work of revision, perhaps

[26] This judgment is based upon internal evidence only. No existing manuscript concludes with John 20:31.

[27] Robert Fortna, *The Gospel of Signs: A Reconstruction of the Narrative Source Underlying the Fourth Gospel* (Cambridge: At the University Press, 1970), pp. 221 ff.

[28] These arguments are not based upon the results of text criticism. For example, 4:54–6:1 seems to represent a corruption of the text prior to the date of the earliest extant manuscript.

even by his unexpected death. Such explanations seem reasonable when applied to the major sections of the book (chapters 15–17, for example), but they are not convincing when applied to smaller sections of material (8:42-47; 7:15-24; 6:60-71; etc.). On the other hand, other interpreters attribute discontinuities in the structure of the Gospel to deliberate rearrangement. Bultmann thinks that the deliberate revision can be ascribed to a group within the church which attempted to supplement the author's understanding of eschatology and the sacraments.[29]

Arguments for some kind of revisionary redaction are impressive. However, each specific proposal remains tentative since no conclusive evidence is available. It is not surprising that no single hypothesis has won general acceptance. Concrete evidence concerning the specific sources of the original work could provide a basis for testing these hypotheses. This evidence is extremely elusive.[30]

Investigation of the literary structure of the Fourth Gospel does not exhaust the quest for internal clues to the writer's message and purpose. C. H. Dodd interprets the Fourth Gospel without reference to the redactionary hypothesis, claiming that a unitary thread of argument is discernible in the present order of the book.[31] Siegfried Schulz suggests that the speeches reflect the author's intention most clearly, even though they reflect the general style of Gnostic litera-

[29] Rudolf Bultmann, "Johannesevangelium," *Die Religion in Geschichte und Gegenwart,* 3rd ed., 3. Band, p. 841.

[30] Bultmann thinks the responsible author (the Evangelist) used three definable sources, namely, a miracle source, a speech source, and a narrative account of Passion Week, *ibid.,* p. 842. This suggestion has won only limited approval.

[31] C. H. Dodd, *The Interpretation of the Fourth Gospel* (Cambridge: At the University Press, 1953). Dodd contends that it is "the duty of an interpreter at least to see what can be done with the document as it has come down to us before attempting to improve upon it" (p. 290).

ture.[32] Eduard Schweizer concludes that the writer's message must be discerned by reference to the present work, since his use of his sources has largely obliterated traces of their earlier form.[33] C. K. Barrett points to the writer's concept of the person of Jesus as the clue to that writer's appropriation of his sources.[34]

In spite of the difficulties which such a theory entails, the hypothesis of literary redaction of an earlier work seems to provide the most acceptable explanation of the discontinuities in the structure of the Fourth Gospel. However, this proposal raises an additional question, namely, where is "John's" theology evident? Does Johannine theology refer to the perspective of the original work, to an intermediate stage between the earlier work and the present Gospel, or to the present Gospel? In other words, is the present form of John's Gospel to be understood as a theological entity or as a history of Johannine tradition?

THE RELIGIOUS-HISTORICAL HERITAGE OF JOHN'S GOSPEL

The Fourth Gospel contains striking parallels and similarities with contemporary religious and secular thought. Indeed, more than any other New Testament writing, John's Gospel seems to reflect Hellenistic first-century religious mentality. However, this mentality is the product of an extensive syncretistic process which encompassed numerous cultures over

[32] Siegfried Schulz, *Die Stunde der Botschaft* (Hamburg: Furche Verlag, 1967), p. 314.

[33] Eduard Schweizer, *EGO EIMI* (Göttingen: Vandenhoeck & Ruprecht, 2. Auflage, 1965), p. 108.

[34] C. K. Barrett, *The Gospel According to St. John* (London: S.P.C.K., 1955), pp. 20-21.

a period of half a millennium. Hence, where Johannine kinship with other patterns of thought is evident, it is necessary to determine both the extent of John's dependence and the stage of the process at which John appropriated the material. Here, too, it is important to remember that John is not merely an eclectic redactor of contemporary religious ideas but rather a witness to the significance of Jesus Christ. As the history-of-religions movement discovered, the author's use of sources is more important than the original meaning of the motif.

The Old Testament

The Fourth Gospel cannot be understood in isolation from the language and religious concepts of the Old Testament. Major Old Testament motifs and themes appear throughout John's Gospel. Frequent reference has been made to the similarity between the opening verses of the book of Genesis and the first verse of John's Gospel. It is not surprising, therefore, that the claim has often been made that the author of the Fourth Gospel used the Old Testament as a direct and primary source, either in the form of the Septuagint (the Greek translation of the Old Testament) or the original Hebrew text.[35]

The occurrence of Old Testament expressions and motifs in the Fourth Gospel does not in itself prove that the author directly appropriated this material from the Old Testament. Judaism—the form of Jewish religious life and thought following the destruction of Jerusalem in 587/86 B.C.—created a rich and varied tradition based upon the Old Testament scriptures. This extensive body of material was available to the writer of the Fourth Gospel and serves to explain the

[35] *Ibid.,* p. 25.

appearances of some Old Testament ideas in John's Gospel.
It is noteworthy that John quotes Old Testament texts
less frequently than the Synoptics. While it is conceivable
that John transformed the concrete ideas of the Old Testament into his sophisticated patterns of symbolism, it is more
reasonable to assume that John's structures of thought preserve the results of an extended process of syncretism brought
about by contact with other modes of thought in the Hellenistic world. Certainly, Johannine dualism is largely alien to
the Old Testament. Thus, even though the Johannine tradition cannot be understood apart from the influence of the
Old Testament, it is highly improbable that the author made
direct use of the text of the Old Testament.

Judaism

As has been indicated, Judaism refers to a distinctive
religious movement which has continued as a living religion
until the present time. The complex nature of first-century
Judaism is evidenced by the variety in its life and thought.
Based upon its confession of one God, Judaism rests upon
the canon of the Old Testament, the Synagogue, and rabbinical instruction.[36] The redaction of the extensive body of
rabbinical instruction into literary form was begun near the
turn of the third century A.D.[37] At the time of writing of
John's Gospel, rabbinical instruction was preserved in oral
form.

Professor Dodd has pointed to similarities between rab-

[36] Werner Foerster, *From the Exile to Christ,* trans. Gordon E. Harris
(Philadelphia: Fortress Press, 1964), pp. 1-8.

[37] The initial compilation (the Mishnah) is generally credited to the
Patriarch Judah who died in A.D. 219. Subsequent rabbinical interpretation
of the Mishnah is contained in the Palestinian (fourth century) and
Babylonian (fifth century) Talmuds.

binical literature and John's Gospel at three significant points, namely, with respect to the understanding of the name of God, the Law, and the Messiah.[38] However, Dodd does not argue for exclusive rabbinical influence in the Fourth Gospel, since he also makes room for Johannine dependence upon such diverse sources as Philo of Alexandria and Egyptian secular Hermetic literature.[39] In reply to Dodd's suggestion, Raymond E. Brown has pointed to the problem of dating the material preserved in rabbinical literature.[40] Kümmel draws the appropriate conclusion in his terse statement that "any kind of familiarity with the views of the rabbis nowhere is evident in John." [41]

Recent discoveries have proved the existence of a sectarian Jewish community (Essene) on the northeast side of the Dead Sea. Parts of the library of this community were first recovered in 1947. (This material is described variously as the Qumran Scrolls or the Dead Sea Scrolls.)[42] Extraordinary parallels exist between the Fourth Gospel and the Dead Sea Scrolls, particularly with reference to dualistic modes of thought (light and darkness, truth and falsehood, above and below, etc.). These parallels assume even greater significance when it is noted that these motifs serve to separate John from other New Testament patterns of thought. To be sure, there are fundamental differences between Johannine and Qumran

[38] C. H. Dodd, *The Interpretation of the Fourth Gospel*, pp. 74-96; cf. also, R. H. Lightfoot, *St. John's Gospel* (Oxford: At the Clarendon Press, 1956), p. 48; David Daube, *The New Testament and Rabbinic Judaism* (London: The University of London, The Athlone Press, 1956).

[39] C. H. Dodd, *The Interpretation of the Fourth Gospel*, p. 133.

[40] Raymond E. Brown, *The Gospel According to St. John*, The Anchor Bible (Garden City, N. Y.: Doubleday & Co., 1966), p. LXI.

[41] Paul Feine, Johannes Behm, and W. G. Kümmel, *Introduction to the New Testament*, trans. A. J. Mattill, Jr., p. 155.

[42] Theodor H. Gaster, trans. and ed., *The Dead Sea Scriptures* (Garden City, N. Y.: Doubleday & Co., 1956).

thought. For example, the Fourth Gospel focuses upon Christology, and the Qumran material emphasizes the observance of the Law as the way of salvation. Nevertheless, these two traditions obviously share major religious perspectives. Professor Brown contends strongly for Johannine kinship with Qumran thought. In his words, "What can be said is that for *some* features of Johannine thought and vocabulary the Qumran literature offers a closer parallel than any other contemporary or earlier non-Christian literature either in Judaism or the Hellenistic world." [43] The basis of Brown's claim lies in the fact that both John and Qumran "have capitalized upon relatively insignificant Old Testament terms and have developed them in much the same way." [44] Although the evidence may not provide conclusive proof of John's direct dependence upon Qumran literature, it seems to show that this material brings us within reasonable proximity to the atmosphere and environment in which the Johannine tradition arose. The differences—the Law and Christology as extreme points of contrast—arose out of the differences between Jewish and Christian orientation.

Hellenism

Hellenism is a term whose exact limits are hard to define. In general it designates that pattern of thought and culture that emerged in the ancient world following the era of Alexander the Great (356-323 B.C.) and his immediate successors. As a result of Alexander's conquests, Greek culture and thought dominated the life-style of the subjugated peoples. At the same time, this amalgamation of Western (Greek) and Eastern (Babylonian-Persian) civilization

[43] Raymond E. Brown, *The Gospel According to St. John*, pp. LXIII-LXIV.
[44] *Ibid.*, p. LXIII.

represented something more than mechanical imposition of the Greek way of life upon oriental culture. In fact, the resilience of the oriental spirit—particularly in the realm of religion—led to a dynamic synthesis of Eastern and Western perspectives. To some extent, this resultant synthesis derived its foundation from Greek rational structures and its animating spirit from oriental religion. Many constellations of religious thought emerged out of this synthesis. Gnosticism is the name that is given to one such pattern which exercised widespread influence during the early centuries of Christian history.

Gnosticism

Although it appropriated its ideas from widely divergent sources, Gnosticism possessed a cohesive set of fundamental concepts (world view) which conferred its distinctive character and served to delimit it from other eclectic systems.[45] Representatives of this perspective were known as "Gnostics," a term derived from the Greek work for knowledge (*gnōsis*). *Gnōsis* occupies a position of key importance in all Gnostic systems of thought. It is instructive to note the distinctive Gnostic connotation of the word, namely, knowledge as a form of divine illumination "from above." This knowledge stands in contrast with information derived from the rational process. The idea of salvation also occupied a place of central importance in all Gnostic systems. This salvation —consisting of revealed knowledge and mediated through the revealer-redeemer who came down from above (the other world)—was identified with an elaborate mythological drama which encompassed total creation. Gnostic thought was expressed in the form of a basic dualism—light and

[45] Cf. Hans Jonas, *The Gnostic Religion* (Boston: The Beacon Press, 1958), pp. 3-99.

darkness, spirit and matter, heaven and earth, good and evil=spirit and matter, etc. Since all material existence was understood per se to be evil, this system of thought contained important points of conflict with the Jewish and Christian confession of God as creator (the creation is, therefore, good).

Since Gnosticism arose out of a complicated process of syncretism, it is possible to define the movement in various ways. Contemporary biblical scholarship is divided regarding the exact meaning and use of the term. At what stage of the syncretism is it appropriate to designate an eclectic system "Gnostic"? To what extent is it necessary for the various constellations of religious ideas to be determined by the explicit concept of *Gnōsis?* Since the "normative" concepts of the movement can be defined in different ways, unity of viewpoint is achieved slowly. Until recently the discussion was hindered by the scarcity of primary literary evidence. This difficulty has been alleviated in part by the unexpected recovery of a rich fund of Gnostic Coptic writings in Upper Egypt (1945). This invaluable collection (Nag-Hammadi) contains fragments from more than fifty separate works. Individual writings have already appeared in translation and plans have been announced for further work in the immediate future.[46]

Rudolf Bultmann has contended for half a century that John's religious heritage is to be traced to the realm of Gnostic thought. He first called attention to impressive parallels between John's mode of thought and that of Mandaean literature. However, this literature is to be dated no

---

[46] Cf. Jean Doresse, *The Secret Books of the Egyptian Gnostics,* trans. Philip Mairet (London: Hollis & Carter, 1960), for a general description of this literature. E. J. Brill (Leiden) has announced the publication of the facsimile edition of this body of material in the near future.

earlier than the beginning of the seventh century A.D. Bultmann solves this problem by claiming that Mandaean texts
preserve a tradition which existed even prior to the first
century A.D.[47] The validity of this thesis regarding Johannine
origins depends upon the acceptance of the claim regarding
the age of Mandaean tradition. Professor Dodd has noted
parallels between Gnostic Egyptian Hermetic (secular)
literature. However, he thinks that both John and the Hermetic authors derived their material from a common earlier
source.[48] Further testimony can be adduced regarding the
kinship of John with Gnosticism. However, the exact character of John's dependence is problematical since so-called
"gnostic" ideas appear in many contexts, including Jewish
and Christian thought.

Gnostic Judaism

The attempt to describe the first-century situation by reference to "Jewish" and "Gnostic" categories as isolated and
independent systems of thought is clearly inadequate. While
such categories do serve to designate basic distinctions—cos-
mology, anthropology, etc.—they often represent unrealistic
abstractions from the actual situation during the first century.
As has been indicated, the world view of the first century
Graeco-Roman culture arose out of a complex eclectic process
which encompassed both Western and oriental cultures. In
spite of attempts to isolate Jewish life and thought from the
influence of this pervasive "spirit of the times," Judaism, too,

[47] Rudolf Bultmann, "Johannesevangelium," *Die Religion in Geschichte
und Gegenwart*, 3rd ed., 3. Band, pp. 846-47; *idem, Theology of the New
Testament*, II. Bultmann describes the background of the Johannine tradition as "oriental Christianity" which is represented by Syrian gnosticizing
Christianity.
[48] C. H. Dodd, *The Interpretation of the Fourth Gospel*, pp. 10-53.

assimilated significant elements of this syncretistic Hellenistic perspective. Strains of Judaism which reflect such Hellenistic influence are called "Hellenistic" or "Gnostic" Judaism. The writings of Philo of Alexandria, the Jewish apologists, and Jewish-Alexandrian philosophers in general represent well-known examples of Jewish religious thought that accommodated its concepts to the pattern of contemporary understanding.

C. K. Barrett suggests that, "The most illuminating background of the Fourth gospel is that of Hellenistic Judaism." [49] While it is easy to agree with Barrett's conclusion, it leaves the issue unresolved, since both "Hellenism" and "Judaism" require further definition. One minimum requirement for this further definition has to do with the recognition that the Hellenistic Judaism with which John's Gospel is related reflects basic ingredients of the Gnostic perspective. At what stage of the Johannine tradition are we to assume the entrance of this Gnostic perspective? Does the author introduce it, i.e., does he "gnosticize" the tradition, or does the Gnostic orientation belong to an earlier stage of the Johannine tradition? If the latter possibility is true, it may be that the author exercised a restraining influence upon the gnosticizing tendency in the tradition by introducing the historical emphasis represented by the historical form of narrative.

THE JOHANNINE INTENTION

Greater certainty concerning the historical situation for which John's Gospel was originally intended would shed further light upon the author's motivation for composing his work. However, in the absence of this information, the con-

[49] C. K. Barrett, *The Gospel According to St. John*, p. 33.

tent and structure of the book seem to supply some clues to the author's interests and concerns, particularly with reference to his dominant purpose.[50]

The Theological Focus of John's Gospel

Christology (teaching about the person and work of Jesus) occupies a place of primary importance in John's Gospel. The author reveals his interest in this subject in various ways. First, the christological theme dominates the first chapter of the Gospel. The prologue to the book (vss. 1-18) presents Jesus as the Word (*logos*) who reveals the Father (vs. 18). The major christological titles that subsequently appear in the book provide the framework for the remaining verses of chapter one: Jesus is Son of God (vs. 34), Lamb of God (vs. 36), Messiah (vs. 41), and Son of Man (vs. 51). It is hardly accidental that the author begins his work by utilizing this fund of titles for Jesus. Also, the writer's use of the "I am" sayings at important junctures in his work (4:25; 6:35; 11:25; etc.) further indicates his concern with the subject of Christology. Second, John concludes his work with a clear indication of his purpose for writing: "In order that you may believe that Jesus is the Christ, the Son of God" (20:31). Third, the distinctive sections of the book—the so-called "discourses"—develop the christological theme in various ways. Finally, the structure of the entire work appears to express the christological emphasis: Jesus is the Revealer who discloses the "glory" (*doxa*) of the Father to the world (chapters 1–12) and to the disciples (chapters 13–20).

---

[50] Hans Conzelmann, *An Outline of the Theology of the New Testament*, p. 322; Rudolf Schnackenburg, *New Testament Theology Today*, trans. David Askew (London: Geoffrey Chapman, 1963), p. 92.

Although the writer of the Fourth Gospel concentrates attention upon the person and work of Jesus, he does not deal with this subject in isolation from the total life of the Christian community. The distinctive Johannine understanding of eschatology, the church, salvation, and the Holy Spirit contributes to the permanent enrichment of Christian thought.[51]

John's Historical Purpose

According to the author, the Fourth Gospel was written, "that you may believe that Jesus is the Christ, the Son of God, and that believing you may have life in his name" (20: 31). To whom were these words addressed? As has been shown, no final answer to this question has been achieved. The general religious and cultural setting of the first century[52] provides a point of contact for answering the question. Within this broad frame of reference, the writer's major emphases supply additional hints regarding the original recipients.

One basis for discovering the intention of the Fourth Gospel has to do with the readers' relation to the Christian faith, i.e., are they believers or unbelievers? [53] If the recipi-

---

[51] C. K. Barrett, *The Gospel According to St. John,* pp. 56-82. Rudolf Schnackenburg, *The Gospel According to St. John,* trans. Kevin Smyth (New York: Herder and Herder, 1968), I, 153-64; Raymond E. Brown, *The Gospel According to St. John.* Brown omits discussion of the subject of Christology. According to Brown, the Johannine emphasis falls upon ecclesiology, sacraments, eschatology, and wisdom (pp. CV-CXXVIII).

[52] Cf. pp. 193-201.

[53] Perhaps an inordinate amount of energy has been expended in the attempt to answer this question solely by reference to the tense of the Greek verb (*pisteuō*) in 20:31. There are numerous difficulties involved in this procedure. First, there is uncertainty concerning the text. If *pisteusēte* (aorist tense) is read, it may suggest that the readers are unbelievers, i.e., *pisteusēte* means to come to belief. If on the other hand, *pisteuēte* (present tense) is read, it can be argued that the readers are

ents are members of the believing community, is the writer concerned to correct erroneous (Jewish or Gnostic?) teaching, or does he hope to stimulate them to greater appropriation of the content of their confession? If, on the other hand, the author addresses unbelievers (Jews or Gnostics?), is his purpose primarily apologetic or evangelistic?

C. H. Dodd argues for the missionary character of the Fourth Gospel. He contends that the writer directs his message to the non-Christian Hellenistic public whose religious perspective is expressed in the Egyptian Hermetic writings. Dodd thinks that similarities of language and thought between John and Hermetic literature show that the Fourth Gospel could have been understood in Egyptian secular circles (or Hellenistic circles in general) even though there had been no previous contact with Christian preaching.[54] While Dodd can point to genuine similarities between John and Hermetic material, these likenesses probably prove nothing more than the syncretistic character of both writings. Furthermore, it is strange that the Fourth Gospel contains no trace of Christian structures of apologetic (cf. Acts 18: 22-31, as an example) with reference to the existence of one God. Other interpreters claim that John's appeal is addressed to unbelieving Jews, perhaps to those who face discouragement and disillusionment following the fall of Jerusalem in A.D. 70.[55] However, it has yet to be shown that significant segments of Jewish people responded to the loss of Jerusalem in this way. Rather, Matthew's Gospel may reflect harden-

---

believers, i.e., *pisteuēte* means to go on believing. Aside from uncertainty regarding the text, it is unwise to allow the author's use of a single word to determine the understanding of the entire book. Also, this approach gives too limited attention to the plan and structure of the entire book.

[54] C. H. Dodd, *The Interpretation of the Fourth Gospel*, pp. 8, 53.

[55] T. C. Smith, *Jesus in the Gospel of John* (Nashville, Tennessee: Broadman Press, 1959).

ing lines of theological opposition between Jews and Christians.

There are undeniable polemical tones in John's Gospel. As early as the second Christian century, Irenaeus claimed that the Fourth Gospel was written to refute the claims of Cerinthus, the Gnostic. Since the close of the nineteenth century, many interpreters have accepted Baldensperger's thesis that the references to John the Baptist represent the clue to the intention of John's Gospel. According to Baldensperger, the author seeks to refute the claims of those who confessed John the Baptist—not Jesus—as the Messiah.[56] Adherents to the Jewish thesis point to John's frequent polemic against the "Jews," the unbelieving opponents (the world) of Jesus (5:16; 7:1; 10:31; 19:7). These opponents are allegedly opponents of the church in John's day whose religious profile is read back into Jesus' situation.

Despite indications of missionary and polemical inclinations in the Fourth Gospel, the work is best understood as hortatory edification to the Christian community. Two considerations give substance to this viewpoint. First, a significant proportion of the material in the book is clearly addressed to believers, particularly chapters 13–17. Second, polemical and missionary interests seem to have played no significant role in determining the structure of the book.[57] The author of the Fourth Gospel assumes the existential stance of the believer—in need, or perhaps in search, of understanding—as the point of contact for his message. His

[56] W. Baldensperger, *Der Prolog des Vierten Evangeliums: Sein polemisch-apologetischer Zweck* (Tübingen: J. C. B. Mohr [Paul Siebeck], 1898). Cf. also, Robert M. Grant, *A Historical Introduction to the New Testament* (New York: Harper & Row, 1963), pp. 152-53.

[57] Hans Conzelmann, *An Outline of the Theology of the New Testament,* p. 332.

work represents a confessional explication of the Christian viewpoint that is designed to "encourage the faith of specific Christians and to strengthen it through polemic defense." [58]

CONCLUSION

The goals of biblical research—the illumination of the biblical message through the application of historical-critical principles of investigation—have been only partially achieved with reference to the Fourth Gospel. Indeed, one consequence of the labor is to be seen in the unusual number of questions that have been raised for which no satisfactory answer has been found. To this extent, the fruits of labor thus far expended may appear unusually limited. However, even unanswered questions can serve to identify areas of primary importance. One significant contribution of research in the Fourth Gospel arises out of its work in clarifying the alternatives that are open to the interpreter.

Historical-critical study has contributed to better understanding of the Fourth Gospel by defining the scope of certain historical issues regarding the origin of this Gospel. In the first place, it now appears that the immediate sources of John's Gospel lie outside the limits of the New Testament canon. This conclusion does not mean that John is totally unrelated to other strata of New Testament tradition. At the same time, this conclusion does set definite limits for earlier claims that the Fourth Gospel represents a redaction of other strata of New Testament tradition, particularly the streams represented by Paul or the Synoptics. Second, in comparison with other New Testament writings, John reflects peculiar

[58] Paul Feine, Johannes Behm, and W. G. Kümmel, *Introduction to the New Testament,* p. 163.

affinity with first-century syncretistic thought in general. The work of identifying the concrete expression of this thought to which John is most closely related has not been accomplished. The task has been undertaken with renewed vigor in the light of new information provided by the Qumran Scrolls and the Nag-Hammadi literature. The extent to which religious-historical perspectives have played a role in influencing Johannine interpretation is reflected by the fact that every major proposal for understanding John's Gospel in this century has been based upon an option derived from the study of the religious-cultural milieu of the era in which John appeared.[59]

Both the achievements and the failures of historical research in John's Gospel point toward the nature of further investigation. For as Professor Kümmel has aptly pointed out, "There is no other access to the understanding of the New Testament writings than the method of historical research." [60]

Books for Additional Reading

1. Raymond E. Brown, *The Gospel According to John* (I–XII), The Anchor Bible (Garden City, N. Y.: Doubleday & Co., 1966), pp. XXI-CXLVI.
2. Ernst Käsemann, *The Testament of Jesus,* trans. Gerhard Krodel (Philadelphia: Fortress Press, 1968).

[59] Paolo Ricca, *Die Eschatologie des Vierten Evangeliums* (Zürich und Frankfurt a.M.: Gotthelf-Verlag, 1966), p. 10.
[60] W. G. Kümmel, *The Theology of the New Testament,* p. 18.

8

The Bible:
The Problem of the Canon

Christians universally recognize the importance of the Bible for their life and thought. However, they have encountered difficult and perplexing problems in their efforts to define the proper function of the Bible in Christian life and experience. There are tensions, perhaps even contradictions, in biblical interpretations. Certain groups insist that statements in the Bible are to be accepted literally as binding regulations for Christian thought and practice. Other equally thoughtful and sincere Christians interpret biblical assertions as religious confessions to be understood in the light of the religious and historical factors that produced them. Also, claims for the normative role of the Bible in Christian life and thought often violate biblical assumptions. For instance, references to the Bible as the *sole* and *final* norm for the church frequently overlook the biblical confession that Jesus Christ alone is Lord (Acts 4:12).

Christian reflection upon the meaning of the Bible for the continuing life and thought of the church has focused attention upon two major concepts: canon and authority. An adequate description of the role of the Bible in the life and thought of the church must be based upon a clear understanding of the issues involved in defining these two concepts.

SCRIPTURE AND THE CANON

Christians have coined numerous terms to express their understanding of the nature of the Bible. Confusion concerning the function of the Bible in the life of the church often arises out of the failure to maintain adequate distinctions in the meaning of these terms. Christians frequently refer to the sixty-six books to which they have ascribed special importance as the "Bible" or as "scripture." "Bible" and "scripture" are frequently used in general discussion as interchangeable and synonymous expressions. Obviously, there are many circumstances in which either term may be appropriately used. Nevertheless, there are significant differences in the concepts of "Bible" and "scripture."

When the Genesis–Revelation collection is described as the "Bible," the individual books in this collection are assumed to be related to one another as parts of a larger unity, i.e., one book. The technical term "canon" suggests this idea. Canon (Greek, *kanon,* meaning standard, rule, or guide) indicates that the church has selected these sixty-six books as the norm for its life and thought. By separating these works from a more inclusive body of Jewish and Christian literature, the church has ascribed peculiar authority to them.

The term "scripture" (Greek, *graphē,* meaning written material) simply refers to biblical literature. In its broadest sense it means religious literature used in the life of the religious community. In the New Testament it refers to all Jewish religious literature (cf. Matt. 21:42; Luke 24:27; II Tim. 3:16; etc.). These and other New Testament references include the so-called Apocrypha and Pseudepigrapha, works which are not classified under the categories of the Law, the Prophets, or the Writings. Later, Christian literature was described also as scripture. Thus, scripture is religious literature that has proved its value for the religious community, without reference to official pronouncements of the church concerning its authority.

Prior to the middle of the second century, perhaps even later, Christians interpreted the function of their religious literature primarily in terms of scripture, a concept inherited from Jewish thought. Since the close of the fourth century (the era in which Christians reached limited agreement concerning a canon of sixty-six books) the dominant emphasis has been placed upon the concept of canon. Either term may be applied appropriately to the Genesis–Revelation collection. However, each term interprets the function of this collection from its own distinctive standpoint. Consequently, consistency is required in interpreting the implications of each perspective, particularly where the question of authority is involved. For example, reference to biblical material as a part of the "canon" indirectly calls attention to the authority of the church which created it. When the same material is described as "scripture," there is an indirect claim for the authority of its testimony to truth. This is the meaning of Luther's emphasis upon the principle of *sola scriptura* (scripture alone), even though he was hesitant to include the Letter of James in the New Testament canon. Thus, the authority of the canon is based upon the correctness of the church's judgment in creating it, but the authority of scripture arises out of its testimony to Christian truth. The discussion in this chapter is concerned with the authority of biblical literature understood from its presence in the canon. Chapter 11 is more directly concerned with the subject of biblical literature understood as scripture.

Since the church possesses its scripture in the form of the canon, it is impossible to define the function of biblical literature in isolation from the question of the canon. Luther has aptly said that the canon is the cradle in which the church receives its scripture.

The existence of the biblical canon raises historical questions since the canon arose as the result of historical decisions on the part of the church. In fact, the church must continue to make historical decisions to receive its scripture in the form of the canon. The recognition of the historical character of the canon does not mean that it can be understood from the historical standpoint only. The church's judgment was also influenced by elements of its own experience and faith. Nevertheless, the church acted in history and was influenced by historical factors in making its decisions. The historical character of the canon, therefore, provides one point of departure for the investigation of its meaning.

THE GOSPEL IN THE EARLY CHURCH

Oral Proclamation and the Appearance of Literary Material

The Bible is a collection of books which were brought together for the purpose of preserving a valid witness to Jesus Christ. Since Christians discerned a unity between their own experience and that of their Jewish ancestors in the faith, the Old Testament was understood to contain an indirect witness to their Lord. Indeed, the life of Jesus was interpreted in retrospect through the testimony of many parts of the Old Testament. Presently, the church has access to the life-death-resurrection-exaltation event of Jesus Christ through the written records which bear testimony to the event.

The church's dependence upon the written form of the tradition about Jesus is somewhat paradoxical and sometimes contributes to a misunderstanding of the nature of the Christian gospel. Clearly, Jesus did not write a single word in the Bible. There is no indication that he instructed his disciples to preserve a written record of his teaching. Indeed, Jesus seems to have rejected current scribal tradition which was understood as the final norm for interpreting the will of God. Rather, his preaching was based on the conviction that God was present and active in the world. He persistently urged his hearers to respond to God who had drawn near in mercy and grace.

The emphasis upon the Word of God as direct personal address was later reflected in the activities of Jesus' disciples. Insofar as can be determined, no book in the New Testament can be attributed to one of the original disciples. When Christians later composed literary works they did not attempt to create a stenographic account of Jesus' words and deeds.

212

Quite to the contrary, they exercised great freedom in altering the form of the tradition which they possessed.

There is evidence that the preference for the oral proclamation of the gospel continued even into the second century. According to the word of Papias, a Christian who lived in the first half of the second century, the "living voice" was preferred over written tradition. It appears that Papias even depreciated the authority of the written word.[1] To be sure, circumstances later made it necessary to preserve written records for the instruction of the church. However, the modern inclination to ascribe final authority to the letter of the written word must be evaluated in the light of the original proclamation of the gospel in oral form.

Paul's letters, composed between A.D. 50 and 55, marked the initial transition from the oral to the literary medium for the spread of the gospel. However, their literary form did not establish their authority in the church. Paul emphasized his desire to preach to the church at Rome (Rom. 1:14-15), even though he was sending an extensive literary work to them. His letters seem to have exercised only limited influence upon the total life of the church for almost four decades after his death. It is also interesting to note that the early leaders of the church in Jerusalem failed to contribute a single book to the canon of the New Testament.

With the exception of Paul's letters and the Gospel of Mark, the books of the New Testament seem to have appeared after the year A.D. 80. The majority of the remaining books in the New Testament were probably written between A.D. 80 and 100. The conditions which prompted this sudden increase in literary activity cannot be described with certainty. It has been suggested that literary activity was stimulated by the desire to provide accurate information concerning

[1] Eusebius, *The Ecclesiastical History*, III:39:4.

Christian origins for succeeding generations. This suggestion represents at best only a partial explanation. It was perhaps to be expected that developing Christian thought would find expression in the precise forms of literary material.

The terminal date for the appearance of New Testament literature cannot be determined with accuracy. Probably a number of books were written between A.D. 100 and 140 (I and II Tim., II Peter, II and III John). Thus, the total material contained in the New Testament canon probably appeared before the middle of the second century.

Norms for Guidance in the Early Church

The earliest Christians did not possess a single fixed collection of literary material to serve as a guide for their life and thought. This indefinite state of affairs created problems that later led to the creation of the canon. In the absence of a specific norm to which they could appeal, various kinds of material were used for guidance and instruction.

Jewish religious literature provided the most accessible source of instruction for the early Christian community. Major collections of this literature circulated in the first century under the titles of the Law, the Prophets, and the Writings. These collections later constituted the Old Testament canon. A second body of literature, the Apocrypha, was also widely used in early Christian circles. By definition, the Apocrypha refer to the books which were present in the Septuagint (a Greek translation of the Hebrew scriptures which was begun in the third century B.C.) but which were not included in the Hebrew canon. Thus, the term represents a Christian rather than a Jewish designation. The status of these twelve books has never been decided with finality in the Christian church. Jerome, who translated the scriptures into Latin (the Vulgate) about A.D. 400, suggested that the canon of the Old Testament should be limited to the thirty-nine books accepted by the Jewish community. His opinion did not prevail in the church as a whole. Luther later separated these works from the Hebrew canon and placed them in a group between the Old and New Testaments. A third body of Jewish religious literature, generally designated as the Pseudepigrapha (pseudonymous writings, or works composed under an assumed name) was also read by early Christians. The name is not an accurate description of the nature of the material, but it has come to be used widely. It refers to Jewish religious literature which is not included either in the Hebrew canon or in the Apocrypha. This extensive mass of material had no specific limits and appeared in various forms among the scattered Jewish communities. Thus, early Christians utilized the Jewish religious material contained in the Hebrew canon, in the Apocrypha, and in the Pseudepigrapha as sources of guidance and instruction. Quotations and references to all three groups appear in the New Testament.

The words of Jesus soon came to constitute a second source of guidance for early Christians. However, since the presence of the Spirit was understood as the continuing presence of Jesus, no rigid distinction was made between the words of the historical Jesus and the words of the Spirit. For example, Paul based his preaching primarily upon his relationship to the resurrected-exalted Lord rather than upon the tradition of the historical Jesus. This tradition of Jesus' words later provided an important source for the authors of the Gospels.

The sayings of the apostles constituted a third source of guidance for the church, especially after the last quarter of of the first century. James, the half brother of Jesus, soon rose to a position of leadership in the Jerusalem church. It is

215

not clear that he was looked upon primarily as an apostle. The apostles in Jerusalem were also recognized as leaders with special authority which was based upon their intimate relationship with Jesus. Paul's claim to be heard was often based upon his position as a "called" apostle of Jesus Christ (Rom. 1:1; I Cor. 1:1; etc.). This deference to the authority of the apostles later constituted one standard for distinguishing false from authentic tradition.

Finally, the early church also appealed to the living word of the Holy Spirit as a source of immediate and direct guidance. The apostle Paul justified his position before the church in Corinth on this basis (II Cor. 2:10). The pronouncements of a specific class of preachers, the prophets (I Cor. 12:28), were understood to possess peculiar authority. However, it proved impossible in actual practice to make adequate distinctions between the message of certain ecstatic enthusiasts (who appealed to the Holy Spirit for the authentication of their message) and the message of Paul. These excesses perhaps explain why the office of prophet was not perpetuated in the life of the church.

Thus, the early church possessed no single objective norm of guidance for its life and thought. The road leading to the recognition of such a norm (the canon) involved an extended and complicated journey. Nevertheless, in the initial phases of that journey a subtle shift in the concept of authority for the church had already begun to take place.

THE DEVELOPMENT OF THE CANON

The historical process by which the biblical canon was created continued more than two centuries after the last book appeared. The Old Testament canon was determined by Jewish rabbis somewhere near the close of the first century

A.D. It was later accepted by Christians. The formation of the New Testament canon was completed in the last half of the fourth century. The following discussion relates primarily to the formation of the canon of the New Testament, but the meaning of the biblical canon also involves the question of the Old Testament.

There is a distinction between the meaning of collection and canon insofar as the problem of authority is concerned. Various collections of Jewish literature (the Law, the Prophets, and the Writings) existed at the time of Jesus' birth. Likewise, Paul's letters seem to have been collected near the close of the first century. However, neither group possessed canonical status: there was no canon of Jewish religious literature in Jesus' lifetime, and Paul's letters were not understood as a canon at the close of the first century. Canon refers to a limited body of material; it represents the exclusive literary norm for the life of the community.

It is impossible to determine an exact date when the idea of canon was first applied to New Testament literature. There were elements of ambiguity involved in the attitude of early Christians toward their literature which make it difficult to discover a clear concept of canon prior to the middle of the second century. It is possible that the idea of a New Testament canon did not clearly emerge until after A.D. 140. This is not to suggest that there were no collections of Christian literature prior to that date. There are references in the apostolic fathers[2] which indicate that the Gospels and Paul's letters were circulated widely in the early part of the second century. There were also frequent references to I Clement

[2] No absolute agreement exists on the exact scope of this literature, but the following books are generally included: Barnabas, the Shepherd of Hermas, two letters of Clement of Rome (the second letter is pseudonymous), the letters of Ignatius of Antioch, the letter of Polycarp, and the Didache or Teaching of the Twelve Apostles.

and The Shepherd of Hermas. Nevertheless, the evidence seems to indicate that the church did not understand these collections as a canon prior to Marcion's creation of his own canon (ca. A.D. 140).

The century following A.D. 150 was decisive for the development of the New Testament canon. A quarter of a century after the time of Marcion, in the time of Irenaeus, the idea of a canon was widely accepted. Irenaeus included thirteen epistles attributed to Paul, Acts, I Peter, and I and II John in his list of acceptable works. He referred to III John, II Peter, James, and Jude as disputed works. The Shepherd of Hermas and the Didache were valued highly, but they were not included in his list of acceptable books. This list corresponds closely to other lists which appeared in the middle of the third century, seventy-five years after Irenaeus' reference to them. From the time of Irenaeus onward, the concept of a limited canon was firmly established. After that period the basic problem concerning the canon related to the distinction between disputed and undisputed books.

The process through which specific books were accepted as a part of the canon continued until the middle of the fourth century. Although no date can be specified to indicate the precise conclusion of the process, the year A.D. 367 is often suggested. In that year, Athanasius, the controversial bishop of Alexandria, wrote his Easter letter to the churches in which he listed sixty-six books which were acceptable. This list is identical with the present biblical canon. Athanasius could lay no claim to universal authority, but his judgment was accepted by various councils of the church within the following half century. However, various groups of Christians (Syrian, Orthodox, and Roman Catholic) have continued to use different canons.

THE NATURE AND AUTHORITY OF THE CANON

Historical factors played a role in determining the limits of the canon. This fact does not mean that all questions relating to the nature and authority of the canon can be answered exclusively from the standpoint of history, but it does mean that it is possible to identify one dimension of the problem. It establishes a limit for certain other exclusive claims that have been suggested. For example, it is impossible to attribute the creation of the canon to the work of the Holy Spirit solely. Such an explanation would exclude historical considerations in principle. Without judging beforehand that the work of the Holy Spirit is to be excluded as a possible basis for explaining the rise of the canon, it is nevertheless legitimate to examine the process for its historical dimensions and their implications for the nature and authority of the canon.

The canonization of specific books to the exclusion of other books raises a twofold claim for canonical literature: it is limited, and it is authoritative. The justification of these claims represents a difficult undertaking. In the first place, the canon expresses the judgment of the church, indeed, it expresses the *historical* judgment of the church. The historical character of the church's judgment raises troublesome questions since all historical judgments are conditioned by the circumstances in which they are rendered. Secondly, it has been impossible to discover a single principle which the church applied consciously and consistently in the creation of the canon. First-century Christians did not sense the need for a canon. The awareness of this need arose first in the second century in connection with the Gnostic controversy. The canon represents historical decisions made by the church in diverse situations. Consequently, the authority of the canon

219

is dependent upon the validity of the church's decision. Various arguments have been used to support such authority.

The early church justified the inclusion of many books in the canon by reference to their apostolic character (derived from or written by an apostle). This standard of judgment represented an effort to distinguish between valid and illegitimate interpretations of the gospel. The argument was often used for works which had proved their value on other grounds (the Epistle to the Hebrews, the Gospel of Mark, and the Gospel of John are notable examples). It was convincing in the context in which it was originally used. However, it is no longer convincing for the following reasons: (1) Modern research has shown that many books which were written in the name of an apostle are pseudonymous. The Pastoral Epistles, Ephesians, and II Peter represent clear examples of this practice. This discovery does not invalidate the message of these books, but it does nullify the early church's argument for including them in the canon. (2) The claim of apostolic authority was based in part upon the assumption that the author's temporal proximity to Jesus constituted a basis for the authenticity of his work. The church did not consistently follow the implications of this assumption. It included works written in the second century, while it excluded others that appeared in the first century (II Peter, ca. A.D. 125, was included, but I Clement, ca. A.D. 95, was excluded). (3) The term "apostle" in the New Testament is ambiguous. The author of Acts and Paul understood the term from different points of view. In fact, there is no singular concept of apostleship which occurs throughout the New Testament. The attempt to establish the authority of the canon upon the basis of its apostolic authorship is unjustified, perhaps even misleading.

The attempt has been made to justify the authority of the

canon upon the basis of its unity. Clearly, unity can be defined from many viewpoints, a fact which explains the rise of numerous proposals. The attempt to establish the authority of the canon upon the basis of its unity has been beset by two major problems. First, it is impossible to discover a definable unity in the teaching of the New Testament. James and Romans, Matthew and John, Acts and Galatians contain differences that cannot be reconciled at the level of historical interpretation, i.e., with respect to the message conveyed to the original recipients of the letters. It is generally conceded that the New Testament contains a multiplicity of theological viewpoints, such as the theology of Paul, the theology of Luke, and the theology of John. Secondly, there is no evidence that the concept of unity played a significant role in the thought of the church which created the canon. Christian literature during the first four centuries is significantly silent at this point. The question of unity can be pursued more appropriately with respect to the meaning of scripture than with regard to the meaning of canon (cf. Chapter 11).

The claim for the authority of the canon as canon is grounded in the authority of the church. However, since the judgment of the church was influenced by historical factors, the claim for the final authority of the canon tends to absolutize the tentative judgment of the church. Also, the authority of the canon cannot be based upon an appeal to the deliberate purpose of the church, since no single standard—historical or theological—was applied in the creation of the canon. However, in spite of the ambiguous motivations that stimulated the church to create the canon, its limits have been defined. General agreement concerning the idea and limits of the canon has existed in the church since the fourth or fifth century. The issue at the present time focuses upon the meaning rather than upon the fact or the limits of the canon.

The conclusions suggested above raise significant questions: (1) Should the canon be rejected, i.e., does it represent a mistake at best and deception at worst? (2) Is the value of the canon at present dependent upon the church's ability to provide logical justification for creating it? (3) Must the meaning and authority of the canon be expressed in the same terms in the twentieth century as in the fourth? (4) Does the correction of the church's defense of the canon invalidate its creation? In my judgment a negative answer to each of the foregoing questions is justifiable. However, the scope of these answers precludes adequate discussion in this work. The historical character of the church's judgment, a judgment whose validity is not dependent upon infallibility, may render a clue.

SCRIPTURE AND TRADITION

The Protestant Reformation framed the question of the authority of biblical literature and its relationship to the extra-biblical tradition of the church. Luther's pronouncements were based upon the concept of scripture rather than canon, i.e., *sola scriptura* rather than *sola regula* (cf. the earlier discussion in this chapter of "scripture" and "canon"). Nevertheless, subsequent discussion of the question has often been encumbered by ambiguity regarding the concepts of scripture and canon and the concept of tradition. The continuing debate between Protestants and Catholics concerning the relative authority of scripture and tradition is well known.

In the broadest sense of the term, tradition refers to information "received from" previous generations. For example, early Christian tradition about Jesus was incorporated in the Gospels as well as in other New Testament literature (cf. I Cor. 15:3). Tradition may be preserved either in oral or written form. Christian tradition includes the total testimony which points toward and interprets the life-death-resurrection-exaltation of Jesus Christ.

In the discussion since the Reformation, tradition has often been identified with Christian testimony outside the biblical canon. Consequently, the discussion concerning scripture and tradition has been understood largely in terms of the authority of canonical material over extra-canonical tradition. However, as Catholic interpreters have rightly insisted, scripture, too, is Christian tradition. The canon contains a part of Christian tradition which has been collected by the church and accorded a position of authority over other Christian tradition. The Gospel of Mark can properly be described as scripture, as a part of the canon, or as Christian tradition. Thus, when scripture and canon are understood as synonymous concepts, the discussion concerning the authority of scripture over tradition becomes involved in overwhelming ambiguities.

The Protestant contention for the superiority of scripture over tradition (*sola scriptura*) calls attention to an important aspect of the nature of scripture. It asserts that the function of scripture is fulfilled in bearing testimony to the meaning of Jesus Christ. Protestants reject as a misunderstanding of the nature of scripture the Catholic contention that the meaning of scripture must be discerned through reference to extra-biblical tradition. A twofold perspective arises out of this stance. First, the question of the relative authority of biblical material over tradition deals with the function of biblical material as scripture rather than with its presence in the canon. Understood as scripture, the authority of biblical material is based upon its valid testimony to Jesus Christ.

223

Understood as canon, the authority of biblical material is grounded in the validity of the church's judgment in including it in the canon. Secondly, extra-biblical tradition is to be accorded its rightful place in the total body of Christian tradition, including biblical tradition. Like biblical tradition, it is to be heard on the basis of its own testimony. Like scripture, its testimony, too, is to be understood within the context provided by the total Christian testimony to Jesus Christ. Thus, the principle of *sola scriptura* understands scripture as testimony rather than as material whose authority is grounded in the decision of the church.[3]

THE LIMITS OF THE CANON

The recognition of the historical character of the canon raises a question concerning the validity of the traditional limits of the canon. The *early* church created the canon; should the *contemporary* church reconsider the validity of the early church's action?

It can scarcely be denied that the demand for the revision of the canon appeals to consistent logic for support. Certainly, the early church possessed no inherent authority that can be legitimately denied to the contemporary church.

Practical reasons can also be given for the revision of the canon. The Bible contains passages that do not express the judgment of Christian conscience. Indeed, in some instances they are repulsive to the sensitive Christian conscience. Certain sections in the Old Testament identify God's will with murder, plunder, and the subjection of innocent victims to numerous indecencies. Paul's estimate of Christian marriage also raises problems. Jesus is alleged to have used the parables to prevent his hearers from understanding and repenting

[3] Gerhard Ebeling, *Word of God and Tradition,* pp. 102-47.

(Mark 4:10-12). Additional problematical passages can be cited which trouble the Christian who is instructed to live according to the principle of love.

Regardless of the voices of logic and pragmatism, the actual work of revising the canon involves insuperable difficulties. In the first place, there is no available standard for revision which is not subject in principle to the same historical limitations that created the present problems. Contemporary Christian insight represents the prejudices of its own time. Revision of the limits of the canon would mean that one historical judgment be supplanted by another of the same character. This does not imply that historical judgments are in principle not subject to review and revision. Rather, insofar as the function of scripture is concerned, the problem of authority cannot be solved by revising the limits of the canon. Second, the work of revising the canon raises procedural problems beyond satisfactory solution. If agreement could be reached concerning a specific body of material to be excluded from the canon, problems would be created which relate to the remainder of the material in the canon. Suppose, for example, that Luther's evaluation of James as an "epistle of straw" was accepted as the basis for excluding it from the canon, despite the fact that James contains material that is superior to other sections of the present canon (e.g., Mark 4:10-12; Matt. 23:3). An attempt to revise the limits of the canon would logically lead to its depletion. Third, there is no unitary standard in the church which can serve as the basis for common judgment. Cultural and political circumstances influence the judgment of Christians who reside in various places in the world. Historical circumstances affect the relevance of biblical material for the Christian community—as the rising or flagging zeal for the book of Revelation in periods of persecution or tranquillity has demonstrated.

The proposal for the revision of the canon is based upon an inadequate understanding of its nature and function, i.e., it implies that the total content of the canon should find universal acceptance in the church. The present content of the Bible has never spoken to Christians universally with the same degree of relevance. The Christians in Jerusalem were agitated by Paul's teaching, and the Gentile Christians were offended by the demands of Jewish Christians. The limited canon is not based upon universal agreement among Christians in each generation. But it does indicate that a specific body of Christian literature provides access to a valid understanding of Jesus Christ.

Books for Additional Reading

1. Kurt Aland, *The Problem of the New Testament Canon* (London: A. R. Mowbray and Co., 1962).
2. Floyd V. Filson, *Which Books Belong in the Bible?* (Philadelphia: The Westminster Press, 1957).
3. Willi Marxsen, *The New Testament as the Church's Book,* trans. James E. Mignard (Philadelphia: Fortress Press, 1972).
4. Alexander Souter, *The Text and Canon of the New Testament,* Studies in Theology; rev. C. S. C. Williams (London: Gerald Duckworth and Co., 2nd rev. ed., 1954), pp. 137-87.

9

The Problem of History:
Jesus of History or Christ of Faith?

A century of investigation of the Gospels has served to focus attention upon the subject of history. Günther Bornkamm summarized the unexpected result of that investigation in the opening statement of his recent book: "No one is any longer in the position to write a life of Jesus." [1]

[1] Günther Bornkamm, *Jesus of Nazareth,* p. 13.

Expressed in other language, this statement means that the material in the Synoptic Gospels does not provide historical information for writing a *biography* of Jesus. Bornkamm's viewpoint is almost universally accepted at the present time and constitutes the logical point of departure for the interpretation of the Gospels. In order to understand Bornkamm's judgment, we must consider the presuppositions upon which it is based. They can be understood best by referral to the major developments in New Testament thought during the past century. The following discussion is devoted to an analysis of some significant aspects of New Testament study since the time of David Friedrich Strauss.

THE ORIGIN OF THE PROBLEM OF HISTORY IN NEW TESTAMENT RESEARCH

David Friedrich Strauss (1808-1874)

Modern study of the Gospels was inaugurated by the publication, in 1835, of *Das Leben Jesu* (*The Life of Jesus*), by David Friedrich Strauss. Strauss proposed a solution for the dilemma that existed in New Testament research at that time.

Interpreters of his generation were divided into two schools of thought, Rationalism and Supernaturalism. Although the conflict between these schools focused upon the interpretation of the miracle stories in the Gospels, it actually reflected two divergent understandings of the Christian religion. The supernaturalists contended that the miracle stories constitute evidence for the authenticity of Christianity and must be interpreted as literal accounts of historical events. The rationalists rejected this position and insisted, rather, that much of the material in the miracle stories owes its existence to first-century believers who preserved and un-

228

critically interpreted these stories. Hence, the rationalists contended that reason and logic must be used in order to distinguish between fact and interpretation.

Strauss was convinced that the entire discussion had reached a stalemate since neither group had been able to establish its position in the light of the objections raised by its opponents. He proposed an alternative solution for the problem of miracles which was based upon a different understanding of the nature of biblical material. According to Strauss, the message of the Gospels is expressed in mythical language and concepts which must be evaluated with respect to the truth of their religious content. From his viewpoint, history does not constitute the norm by which religious truth is to be judged, i.e., a statement may be religiously true and historically inaccurate.

Strauss found his thesis violently rejected by the majority of his contemporaries, but he raised questions that demanded answers. Unfortunately, Strauss made few direct contributions to the solution of the historical problems which he raised. His proposal was prompted by philosophical (the dialectical thesis of Hegel, expressed as thesis, antithesis, and synthesis) rather than by historical considerations. His position had to be tested ultimately by the use of methodology which had not been developed at that time (cf. source, form, and redaction criticism). However, his suggestion provided one stimulus for the development of those methods of research.

Ferdinand Christian Baur (1792-1860)

Ferdinand Christian Baur initiated the modern period of historical study of Christian origins. His contact with earlier studies of Greek and Roman history convinced him of the importance of historical study for understanding Christianity. Two of Baur's works set the stage and provided the impetus for further development of this method. They were *Die Christuspartei der korinthischen Gemeinde* (*The Christ-Party in the Corinthian Church*), in 1831, and *Paulus, der Apostel Jesu Christi* (*Paul, the Apostle of Jesus Christ*), in 1845.

Baur insisted that events must be understood from the standpoint of the historical contexts in which they occur. He interpreted the development of Christianity in the first century as an expression of the conflict between Jewish and Gentile Christians, represented by Peter and Paul respectively. In accordance with his acceptance of Hegel's scheme for understanding history, he suggested that Jewish Christianity represented the thesis, Gentile Christianity represented the antithesis, and the church of the second century represented the synthesis. Baur dated New Testament literature according to the stage of the conflict which it seemed to reflect. Thus, the famous "Tübingen School" of thought was born.

Unlike Strauss's proposal, Baur's suggestion was received enthusiastically by his contemporaries. New Testament students accepted his basic conclusions and for half a century used them as the foundation for their work.

Two implications of Baur's thought were influential in shaping the course of New Testament study during the latter half of the nineteenth century. First, Baur's proposal that Jewish and Christian history are to be understood in the light of their historical antecedents led to the rise of the so-called history-of-religions approach to the interpretation of Christian history. (Christianity represents one of the religions of the world. Its origin can be explained as a historical event which was stimulated by earlier religious movements.) According to the explanation given by the history-of-religions school of thought, Christianity represents the amalgamation (synthesis) of Jewish and Gentile religion. It seemed, then, that a logical explanation had been found for the presence of Jewish and Greek ideas in the New Testament. Second, Baur's emphasis upon the necessity of historical interpretation led to intensified research in the life of Jesus. The reconstruction of the historical life of Jesus was accepted as a primary task in New Testament study. This definition of the work of New Testament investigation led to innumerable attempts to write a biography of Jesus which would portray him "as he actually was."

The intensive study of the Gospels which resulted from these efforts soon revealed that the Gospels contain a great deal of material that cannot be assimilated into a biographical sketch of Jesus' life and thought. Critical study of the accounts in Matthew, Mark, and Luke revealed that important elements must be attributed to the early Christian community. Consequently, it became necessary to devise methods of analysis by which distinctions could be made between historical and interpretative material. The discovery of this problem led to the revision of the basic understanding of the nature and message of the Gospels, particularly with respect to their function as historical documents.

Nineteenth-Century Thought Subsequent to Strauss and Baur

The theses of Strauss and Baur stimulated an era of unprecedented activity in New Testament research. Their proposals were related to issues which called for the expansion of the entire discipline of New Testament study. Crucial problems arose concerning the history of Christianity in the first century. For example, the historical positions of Jesus and Paul were studied intensively. This study revealed the contrast between the content of Jesus' preaching and Paul's thought. Based upon certain elements of the material in the Gospels, it was generally believed that Jesus' central emphasis concerned man's obligation to love God and his fellowman (Matt. 5:43). However, Paul focused attention upon the significance of Jesus' person and work (the meaning of cross-resurrection, pre-existence, atonement, judgment, etc.; cf. Phil. 2:5-11). Thus, two concepts of religion were traced to Jesus and Paul which could scarcely be reconciled. The suggestion arose that a choice between Jesus and Paul was necessary. Obviously, the majority of the proponents of this "Jesus *or* Paul" perspective relegated the thought of Paul to a place of secondary importance. At the same time, other students of the problem praised Paul as the intellectual genius, the real founder of Christianity who had dealt seriously with issues which Jesus' simple religion of love had overlooked.

Research in the life of Jesus raised additional problems concerning Jesus' understanding of religion. The Gospels seemed to point to Jesus' emphasis upon love as the basic principle of life. However, in using the Gospels to create this kind of portrait of Jesus, interpreters had consistently overlooked other emphases in the Gospels. For example, Jesus' eschatological teaching was ignored or subordinated to his ethical emphasis. Nevertheless, crucial passages in the Gospels suggest that eschatology may have represented Jesus' primary concern (cf. Mark 1:14-15). In this context, the question of Jesus' understanding of the kingdom of God became a primary issue.

Prior to the time of Johannes Weiss,[2] Jesus' announce-

[2] Johannes Weiss, *Jesus' Proclamation of the Kingdom of God,* trans., ed., and introduction by Richard Hyde Hiers and David Larrimore Holland (Philadelphia: Fortress Press, 1971).

ment of the nearness of the Kingdom was generally interpreted as one form of his ethical summons to live by the principle of love. Weiss rejected the identification of these two concepts. He suggested that Jesus' eschatological preaching was rooted in Jewish apocalyptic views which expected the sudden, cataclysmic end of history. Again, historical research seemed to have discovered two radically contrasting aspects of Jesus' thought. His ethical teaching suggested principles by which men were to live in a continuing historical order; his eschatological preaching indicated the immediate end of history.

Obvious problems arose from the efforts of historians to reconstruct the history of the rise and development of early Christianity; Paul and Jesus appeared in sharp contrast to each other, indeed, Jesus' own concepts seemed to stand in tension with each other. These results of historical research could be understood as discrediting Christianity. But they could also point to the necessity of a re-evaluation of the research which had created this kind of historical interpretation. For this, events at the close of the nineteenth century opened the way.

While theologians were struggling with historical problems in biblical literature, historians were revising their concepts of history. The results were new insights concerning the nature and goals of scientific historical research. Scientific methodology was developed originally in close correlation with the subject matter of the exact sciences. In accordance with the goals of those sciences, historians defined truth in terms of the kind of objectivity which their work required. The procedure of repeated experiments produced objective facts free from the "subjective" influence (perversion) of the interpreter. Historians had accepted those assumptions during the earlier stages of the development of scientific historical research. However, further reflection upon the nature of historical truth showed the definition of historical truth as "objective facts" to be fraught with serious limitations and misconceptions. Historical events, unlike the subject matter of the exact sciences, cannot be subjected to repeated experiments. They belong to the past and can be understood only through reports which are both subjective and interpretative in character. Furthermore, the meaning of a historical event is not evident at the time of its occurrence. Rather, its meaning is related to the future course of events which brings its possibilities to expression. For example, the Declaration of Independence has become meaningful because the movement that supported it succeeded. If the American Revolution had failed in its purposes, the Declaration of Independence would be understood quite differently at the present time. When the distinctive dimensions of historical truth are overlooked or sacrificed in subservience to the demand for objective facts, historical truth becomes a meaningless concept. Indeed, Christianity's claim to be a historical religion would only discredit it.

Recognition of the distinctive dimensions of historical truth enabled historians to develop methods of historical research appropriate for the subject matter with which this kind of research is concerned. Consequently, the problems that had plagued historians and theologians could be understood in a different light, and the goals and problems with which interpreters of the New Testament had been concerned for half a century could be redefined.

The insights of Martin Kähler, William Wrede, and Albert Schweitzer could have terminated the efforts to reconstruct the historical life of Jesus from the material in the Synoptic Gospels. Kähler showed that the Gospels proclaim the resurrected-exalted Lord—not Jesus of Nazareth as a historical figure in isolation—as the object of Christian faith.[3] Wrede traced the idea of the "messianic secret" in the Gospels to the author of Mark's Gospel.[4] Schweitzer showed that previous efforts to write a biography of Jesus had all ended in failure.[5] Yet Schweitzer perpetuated the approach of nineteenth-century scholars by writing another life of Jesus! The distinction lay in the fact that he accepted the theme of eschatology as his point of departure. To be sure, the evidence which these men produced did not eliminate the problem of history from theological thought. However, it did enable theologians to deal with the concept of history from a more adequate perspective. Specifically, it shifted the attention of twentieth-century research away from efforts to write a biography of Jesus (cf. Bornkamm's statement, p. 124).

THEOLOGY AND HISTORY

It may seem strange that the subject matter of history and theology is related so intimately that changes in the understanding of the concept of history are reflected in theological thought. This intimate relationship is grounded in the fact that Christians point to a historical person, Jesus of Nazareth, as the focus of God's redemptive action. Furthermore, the gospel proclaims Jesus Christ as the judge and Lord of the whole world, thereby indicating his meaning

[3] Martin Kähler, *The So-Called Historical Jesus and the Historic, Biblical Christ.*

[4] William Wrede, *The Messianic Secret.*

[5] Albert Schweitzer, *The Quest of the Historical Jesus.*

and relevance for man's historical existence. Indeed, Christ is described as the clue to the meaning of the entire historical process (Matt. 25:31-46). However, the terms "history" and "historical" are used with varying connotations in contemporary discussion. When Christians refer to the historical Jesus, historical revelation, and the historical character of Christianity, they are obligated to define the concept of history involved in these references.

In spite of the intimate relationship between historical and theological thought, the decisive affirmations of Christian faith cannot be substantiated by the results of historical research. In fact, the Gospels are not historical documents in the strict sense of the term. To be sure, they employ the form of historical narrative, but they incorporate a principle of explanation which distinguishes them from the historical narrative. For example, the Gospels affirm that God exalted Jesus to a position of authority and power at his own right hand where he reigns as Lord of the universe (Matt. 28:18. Cf. also Heb. 1:1-4; Phil. 2:5-11; etc.). These claims express convictions of faith and are not historical statements, since there is no verifiable historical evidence that can be presented as proof (historical evidence is limited to empirical evidence in this world and is subject to examination as the basis for verification). Thus, the Gospels refer to Jesus as Lord, Son of God, and Son of Man; but these are not references to be understood as historical statements. Since they transcend the realm of observable human experience for interpreting the meaning of Jesus' life and death, the Gospels are no longer historical documents in the strict meaning of the term. This definition of historical literature and historical evidence does not imply that truth must be interpreted solely in historical terms. But this definition is necessary in order that the distinctive dimensions of the Christian witness to truth become evident.

The problem of history in the Gospels cannot be solved through rigid classification of historical and confessional material (material which arises out of the convictions of faith). Historical and confessional statements in the Gospels do not appear in isolation from each other. Rather, there are often historical and confessional dimensions in the same statement. There is no reference to Jesus of Nazareth which does not assume his crucifixion and resurrection. Likewise, there is no theoretical discussion of the meaning of resurrection apart from its direct reference to Jesus of Nazareth. For example, when the Gospels refer to Jesus' return to the city of Nazareth they assume that this man was later crucified and resurrected. Similarly, when the Gospels refer to the appearances of the resurrected One, they assume that he once entered the city of Nazareth as a Palestinian Jew. This relationship between historical and confessional perspectives constitutes the point of departure for the interpretation of the Gospels.

The present stage of the discussion concerning the problem of history in the Gospels cannot be described accurately by pointing to specific assured results of investigation. (The concluding section of this chapter indicates some alternatives that have been presented.) But some basic theses may be guidelines to further discussion. First, the historical foundation of the Christian gospel in Jesus of Nazareth has been firmly established by research. Jesus, a Jew, lived in Palestine during the first half of the first Christian century. It is no longer necessary to give serious attention to suggestions that the figure of Jesus in the Gospels represents a fictitious character created out of the religious expectations of the first century. A great deal can be said with

237

reasonable certainty concerning his general religious attitude, his behavior, and his relationships with his contemporaries. Thus, the problem of history has become a permanent responsibility for Christian theology. Secondly, the fruitfulness of historical research for Christian thought has been demonstrated. It is no longer necessary for theologians to apologize for the "subjective" results of historical research in biblical material. Historical-critical research constitutes an indispensable tool for understanding biblical material. Third, the Christian gospel cannot be understood solely by reference to historical norms. Christian confession clearly contains an integral element of faith.

These statements do not exhaustively describe the results of historical Gospel studies. They may even seem to represent a miserly reward for extensive labor. However, they indicate the direction in which the interpreter of the Gospels may pursue his work. In this instance, direction is more important than assured results in the realm of factual information.

THE CRISIS OF THE PROBLEM: JESUS OF HISTORY OR CHRIST OF FAITH?

Since the time of Martin Kähler (cf. note 3) the problem of history in the Gospels has been expressed by the question, "Jesus of history or Christ of faith?" This question calls attention to two divergent interpretations of the Gospels. The phrase "Jesus of history" identifies the Gospels as sources of reliable historical information concerning the life of Jesus. ("Jesus of history" in Kähler's work describes the portrait of Jesus which emerged out of the efforts to write a biography of Jesus.) It does not necessarily assume that the Gospels contain history only. The phrase "Christ of faith" rejects the idea that the Gospels can be used primarily as authentic historical sources, particularly in relation to the thought of Jesus, the development of his life, and the interpretation of his death. It does not claim that the material arose independently from historical events, or that its references to historical circumstances are entirely fictitious. Rather, it points to the fact that the Gospels were formulated in the service of faith which subordinated history to its own purposes.

The question "Jesus of history or Christ of faith?" expresses basic options for understanding the significance of history in the Gospels. The debate over the "biography" of Jesus has frequently been interpreted as created by curiosity, i.e., as a dispute over how much can be known about Jesus. However, historical evidence for or against the veracity of isolated references to Jesus' life can hardly be decisive for the message of the Gospels. For example, if it could be proved that Jesus was born in an unknown Jewish village rather than in Bethlehem, that his childhood was spent in Capernaum rather than in Nazareth, or that he did not live in Egypt as a child, the Christian understanding of the cross and resurrection would hardly be jeopardized. But the problem of history in the Gospels as well as in the remaining literature of the New Testament is not concerned merely with the number of historical facts which can be substantiated about the life of Jesus.

"Jesus of history or Christ of faith?" involves the standpoint from which the authors of the Gospels composed their works. Is the portrait of Jesus Christ in the Gospels based upon the life of Jesus of Nazareth, or is it determined by the concept of resurrection-exaltation? In other words, the question is: Is the confession of Jesus Christ as Savior

239

and Lord formulated to explain the historical dimensions of Jesus' life, or is it formulated to describe Jesus' historical life in dimensions derived from his status as resurrected-exalted Lord? Thus, the problem of history in the Gospels is concerned with the extent to which the authors of the Gospels, in unity with early Christians generally, interpreted the life of Jesus in accordance with strict historical principles. Contemporary thought on the subject varies widely, but the general viewpoint is indicated by these basic alternatives.

Rudolf Bultmann

Rudolf Bultmann, emeritus professor of New Testament at the University of Marburg, has raised decisive theological issues in this century. Much of his thought has been concerned with the problem of history in Christian thought. Although entire books have been devoted to the discussion of his interpretation, his basic emphasis may be indicated in a summary statement.

Bultmann asserts that "the message of Jesus is a presupposition for the theology of the New Testament rather than a part of that theology itself." [6] This is Bultmann's graphic way of emphasizing that the biblical writers did not understand the Christian gospel as a simple repetition of Jesus' preaching. Jesus announced the nearness of the kingdom of God (Mark 1:14-15), whereas the biblical authors pointed to the meaning of Jesus' person as the central content of the gospel message (I Cor. 1:2; Rom. 10:9; Acts 4:12). At this point one of the fundamental problems of Christian theology emerges. It is clear that the biblical authors have incorporated their interpretation of the *meaning* of a historical event (Jesus of Nazareth) as an integral part of the Christian

[6] Rudolf Bultmann, *Theology of the New Testament,* trans. Kendrick Grobel (New York: Charles Scribner's Sons, 1951), I, 3.

gospel. Furthermore, it is evident that the "name" of Jesus (Acts 4:12) refers not only to the historical figure of Jesus but also to his position as exalted Lord. How did the biblical writers interpret the historical figure of Jesus of Nazareth when they proclaimed Jesus Christ as Lord? This is one way of stating the problem of history in the Gospels.

Bultmann has insisted that the biblical writers wrote from the standpoint of the cross-resurrection event, i.e., they proclaimed as Savior the crucified-resurrected Lord, not the historical Jesus. While it was Jesus of Nazareth who had been exalted to the right hand of the Father by the resurrection from the dead, the relationship between Jesus of Nazareth and the exalted Lord in Christian preaching remains problematic. Obviously, more is affirmed regarding the exalted Lord than can be claimed for Jesus of Nazareth.

Bultmann has defined this problem in the form of a question about the *nature of the continuity* between Jesus of Nazareth and Jesus Christ. According to Bultmann, the New Testament does not proclaim *historical* continuity between Jesus of Nazareth and Jesus Christ. While he agrees that the confession "Jesus Christ" (Jesus is Messiah) affirms continuity between Jesus of Nazareth and Jesus Christ, he rejects the idea that this continuity is to be understood purely historically. Rather, this continuity must be traced to the resurrection-confession of the early Christian community. Historical evidence (evidence subject to historical investigation) points to Jesus of Nazareth, not to Jesus Christ, and Bultmann considers an appeal to historical evidence in support of the Christian message inappropriate and misguided.

Thus, from Bultmann's viewpoint, the quest for historical information about Jesus cannot represent the primary concern of theology. He does not deny the existence of the historical Jesus, nor does he hold that nothing can be known

241

concerning the historical life of Jesus. Rather, he contends that the Christian confession is not based upon an appeal to historical evidence in the life of Jesus, i.e., historical evidence did not provide the principle of interpretation for the biblical writers.

Ernst Käsemann

While Bultmann has been an influential scholar, he has also been a controversial one. His views on the subject of history in Christian thought have occasioned widespread dispute. Professor Ernst Käsemann, Bultmann's former student and currently professor of New Testament at the University of Tübingen, has been an influential exponent of a different viewpoint.

In an article published in 1954, Käsemann contends that continued investigation of the life of Jesus is not only relevant and possible, but that it is required by the nature of the Christian gospel itself, lest Christians accept a myth as substitute for the historical Jesus.[7] He supports his position by pointing to those strata of the tradition in the Gospels which cannot be reasonably attributed either to Jewish or Christian influence. In his judgment, when allowance has been made for Jewish and Christian influences upon the material in the Gospels, the remaining material can provide access to Jesus' actual teaching. He cites the first, second, and fourth sayings in the Sermon on the Mount as examples of material that has come directly from Jesus (Blessed are the poor in spirit; Blessed are those who mourn; Blessed are those who hunger and thirst for righteousness). Thus, Käsemann is concerned

[7] Ernst Käsemann, *Essays on New Testament Themes,* Studies in Biblical Theology No. 41; trans. W. J. Montague (London: SCM Press, 1964), pp. 15-47.

with historical information regarding Jesus' life and teaching.

Käsemann's concern with the subject of history in the Gospels should not be understood as a renewed attempt to write a biography of Jesus. He concedes that the Gospels contain the results of the early Christians' interpretation of Jesus' life. Each generation of Christians has "shattered" (altered) the form of the tradition which they received. He does not suggest that the Gospels in their present forms should be accepted as factual reports of Jesus' life with no traces of early Christian interpretation.

Käsemann is especially concerned with the lack of historical continuity between Jesus of Nazareth and Jesus Christ in Bultmann's thought. He argues that historical continuity does not consist in maintaining exact records of past events from generation to generation. Rather, historical continuity is preserved through material that interprets the meaning of the past, thereby keeping the voice of the past alive in the present. Each generation must interpret the tradition it receives, "shattering" (altering) its previous form. In Käsemann's own words, "history is only accessible to us through tradition, and tradition is only comprehensible through interpretation." [8] Hence, historical continuity with the past is maintained through a living tradition that must assume new forms in order to mediate its message.

In a later essay, Käsemann writes of the theological necessity of historical research. He calls attention to the function of historical investigation to restrain the illusions fostered by an ecstatic mentality, by those who desire to glorify tradition and by the supporters of established institutional forms of religion.[9] Käsemann's point is well taken where he discusses

[8] Ernst Käsemann, *Essays on New Testament Themes,* p. 18.
[9] Ernst Käsemann, "Vom theologischen Recht historisch-kritischer

historical studies of the tradition of the church. It is not so relevant where he analyzes the nature of the original Christian confession.

Käsemann has been the foremost exponent for the necessity of historical study of the life of Jesus. He has been supported in various ways by such influential scholars as Ernst Fuchs[10] and Günther Bornkamm[11] in Germany, and James M. Robinson[12] in America.

Alternative Proposals

The foregoing discussion calls attention to significant issues which should be evaluated in the light of alternative approaches to the problem of history in biblical literature.

Professor C. H. Dodd has written extensively concerning the subject of history in biblical thought. Dodd has rejected Bultmann's claim that New Testament research has little interest in historical information concerning the life of Jesus. He claims that the authors of the Gospels, particularly the author of Mark's Gospel, exercised considerably less influence upon the structure of the Gospel than the proponents of redaction criticism have assumed.[13] Dodd contends that a comparative study of Mark and Q can yield a reliable

---

Exegese," *Zeitschrift für Theologie und Kirche*, 64, Jahrgang 1967, Heft 3 (Tübingen: J. C. B. Mohr [Paul Siebeck]), p. 259.

[10] Ernst Fuchs, *Studies of the Historical Jesus* Studies in Biblical Theology No. 42; trans. Andrew Scobie (Naperville, Illinois: Alec R. Allenson, 1964), pp. 11-31.

[11] Günther Bornkamm, *Jesus of Nazareth.* In half a century, Bornkamm has written the first work which can rightly be called a life of Jesus. In this work Bornkamm has incorporated the basic results of the discussion of the historical problem. It is not, however, a life of Jesus like the older attempts at a biography of Jesus.

[12] James M. Robinson, *A New Quest of the Historical Jesus.*

[13] C. H. Dodd, *New Testament Studies* (Manchester: Manchester University Press, 1953), Chap. 1.

picture of the ministry of Jesus.[14] In his judgment, the preaching of the early church consisted in the "announcement of certain historical events in a setting which displays the significance of those events." [15] Dodd's viewpoint regarding Jesus' understanding of eschatology became the object of widespread discussion. In his work on the parables[16] he espoused his thesis of so-called "realized eschatology," i.e., Jesus proclaimed the coming of the Kingdom within his earthly ministry. Dodd's concept of history is related to the idea of "sacred history" which raises problems concerning this use of the term history ("history is to be judged not as a single succession in time, but as a process created by the act of God vertically from above").[17]

Professor Oscar Cullmann has interpreted history within the context defined by his theory of "salvation-history" (*Heilsgeschichte*).[18] Cullmann contends that the Christian concept of redemption is rooted in a distinctive understanding of time. In his judgment, New Testament thought identifies the Christ-event (including crucifixion-resurrection) as the midpoint of time from which all history is to be understood and judged. This event constitutes the focus of a special limited process encompassing the total scope of temporal succession. Cullmann asserts that New Testament thought recognizes the absolute revelation of God only in this limited process, the so-called "Christ line." Cullmann has perhaps been criticized most for his definition of eternity as the

[14] C. H. Dodd, *History and the Gospel* (London: Nisbet & Company, 1938), pp. 85-86.

[15] C. H. Dodd, *According to the Scriptures* (London: Nisbet & Company, 1952), p. 11.

[16] C. H. Dodd, *The Parables of the Kingdom* (London: Nisbet & Company, rev. reprint; 1936).

[17] C. H. Dodd, *History and the Gospel,* p. 181.

[18] Oscar Cullmann, *Christ and Time,* trans. Floyd V. Filson (London: SCM Press, rev. ed., 1962).

unending succession of God's time. He seems to overlook the fact that the salvation-history to which he alludes is itself a product of Christian faith and can scarcely be related to a concept of history that does not take its point of departure in faith.

Wolfhart Pannenberg's interpretation of history has become a focus of discussion in recent New Testament scholarship. Pannenberg rejects the claim that revelation is to be understood as a supernatural occurrence perceived in faith. Rather, revelation is to be understood as the language of historical facts, interpreted in terms of historical relationships. As such, the revelation of God possesses universal character and is evident to all who have eyes to see. Obviously, this proposal is based upon assumptions that transcend the subject of history. However, his understanding of history seems to point to a new direction in theology.[19]

CONCLUSION

General agreement has not been reached in many areas of the problem of history in Christian thought. Perhaps some of the current discussion may be compared with the experiences of travelers in a railway station—they see faces and hear voices, but they have no unified theme of conversation.

[19] Wolfhart Pannenberg, et al., "Dogmatic Theses on the Doctrine of Revelation," Revelation as History, trans. David Granskow (New York: The Macmillan Company, 1968), pp. 125-81; "Hermeneutics and Universal History," History and Hermeneutic, Journal for Theology and the Church (New York: Harper & Row, 1967), IV, 122-52. Cf. also, Wolfhart Pannenberg, "The Revelation of God in Jesus of Nazareth," Theology as History, New Frontiers in Theology, ed. Robinson and Cobb (New York: Harper & Row, 1967), III, 101-33.

A great deal of the recent discussion has been related in one way or another to Bultmann's suggestion concerning the nature of the continuity presupposed in the Christian confession of Jesus of Nazareth and Jesus Christ. The problem does not concern the continuity which can be objectively shown to have existed between Jesus and Jesus Christ but concerns the assumptions of those who formulated the confession. The resurrection provided one dimension of those assumptions.

This does not imply that early Christian tradition about Jesus was unrelated to Jesus' actual historical existence. It simply calls attention to one element which played a role in the rise of the tradition about Jesus. Further, it suggests that the tradition about Jesus was animated from the beginning by the presupposition of his resurrection. The tradition about Jesus, then, cannot be understood either in purely historical or purely transcendental terms. The effort to isolate distinct historical and distinct confessional traditions must inevitably end in failure since both perspectives relate to the same tradition (before the resurrection there was no *Christian* understanding of Jesus' life. After the resurrection there was no purely *historical* understanding of his life, i.e., an understanding that did not involve the resurrection).

Professor Hans Conzelmann has advanced the present stage of the discussion by his recent suggestion that the primary question in New Testament theology is not, "How did the proclaimer, Jesus of Nazareth, become the proclaimed Messiah, Son of God, Lord? It is rather, why did faith maintain the identity of the Exalted One with Jesus of Nazareth after the resurrection appearances?" [20]

[20] Hans Conzelmann, *An Outline of the Theology of the New Testament,* p. xviii.

A summary statement about the problem of history in the Gospels may identify some foundations for future thought on the subject:

1. The Gospels were not composed as records of the historical life of Jesus, even though they relate to his life and reflect the forms of historical narratives.

2. The resurrection-exaltation of Jesus constituted the animating dynamic for the rise of the Christian tradition about Jesus.

3. The historical and transhistorical elements in the Christian confession of Jesus Christ must be understood in such a way that neither dimension is eliminated, i.e., Jesus of Nazareth must not become a fictitious character, and history must not become the final arbiter for Christian truth.

4. Christianity does not proclaim its message through norms that obligate it to "prove" its validity in ways alien to its own nature. Historical investigation is willingly accepted as an ally. But those dimensions of the Christian confession which do not appeal to historical norms for verification are to be understood from their own peculiar perspective.

Books for Additional Reading

1. Günther Bornkamm, *Jesus of Nazareth,* trans. Irene and Fraser McLuskey with James M. Robinson (New York: Harper & Row, 1960).
2. Rudolf Bultmann, "The Primitive Christian Kerygma and the Historical Jesus," *The Historical Jesus and the Kerygmatic Christ,* trans. and ed. Carl E. Braaten and Roy A. Harrisville (Nashville: Abingdon Press, 1964), pp. 15-42.

3. Joachim Jeremias, *The Problem of the Historical Jesus,* trans. Norman Perrin (Philadelphia: Fortress Press, 1964).
4. Norman Perrin, *Rediscovering the Teaching of Jesus* (New York: Harper & Row, 1967), Chapter V.
5. James M. Robinson, *A New Quest of the Historical Jesus,* Studies in Biblical Theology No. 25 (Naperville, Illinois: Alec R. Allenson, 1959).

10

The Problem of Interpretation:
The Function of Biblical Language

It is somewhat paradoxical that a crisis should arise in the field of biblical interpretation at the close of a century of intensive study of the Bible. Nevertheless, biblical interpreters have struggled for a quarter of a century with questions which relate to the basic principles of their work. This crisis has arisen in part as an expression of the intellectual problems of the present time. Also, a century of research in biblical literature has contributed to the rise of new problems. Biblical interpreters have been forced to reconsider the adequacy of the assumptions that have previously guided them in their work. At any rate, the attention of biblical scholarship is focused at the present time upon the question of hermeneutics. It may be helpful to relate this question to the events and movements which have contributed to its present form.

THE MODERN CRISIS IN MAN'S SELF-UNDERSTANDING

Political Turmoil

One cause of the present sense of uncertainty which characterizes modern man can be found in the atmosphere of political instability which has permeated recent world history. The centuries preceding the present one have been marked by the emergence and collapse of numerous world powers. Every major segment of the human race has been affected in one way or another by these events. Not even a prophet would dare to predict the shape of the world political community at the close of the present century.

Of course, political change represents no new phenomenon in Western history. Since the fall of the Persian Empire at the hands of Alexander the Great (fourth century B.C.) history in the Western world has been written largely from the standpoint of the changing fortunes of political empires.

Although men of the twentieth century are able to recognize certain parallels between their own experiences in the collapse of empires and those of men in previous periods of history, there are dimensions of human experience to which historical literature often speaks only superficially. Despair

251

and frustration accompany the collapse of every political empire and the dissolution of national and political bonds. The cry of the unknown Jewish exile in Babylon seems to echo the anguish of all of them, "How shall we sing the Lord's song in a foreign land?" (Ps. 137:4.) At the same time, each catastrophe contains elements of human despair and fear which are not preserved in the historical accounts of the fall of an empire. Political structures are built upon fundamental concepts of meaning and value which animate and sustain them. When these structures collapse, for whatever reason, meaning and value are called into question. The altered social and political circumstances of life in the new situation often require re-evaluation of earlier moral and religious beliefs. There are no hereditary landmarks which provide a sense of security for men who have suddenly become vagabonds in the universe of moral and religious values. Thus, the uncertainty and instability which threaten society in this generation are produced and sustained in part by the transitional character of the modern-world political community.

Intellectual Revolution

Obviously, the intellectual revolutions of the modern era are related to the political upheavals within which they have taken place. In many respects, neither phenomenon could have occurred apart from the other. For example, the emergence of a spirit of freedom and self-reliance has disrupted static political orders and replaced them with other forms of government. Likewise, the rise of political powers that have permitted freedom of expression has fostered creativity and progress. The attendant processes of change have contributed to a crisis in modern man's understanding of himself and of his situation.

Paul Tillich has described the intellectual revolution in modern times as the "shaking of the foundations." He has called attention to the radical degree to which modern thought has challenged traditional standards and concepts. The scientific revolution has played a major role in this challenge. The mass of information produced through the use of the experimental method has resulted in basic changes in man's understanding of his place and role in the world. For example, so long as the earth was understood to be the center of the universe it was possible to attribute focal significance to man's position in it. This interpretation of man's importance has been called into question by the discovery that the earth is only a minor planet among a multitude of galaxies of planets.

The ultimate questions confronting man cannot be answered through the use of the experimental method. These questions concern the problems of meaning and purpose. It is in this realm of moral values where the most troublesome questions have arisen in the modern era.

Modern man's experiences in an age of political and intellectual revolution have crystalized in the form of a crisis in self-understanding. The clearest evidence of this crisis is seen in the uncertainty and frustration with which he confronts the questions that concern the ultimate issues of his existence; namely, who he is, what the source and nature of his obligations and responsibilities are, and in which direction he may find confidence and hope.

In many respects, modern man is often immobilized by his sense of estrangement and "lostness." The landmarks and guideposts by which he was able earlier to chart his course seem to have vanished in the process of the "shaking of the foundations" which now threatens his sense of security and certainty. Although medieval man lived according to a world view whose structures now seem incredibly naïve, modern man evidences traces of nostalgia for medieval man's simplified understanding of existence. At least, his existential questions arose within stable landmarks. Nagging questions about the nature of religious and political authority had not become crucial. Modern man's intellectual sophistication has complicated his quest for a sense of "at homeness" in the universe.

Biblical interpretation in the present generation cannot be undertaken in isolation from current issues and problems but involves the obligation to speak responsibly to these issues in the name of the Christian faith. Biblical interpretation must incorporate the problems of the world into the framework of its own obligations. The following discussion defines some aspects of modern thought within which the biblical interpreter is called to do his work.

THE MODERN PERSPECTIVE
AND BIBLICAL INTERPRETATION

Philosophy

In Western culture philosophy has traditionally assumed responsibility for the interpretation of the nature of the human situation. Philosophers have created complicated systems of thought through which they have proposed answers for the basic human questions. These answers have been concerned with such issues as the origin and structure of the universe, the nature and destiny of man, the nature of good and evil, the meaning and purpose of history, the nature of knowledge, and even the nature of God (ultimate reality, Being, first principle, etc.). Understood from this perspective, philosophy has been called metaphysics (Greek, *meta phusika,* after or beyond nature or physical things).

Western men have ordinarily depended upon philosophical answers in these areas of thought as a source of guidance for ordering their lives in the world. So long as philosophy's prerogatives remained unquestioned, men lived their lives with a sense of certainty and assurance.

Although it is not possible to speak categorically at this point, Western philosophy has generally based its pronouncements upon two fundamental assumptions. First, it has assumed that human reason possesses adequate resources for acquiring knowledge of truth. René Descartes (1596–1650) expressed this conviction in his famous statement *Cogito ergo sum* (I think, therefore I am). Further, philosophy has generally assumed that human language, adequately understood and intelligibly used, is a reliable instrument for communicating human knowledge acquired through the rational process.

Philosophy's traditional assumptions concerning reason and language have been seriously questioned in the modern era, even within the field of philosophy itself. First, the capacity of human reason to provide immediate access to reality has been challenged. After all, reason is human reason and remains subject to the limitations imposed by the conditions of human existence. Secondly, the nature and function of language as a medium for conveying knowledge have been subjected to thoroughgoing analysis. In spite of the claims of some schools of philosophy (e.g., Positivism) that language can be used as an exact scientific instrument, other (symbolical or analogical) dimensions of language are evident. Consequently, philosophical descriptions of reality must be understood as the "way things appear" from a specific human perspective. It is impossible in principle to transcend the limitations of this perspective. Hence, the metaphysical prerogatives of philosophy have been seriously questioned. A

255

the present time there are few defenders of this traditional role of philosophy.

The changing role of philosophy is reflected in biblical interpretation. For example, theology no longer attempts to "prove" the existence of God since the philosophical foundations of these proofs have been discredited. Also, biblical interpreters have become concerned with the problems related to the nature of the knowledge which language is able to convey.

Science

Science has produced spectacular results that have transformed the environment in which modern man lives and works. Its conquests over space, its victories over suffering and disease, and its creation of more comfortable standards of living for millions of people have tended to create unbridled confidence in the ability of science to guarantee man's future happiness and well-being. At the same time, the society that has arisen as a result of the scientific revolution has tended to depersonalize man. Scientific research has provided the instruments through which demagogues have been able to inflict mass destruction upon countless numbers of innocent and helpless people. The moral implications of the scientific revolution threaten to discredit it as a benefactor of the human race. But modern man lives his life in an era produced by the scientific revolution. There are strange and uncanny dimensions of this era which have affected man in many realms, including those of his society and his religion.

The scope of influence which the scientific revolution has exercised upon man's understanding of the universe can be seen by comparison with first-century concepts. The earth was thought to be the center of the universe. It was conceived as a flat, four-cornered expanse of land whose boundaries were determined by the chaos that existed beyond it. The visible planets were supposed to define the limits of space. Each planet was thought to be the seat of authority for powers exercising absolute sovereignty over man's life and destiny. Efforts were made to avoid the displeasure or placate the anger of those powers (gods or demons) through offering various types of sacrifices and through participating in acts of ritual worship. Sickness, disease, and misfortune were commonly attributed to the activity of demonic spirits living in the atmosphere. When God as the supreme power was conceived as playing a role in the world view, he was said to inhabit the realm beyond the stars. Satan, the ruler of evil spirits, was sometimes thought to dwell in the lower regions of the earth, in the sea, or in the upper spheres of the atmosphere. Salvation was interpreted in accordance with the prevailing concept of evil. In the Gnostic systems of thought salvation consisted in acquiring knowledge of the secrets of the universe which would enable the disembodied spirit at death to make its way past the barriers of the guardian powers attempting to impede its journey to paradise.

It is unnecessary to describe the contrast between the understanding of the world in the first and twentieth centuries. School children are able to perform that task. The average man now plans his daily schedule upon the basis of a world view which nullifies the total first-century viewpoint.

Expanded knowledge of the universe, instead of contributing to man's sense of certainty and security in it, has intensified his feeling of insecurity. Although science has provided reasonable answers to the preliminary questions, it has deepened the mystery beyond the limits of its knowledge. To be sure, many ancient puzzles no longer fascinate modern man. However, he discovers that he exists in a universe of almost unlimited proportions in which the old questions which haunted his predecessors recur in a more complicated form. What is the nature of human existence? Is it possible to speak of purpose and meaning in a universe which seems to be indifferent to man's deepest longings? What are the crucial dimensions of man's choices? The list of questions can be extended to include the total scope of man's existence. Clearly, scientific knowledge provides no conclusive answers to these queries.

Modern man's changed view of the world is reflected in his religious questions. This world view becomes a primary point of concern when an attempt is made to understand the Bible. Man's answers to the ultimate questions arise out of the religious dimensions of his experience. When he tries to express the nature and meaning of his religious experience, he naturally utilizes concepts and language which are germane to his understanding of the universe and of his place in it. It is at this point that serious difficulties arise for the twentieth-century man who turns to the Bible for guidance. Clearly, the Bible speaks the language and presupposes the concepts of the first-century mentality. No other medium was available for first-century Christians. Twentieth-century men neither understand nor accept these concepts. This fact raises a question concerning the relationship between the content of the biblical message and the form in which it is expressed. It is certain that the biblical writers did not intend to convince their readers that the world view of their day was correct—since both writers and readers accepted that world view. Rather, the writers were concerned with the truth about man's situation, his problems, and his hope in that world.

A basic question emerges for biblical interpreters who confront such problems. Is it necessary to accept the world view reflected in biblical literature in order to appropriate its message of forgiveness and salvation? If the answer is yes, the prospective believer confronts a twofold decision: He is called upon to make a religious decision concerning faith in Jesus Christ, but at the same time he cannot exercise faith without making an intellectual decision to accept the world view of the first century. If the answer is no (i.e., the Christian message is not indissolubly bound to biblical modes of expression), what modern form is available and appropriate for the expression of the biblical message? Thus, the interpreter must both remove the restrictions involved in the first-century world view and provide adequate channels for understanding the message in the modern age.

Theology

Theology and biblical interpretation were once conceived as separate and distinct disciplines. Biblical interpretation was defined as an exercise in exegesis (explaining what the text actually intended to say to the original readers). Theology was supposed to utilize the results of biblical exegesis in interpreting its meaning for the current situation. Historical investigation of the New Testament has made it clear that this division of labor was based upon a misunderstanding of the nature of New Testament literature (cf. Chapters 2–5). In the first place, theological thought does not begin after the content of the biblical message has been determined. Indeed, the texts themselves can only be understood as theological statements since they were concerned with the question of meaning. Secondly, the interpreter in each generation illumines the text to men of his own generation. There is no objective meaning of the text apart from its meaning in a particular historical situation. Otherwise, interpretation would become an exercise in curiosity about what the text

259

had to say to an ancient group of unknown readers. Biblical interpretation is no longer concerned solely with the quest for information about the ancient texts. Rather, it allows those texts to speak their message to man in his contemporary situation. This insight has major significance for other theological disciplines such as church history, systematic theology, ethics, and practical theology.

The insights contributed by the total family of theological disciplines provide the background for biblical interpretation. The interpreter brings this heritage as a part of his equipment for his task. This specific heritage is clarified, expanded, and corrected in the light of the text. An attempt to describe the current theological concern would lead far beyond the limits of this work. However, it cannot be overemphasized that biblical interpretation must be understood within the context of theological understanding. Indeed, interpretation is itself a theological endeavor.

THE NATURE OF BIBLICAL LANGUAGE

Current biblical interpretation focuses upon the problem of language. This focus represents the crystalization of the influence of modern perspectives (cf. the discussion in the preceding section).

The Problem of Demythologizing the New Testament

The question concerning the nature of biblical language was posed in a crucial form by Professor Rudolf Bultmann. Bultmann formulated his proposal in an essay which appeared in 1941.[1] According to Bultmann, it is necessary to

---

[1] Rudolf Bultmann, "New Testament and Mythology," *Kerygma and Myth,* I, 1-44.

"demythologize" (German, *entmythologisieren,* literally, unmythologize) the language of the New Testament in order that it may be understood by modern man. Mythology, as defined by Bultmann, is "the use of imagery to express the other worldly in terms of this world and the divine in terms of human life, the other side in terms of this side. For instance, divine transcendence is expressed as spatial distance." [2]

The program of demythologizing has evoked discussion of every major facet of biblical thought, although the original emphasis was most directly concerned with the problem of biblical language.

Bultmann pointed to the problem of language as the essential issue in New Testament interpretation in the modern era. He proposed to solve the problem on the basis of the following assumptions. First, New Testament language expresses the mentality of the first century which was not informed by scientific investigation. This language occasioned no problems for the original recipients of the biblical material since they also thought in these categories. However, this language raises crucial problems for the modern reader who neither understands nor accepts these concepts. Secondly, biblical thought is expressed in language that was normally used to refer to objects in this world whose existence and structure could be verified by observation. However, when this kind of language was used to refer to God who transcends the realm of empirical observation, it was called upon to render service for which it was basically unqualified. Third, first-century mentality conceived spiritual reality in objective terms analogous to the world of daily experience. (This tendency to objectify reality which cannot be con-

[2] Rudolf Bultmann, "New Testament and Mythology," *Kerygma and Myth,* I, 10, n. 2.

ceived in objective categories has been described by Bultmann as a mythological mentality.) Their gods, demons, and spirits were conceived by analogy with the objects and persons of everyday experience. But—God cannot be conceived in such terms. Fourth, this mythological language appears not only in the peripheral pronouncements of the New Testament. First-century man used it to indicate his understanding of his situation, including his basic religious problems. Consequently, mythology appears in the description of the person and work of Christ, the character of Christian salvation, and the Christian hope for the future.

On the basis of these assumptions, Bultmann concluded that the language of the New Testament is both an inappropriate and inadequate vehicle for expressing the message of the gospel in our generation. It is inappropriate because it can no longer be understood in its original intentions. It is inadequate because it is basically unsuited for expressing the total dimensions of the gospel. Bultmann pointed to the Gospel of John as evidence that the writers of certain New Testament works had already sensed this inadequacy (in John's Gospel the cross is interpreted as the exaltation of Christ, Jesus' presence in the world is described as the judgment, and the coming of the Holy Spirit is related to the hope of an early return of Christ).

Bultmann's method is based upon his conviction that it enables the interpreter to avoid the fundamental error of nineteenth-century interpreters. Whereas those interpreters suggested that the mythological elements in the Bible should be *eliminated* through the use of rational judgment, he proposed to retain this language and *interpret* it for modern man.

Bultmann was aware that the process of demythologizing involves a twofold procedure; namely, the interpreter must demythologize the language, and he must also clothe the ideas in new forms of thought. He suggested that modern existentialism provides the most accessible medium for expressing the message of the gospel. In his judgment, Martin Heidegger's analysis of the structure of human existence is most appropriate for this task.[3] In using Heidegger's thought, Bultmann did not propose a permanent identification of Christian thought with existentialist philosophy. Rather, he suggested that Heidegger's philosophy provides the most usuable vehicle for interpretation in this generation.

Bultmann's viewpoint has called forth a violent storm of protest from many quarters. His opponents have accused him of overlooking or eliminating fundamental elements of the biblical message because they cannot be readily accommodated to the structures of existentialist thought. They have objected that he has propagated an unbiblical doctrine of man, and that he has surrendered the distinctive biblical claim to revelation by subordinating it to the standards of philosophical thought.

Bultmann's reply to his critics can be found in the extensive material that has come from his pen. He has steadfastly maintained that his method of interpretation is based upon the nature of biblical material. His opponents have experienced some difficulty in their efforts to arrive at a unified conclusion regarding the basic fallacy in his suggestion. Their arguments often tend to nullify one another.

In conclusion, we must concede that Bultmann's proposal for demythologizing the New Testament has never been refuted. The language and mentality of the New Testament do constitute a formidable barrier for modern men. The

---

[3] Martin Heidegger, *Being and Time,* trans. John Macquarrie and Edward Robinson (New York: Harper & Row, 1962).

total New Testament perspective cannot be mechanically transposed into twentieth-century thought. The fear that some emphases in New Testament thought may be overlooked in the effort to translate its message into modern thought is well founded. Nevertheless, this risk must be accepted as an inherent element in the total work of translation and interpretation. In fact, this problem arises out of the acceptance of an ancient document as the authority for succeeding generations of Christians. Even when the text is translated as literally as possible, the modern reader misses important emphases of the language. Hence, biblical interpretation involves the responsible acceptance of the risk that arises in the effort to reiterate truth in the midst of changing historical circumstances. In this respect, biblical interpretation shares in the problems of all attempts to understand the nature of knowledge and the character of truth.

Beyond Demythologizing

After a quarter of a century, the demythologizing controversy no longer claims the primary attention of biblical interpreters. The shift in interest and emphasis can be explained from various standpoints. First, biblical interpretation, as well as theological discussion in general, is not a static enterprise. Theological and biblical issues arise as an expression of problems that emerge within a specific historical context. In each instance they reflect the stage of development to which the disciplines have arrived. The demythologizing proposal represented a pertinent formulation of the problems which confronted biblical interpreters at that time. The discussion that ensued regarding those problems further clarified and defined them. Hence, the earlier statement of the issue has in some sense become inadequate. Secondly,

Bultmann's proposal did not formulate the issue (language) in its decisive form. In pointing to the impasse which confronts the modern reader of the Bible, he identified one aspect of the problem of religious language as a whole. However, the problem of religious language cannot be solved in isolation from the larger issues which relate to the nature and function of human language. Third, Bultmann's suggestion raised attendant theological and historical problems of comprehensive importance. These questions have resulted in an expansion of the theological discussion in general. Bultmann's suggestion is no longer entirely appropriate within this discussion. Fourth, continuing philosophical occupation with the problem of language has required that the questions concerning biblical language be restated in accordance with the results of philosophical investigation.

The problem of hermeneutics has become the primary problem in theology. It has crystalized in the form of the question about the nature and role of language in human experience. The scope of the discussion has expanded to the extent that language has become a subject of primary interest in biblical interpretation, systematic theology, and philosophy.

The theological context in which the question of language became crucial was created in part by the consistent application of the principles of historical-critical methodology. This methodology, supported at times by an inadequate understanding of the doctrine of *sola scriptura,* focused attention upon the scripture as the object of interpretation. Consequently, it became easy to identify the content of scripture —objectively investigated!—with the Word of God. Hermeneutics became synonymous with objective, scientific investigation (exegesis) of the message of scripture. The recovery of what Paul "intended" to say to his contempor-

265

aries became the final goal of biblical interpretation. The Word of God, identified with the message of scripture which is accessible to the methods of historical investigation, did indeed appear to be an isolated historical phenomenon. That such problems could arise through the use of historical-critical methodology does not mean that this method of study is to be rejected, or that scripture fulfills its function apart from such an approach. Rather, these problems have become the occasion for a more comprehensive understanding of the implications of historical research in biblical literature.

Martin Heidegger's understanding of the nature of language has stimulated theological reflection upon the nature and function of biblical language. His analysis of the phenomenon of language is related to his understanding of the nature of thought. According to Heidegger, thinking arises out of being's gift of itself to man in self-disclosure. This "givenness" eventuates in language, man's response to the "silent toll" of being. Consequently, language is not an "instrument" at man's disposal for the articulation of previously existing rational concepts. Rather, language is the occasion where meaning arises through being's gift of itself to man. In this occurrence man becomes man, the focus where being is brought to clarification. (Such an occurrence is described as "authentic language," i.e., the clarification of being. Heidegger also allows that language may fail in this function, particularly when it uses traditional language without perception of its ultimate dimensions.) [4]

Heidegger's perspective is theologically reflected in the

[4] Martin Heidegger, *Existence and Being* (Chicago: Henry Regnery Company, 1950). Also, Martin Heidegger, *Unterwegs zur Sprache* (Pfullingen: Verlag Günther Neske, 1959). Cf. James M. Robinson, "The German Discussion of the Later Heidegger," *The Later Heidegger and Theology,* New Frontiers in Theology, ed. Robinson and Cobb (New York: Harper & Row, 1963), I, 3-76.

works of Gerhard Ebeling and Ernst Fuchs who have played leading roles in the discussion of the hermeneutical problem in biblical interpretation. Ebeling, a systematic theologian, has pointed to the limitations of the view which overtly identifies the content of scripture with the Word of God. He understands the text of scripture as "word event" (*Wortgeschehen*), which is the occasion for the Word of God, the subject matter of the text, to come to expression. Consequently, the "words" of scripture do not function as a restraining agent to conceal "information" which must be wrested from the text by scientific investigation. On the contrary, scripture is to be understood as language event which performs an interpretative (revealing) function in bringing the Word of God to expression. Scripture is described as interpretative event (*Auslegungsgeschehen*).[5] Furthermore, the word of scripture fulfills its inherent function only when it leads to further proclamation. Thus, scripture and preaching are bound together by their common nature as word event.[6] While Ebeling's work has been done more directly in relation to the context of the Reformation, Fuchs has dealt with the problem of language as word event (*Sprachereignis*) as it concerns the scripture and preaching. According to Fuchs, the language of scripture is the place where God "announces" himself. Scripture is the continuation of God's "announcement" in Jesus. In the words of Fuchs, "Jesus has made God present for me. And how has he done that? Through his words. . . ."[7] Furthermore,

[5] Gerhard Ebeling, *Theology and Proclamation*, trans. John Riches (Philadelphia: Fortress Press, 1966), p. 28.

[6] Gerhard Ebeling, *The Nature of Faith*, trans. Ronald Gregor Smith (Philadelphia: Muhlenberg Press, 1962), Chaps. II, VII, and Appendix. Also, Gerhard Ebeling, *Word and Faith*, trans. James W. Leitch (Philadelphia: Fortress Press, 1963), pp. 305-32.

[7] Ernst Fuchs, "The New Testament and the Hermeneutical Problem," *The New Hermeneutic*, New Frontiers in Theology, ed. Robinson and Cobb (New York: Harper & Row, 1964), II, 130.

Fuchs reverses the traditional understanding of the relationship of the interpreter to the text, i.e., rather than the interpreter interpreting the text, the text is said to interpret (illumine) the situation of the interpreter who hears the text as Word of God. This Word of God calls for response (faith).[8] Thus, biblical interpretation involves the recognition of language as a phenomenon in which man becomes man through the disclosure of God in language. Ebeling and Fuchs understand their work as a correction of a limitation of demythologizing, since it points toward a more profound grasp of the nature of language.

Amos N. Wilder presents an alternative to the viewpoint just described. Wilder applauds the progress that has resulted from the approach made by Ebeling and Fuchs, but he questions the presuppositions upon which they have proceeded. In Wilder's judgment, the circle of thought which is related to Heidegger (existentialism) is limited by its abstract anthropology (doctrine of man). Existentialism is said to interpret human existence in terms of a universal, generalized conception of man rather than in terms of man's concrete situation. Consequently, Wilder thinks that the historical circumstances of man's life as a social-psychic being are inadequately understood. For example, he thinks that the exponents of "language event" have placed disproportionate emphasis upon man as a choosing-willing agent. Wilder calls for larger recognition of the content of the message to which faith responds.[9] In contrast with Ebeling

---

[8] Ernst Fuchs, *Studies of the Historical Jesus*, pp. 65-83; 207-12.

[9] Amos N. Wilder, "New Testament Hermeneutics Today," *Current Issues in New Testament Interpretation*, ed. Classen and Snyder (New York: Harper & Brothers, 1962), pp. 38-52. Also, Amos N. Wilder, "The Word as Address and Meaning," *The New Hermeneutic*, New Frontiers in Theology, ed. Robinson and Cobb (New York: Harper & Row, 1964), II, 198-218.

and Fuchs, Wilder calls for consideration of the psychological, sociological, and historical dimensions of the phenomenon of language as clues to its message and function.
In his judgment, the basic questions are: "How does the
whole phenomenon of language, speech, communication,
rhetoric present itself in the rise of Christianity? What
modes of discourse are specially congenial to the Gospel?
What is the special role of oral as against written discourse?
What is the theological significance of particular rhetorical
patterns used or neglected in the early Church?" [10] Wilder's
study of literary forms (dialogue, story, parable, poem) calls
attention to literary form and content in biblical literature.
His thought has stimulated further serious reflection on this
issue, including two works which deserve to be mentioned
in this context.[11]

CONCLUSION

The basic hermeneutical questions that confront biblical
interpreters are rooted in Christian claims regarding the
historical character of the faith. On one hand, the church's
acceptance of the scriptures—themselves historical documents—as the norm for its life and thought establishes one
point of reference for interpreting the Christian witness. On
the other hand, the church's acknowledgment of the authority
of the scriptures—regardless of the form in which the concept of authority is expressed—involves implicit recognition
of the obligation to say what these historical documents
"mean" for the contemporary situation. This claim for

[10] Amos N. Wilder, *The Language of the Gospel,* p. 11.
[11] Robert W. Funk, *Language, Hermeneutic, and Word of God* (New
York: Harper & Row, 1966) ; William A. Beardslee, *Literary Criticism
of the New Testament.*

present relevance of *historical* documents constitutes the framework of the structure in which the Christian community seeks to discharge its hermeneutical responsibility. Without falling victim to the temptation to "define" the hermeneutical task, it may be possible to point to some clues regarding the nature of the endeavor.

1. The attempt to understand the scriptures historically, i.e., within the structures of understanding of the original recipients, still represents the necessary point of departure for biblical interpretation.

2. Hermeneutics fulfills its total responsibility, however, only to the extent that it succeeds in translating the biblical witness into appropriate contemporary categories and modes of understanding.

3. Scientific hermeneutical principles constitute the legitimate instrument for understanding the biblical message, i.e., the religious character of biblical literature does not call for "special" hermeneutical principles.

4. Biblical interpretation inevitably reflects philosophical assumptions—implicit or explicit—regarding the phenomenon of human language. Consequently, evaluation of the alternatives—for example, positivism *versus* existentialism—represents an integral part of the work of interpretation.

Books for Additional Reading

1. Hans Werner Bartsch, ed., *Kerygma and Myth,* trans. R. H. Fuller (London: S.P.C.K. Press, 1953), I.
2. Rudolf Bultmann, *Jesus Christ and Mythology* (New York: Charles Scribner's Sons, 1958).
3. Amos N. Wilder, *The Language of the Gospel* (New York: Harper & Row, 1964).
4. William A. Beardslee, *Literary Criticism of the New Testament,* Dan O. Via, Jr., ed. (Philadelphia: Fortress Press, 1970).

11

The Scriptures:
The Problems of Unity
and Authority

The previous chapters have described some techniques and aspects of contemporary biblical scholarship. This description has shown that current understanding of the biblical message is achieved through the use of historical-critical methodology.

Historical-critical methodology has contributed to a better understanding of the message of the scriptures. This enriched understanding has in turn revealed limitations in earlier concepts of the nature and function of the scriptures. Traditional concepts of the unity and authority of the scriptures have had to be revised. For this reason, historical-critical methodology as an approach to understanding the scriptures has sometimes been rejected.

CRITICAL RESEARCH AND BIBLICAL INTERPRETATION

The value of scientific biblical study has been challenged since the time of its inception. Opponents of critical methodology have pointed to its alleged negative and destructive tendencies. They have charged that this methodology raises irrelevant questions that cannot be answered through study of the scriptures. Also, they have condemned critical scholars for challenging cherished doctrines. In short, the critical approach to the interpretation of the scriptures has been said to jeopardize biblical truth.

Admittedly, critical methods of study have raised new problems in biblical interpretation. Also, these methods have not provided final answers for all the old questions. But we must remember that critical methodology arose in response to unanswered questions. The issue cannot be decided solely upon the basis of demonstrated ability to answer existing questions. The value of a specific approach to biblical interpretation can be seen best in its ability to *identify* important questions. Here, critical methodology has rendered its most valuable service.

One major weakness of the uncritical approach to biblical interpretation lies in its inclination to rely upon faith for answers to questions that require rational investigation. This kind of reliance distorts faith's proper function and obscures its legitimate role in religious experience.

A realistic evaluation of the function and limits of critical research is mandatory lest extravagant and unjustified claims for its results imply that faith itself is dependent upon the conclusions of research. Rightly understood, critical research clarifies the nature and scope of faith's decisions. For example, the question concerning the authorship of II Peter can be investigated rationally through the use of techniques developed in scientific biblical study. Any attempt to substantiate a conclusion in this question by an appeal to faith denies the legitimate function of reason. On the other hand, the affirmation that the cross is a symbol of God's redemptive love for sinful man expresses a Christian conviction that arises in faith, and an attempt to provide rational foundations for this confession obscures the nature of faith.

The validity of critical methodology must be judged from within as well as from beyond its scope. That its conclusions have appealed to the majority of Christian scholars is one basis for its continued application. The history of the debate with its opponents reveals a gradual retreat on the part of these opponents at points which they once contended were crucial and decisive. Furthermore, critical scholarship has provided insights regarding the meaning of the gospel which have constituted an incisive response to modern opponents of the Christian message.

THE UNITY OF THE SCRIPTURES

The "unity of the scriptures" is a phrase that occurs frequently in discussions about biblical literature. It has become a kind of slogan which suggests that there is a discernible unity in viewpoint or teaching in the books of the Bible. The "unity of the scriptures" expresses a general idea which has led to a variety of interpretations. Like other slogans, the "unity of the scriptures" is often accepted as a self-evident statement of fact. If questions are raised concerning the exact meaning of the phrase, they are often branded as covert attempts to discredit the scriptures. Nevertheless, critical investigation has discredited the idea of the "unity of the scriptures," particularly in the forms in which it has been commonly understood.

The scriptures do not express a unified religious viewpoint. Old Testament literature preserves a tradition that developed over a period of more than one thousand years. It testifies to various stages of that developing tradition and reflects changes in the understanding of the nature and obligations of religion. For example, Old Testament literature contains divergent interpretations of the meaning of the Law and the Covenant, the form and obligations of worship, and the nature of ethics. Likewise, there are obvious differences in the teaching of the New Testament books. For instance, James and Hebrews do not reflect Paul's teaching on justification by faith. The understanding of faith in John's Gospel is not paralleled elsewhere in the New Testament. Differences in religious perspectives become even more crucial when the Old Testament claims for the Law are compared with the New Testament reinterpretation or rejection of that Law.

The "unity of the scriptures" has been understood as an alleged unity of teaching. This interpretation is untenable for many reasons, two of which may be indicated here. First, the scriptures do not reflect unified historical expectations. This is most evident when the Old Testament hope for an earthly political Messiah is compared with the New Testament confession of Jesus as the Messiah. Also, Paul seems to have expected the return of Christ within his lifetime. Luke wrote his Gospel and the book of Acts to interpret the meaning of the gospel when Paul's expectation was abandoned. Paul's expectation seems to have exercised little or no influence upon the thinking of the authors of many other New Testament works (cf. Hebrews, John's Gospel, and Ephesians). Secondly, the scriptures do not express unified theological concepts. The Gospel of Mark interprets Jesus as the divine Son of God whose presence upon the earth represented God's challenge to the demonic lordship over the world. In contrast, the Gospel of Matthew refers to Jesus as the fulfillment of Jewish expectations. Further differences appear in connection with such important concepts as the church, the meaning of the Law for Christians, and the concept of apostleship.

Arguments for the "unity of the scriptures" were formulated originally in support of the authority of the scriptures. Such arguments were designed to show that the scriptures contain an authentic witness to Jesus Christ. They were influenced by the accepted historical norms of the era. According to those norms, authentic historical tradition must maintain an unchanging form in order to preserve the tradition. Hence, it seemed necessary to show that the tradition about Jesus Christ had begun as a unity and that it had remained relatively unaltered from the beginning. This kind of argument doubtless appeared necessary and convincing to the generation that created it.

Developments in modern times have robbed the arguments for the "unity of the scriptures" of much of their original plausibility. In the first place, critical research has shown that the alleged unity does not exist (cf. Chapters 3–

275

5 and the previous discussion in this chapter). Second, the norms of evaluation for authentic historical tradition have been revised in the light of more comprehensive understanding of the nature of historical truth. Each generation alters the form of its received tradition precisely in order to preserve the truth of the tradition. Finally, the authenticity of the Christian tradition cannot be measured solely by historical norms. There are dimensions of the Christian confession to Jesus Christ which are not subject to historical verification (cf. Chapter 9).

The idea of the "unity of the scriptures" no longer adequately testifies to the authenticity of the scriptural witness to Jesus Christ. The question concerning the *continuity* of the scriptural witness with the original Christian confession has supplanted that of the unity of the scriptures. Here the aim is to show that the witness of the scriptures stands in vital and essential continuity with the original Christian confession to the resurrected Lord, even though the external form of that confession was altered in the process of preserving it.

THE AUTHORITY OF THE SCRIPTURES

Christians universally recognize the authority of the scriptures. Questions relating to the nature and scope of that authority have been debated by Protestants and Catholics since the time of the Protestant Reformation. No single statement has succeeded in winning the approval of more than a segment of the total Christian community.

The problem of scriptural authority is rooted in the ambiguity of the idea of authority itself. In its most general meaning authority connotes the right to control or determine actions or beliefs. For example, a book on history may be described as an authoritative book, and learned men are said to be authorities in their specialized fields of study. However, guards in penal institutions exercise authority over prisoners, parents possess legal authority over minor children, and men are said to possess authority over their own wills. In what sense, to what degree, and in what areas may the scriptures be said to possess authority? It is exceedingly difficult to answer these questions.

We must be clear from the outset that we are concerned with the authority of the *scriptures,* in distinction from the authority of the *Bible.* The importance of the Bible (canon) as a historical instrument for preserving the scriptures for the church has already been discussed (Chapter 8). However, the authority of the canon is based upon the church's right (or correctness in judgment) to create the canon. Hence, this discussion focuses upon the authority of the message of the scriptures rather than that of the collection (canon) in which the scriptures have been preserved.

The Claim for Absolute Authority of the Scriptures

The scriptures are frequently described as the "sole," "final," or "absolute" authority for the church. Such statements properly recognize the importance of the scriptures. But they raise difficult questions. In the first place, only God, the Creator and Lord, possesses sole, final, and absolute authority. The use of such words to define the authority of the scriptures has often led to an improper reverence for them which can scarcely be distinguished from bibliolatry (worship of the Bible). In point of fact, the scriptures do not possess authority that equals or supplants God's authority.

277

The dilemma is not solved by the suggestion that God has "bestowed" such authority upon the scriptures. This kind of bestowal would amount to abdication. It should perhaps be remarked in passing that men, rather than God, have attributed "sole," "final," or "absolute" authority to the scriptures.

It is impossible to speak cogently of the authority of the scriptures as a whole. Such statements more appropriately concern the authority of the canon. The reader cannot approach the message of the scriptures as a whole, nor can he grasp it in this form. He can understand the message of the various parts of the Bible only in the form of verses, chapters, and books. These parts or sections do not all express the same message, nor do they reflect the same degree of spiritual maturity (some passages identify hatred, plunder, and murder with the will of God. Even Paul's teaching on marriage scarcely represents the same level of insight as his doctrine of the cross). Since the individual parts of the scriptures vary widely in their level of perception, it is logically impossible to attribute absolute—or even sole or final—authority to every segment.

The attempt to describe the nature and scope of scriptural authority inevitably limits and qualifies that authority. Hence, the word "absolute" cannot appropriately describe scriptural authority (although "sole" and "final" do not carry the identical implications of "absolute," the terms are often used with the same connotations). A discussion can involve only the nature of limited authority of the scriptures.

The Nature of Scriptural Authority

The limited authority of the scriptures is sometimes defined as authority in "religious" matters. This description rightly indicates that the scriptures are not to be understood as an encyclopedia for all kinds of information. However, the scriptures do not recognize a special realm of man's life which it defines as "religious." Man's total life is conceived in terms of the religious dimension, and the scriptures possess authority for man's total existence in the world.

A single definition of scriptural authority will hardly be universally satisfactory. That does not mean that the idea of scriptural authority is altogether nebulous. Rather, it suggests that the claim for scriptural authority is such that it is not amenable to objective formulation, isolated from the experience of those who hear the testimony of the scriptures. Scriptural authority is not imposed but accepted by personal decision in response to the compelling nature of the scriptural witness to truth. Certain intangible factors, such as experience and training, inevitably play a role in the interpretation of scriptural authority. Hence, any specific description of that authority may seem to some readers to oversimplify the issue, while it may appear abstract and irrelevant to others.

The claim for the authority of the scriptures is grounded in experience. Christians who have heard and heeded the message of the scriptures have confirmed the validity of this message in their own experiences. But while it is based upon evidence from past experience, it must at the same time assume the form of a promise for the present and future. The attempt to provide absolute proofs and guarantees for the present and future by an appeal to the authority of the scriptures misconstrues the meaning of scriptural authority. For example, a guide who is able to direct travelers to a place of safety after they have lost their sense of direction in the wilderness has "proved" his authority as a guide in a particular set of circumstances. However, those travelers cannot use this evidence as absolute proof if they should become lost again in the wilderness and face the necessity of risking their lives in following the same guide again. To be sure, experience would dictate the wisdom of reliance upon the judgment of the guide who had previously demonstrated his ability. Nevertheless, proof of the certainty of his knowledge can come only at the successful conclusion of the journey to a place of security. Likewise, the experience of countless Christians with the scriptures provides great encouragement to rely upon their testimony in making decisions in the present time. But a claim for the authority of the scriptures which omits the element of faith contains an inherent contradiction.

The claim for the authority of the scriptures must be properly related to the nature of human experience. There are unique dimensions of human experience which cannot be recorded in literary documents. We cannot expect the scriptures to provide an exact replica of all human experiences. For example, other travelers will not exactly reproduce the experiences of the travelers mentioned above, i.e., they may be lost but not in the same place, with the same problems, etc. The scriptures do not contain a mosaic of all possible human situations; they cannot serve as a handbook of instructions on how to act in every circumstance. Paul faced problems in his Gentile environment which Jesus did not confront in Palestine. The authority of the scriptures means that they function as an arrow to indicate the proper direction, or as a light to illumine the nature of the situation.

The effort to define the authority of the scriptures may be an unfortunate undertaking. The inadequacy of existing definitions could point to that conclusion. At any rate, previous failures cannot be overcome by more intensive efforts to define the concept. We must remember that Christians have applied the concept of authority to the scriptures in order to emphasize their importance. At the same time, it remains questionable whether the idea of authority is fully adequate to express all that Christians intend to say about the scriptures. In the first place, the concept of authority is ambiguous (cf. the discussion above). Second, the idea of authority is often colored by its association with the concept of a legal, externally imposed right to control thought and actions. This idea is foreign to a mature understanding of the role of the scriptures. Nevertheless, numerous definitions of scriptural authority have reflected it. Finally, the scriptures do not contain a clearly enunciated claim for authority. To be sure, they are said to be "inspired" and "useful" (II Tim. 3:16-17, Am. Bible Soc.; the reference in this passage concerns Jewish religious literature, including material in the present canon of the Old Testament). However, the words "inspired" and "useful" do not contain many elements of modern concepts of scriptural authority. The suggestion that the concept of authority may be inappropriate to describe the role of the scriptures does not deny their primacy. It only reflects upon the inadequacy of the concept of authority to interpret the nature of that primacy.

Perhaps the nature and function of the scriptures can be expressed best in terms of "witness," "testimony," or even "call." They preserve a variety of Christian testimony articulated prior to the middle of the second century. These witnesses point to a common experience of the redemptive love of God which was mediated through Jesus Christ. Further, they iterate the conviction that this love encompasses the whole of humanity. From the standpoint of modern man who is confronted by the testimony of the scriptures, the scriptures function as "call" and "promise." To be sure, the hearing of that call through the specific human media of the first two centuries raises questions to which logic provides only partial answers. This rational dilemma points to another dimension: The scriptures provide access to the originative event of faith which also sustains faith, the life-death-resurrection of Jesus Christ. Faith acknowledges continuity between Jesus Christ and its own experiences and lives in the scriptural dialectic of witness and call.

CONCLUSION

The scriptures mediate promise and hope to man by illuminating the contours of the situation in which other men encountered the call to faith. Herein the glory of the scriptures appears. However, this glory becomes visible only in response to him to whom the scriptures testify—Jesus Christ, the living Lord. If the scriptures mediate the event of Jesus Christ in such a way that they lead to further proclamation of that event, they also anticipate the rekindling of a faith akin to that from which the scriptures arose.

Each attempt to delineate the meaning and function of the scriptures can achieve only partial success. The inability to "tell the whole story" about the scriptures is testimony to the scope of their significance. In some sense, what remains to be said but what cannot be said identifies the nature of the mystery toward which the scriptures point. An early Christian bore testimony to this dimension of scripture when he wrote: Above all else, however, remember this: no one can explain, by himself, a prophecy in the Scriptures. For no prophetic message ever came just from the will of man, but men were carried along by the Holy Spirit as they spoke the message that came from God. (II Peter 1:20-21, Am. Bible Soc.)

Books for Additional Reading

1. L. Harold DeWolf, *A Theology of the Living Church* (New York: Harper & Row, 1953), pp. 63-86.
2. C. H. Dodd, *The Authority of the Bible* (London: Nisbet & Company, 1948), pp. 1-31; 289-300.
3. Herbert H. Farmer, "The Bible: Its Significance and Authority," *The Interpreter's Bible* (New York and Nashville: Abingdon-Cokesbury Press, 1952), I, 3-31.

Scripture Index

Matthew

3:7-10	85
3:7-12	85
3:11-12	84-86
3:13-17	77, 82-86
3:14	118
3:14-15	134
3:15	118, 123
4:23	136, 137
4:23-25	136
4:23–9:35	136
5–7	71, 75, 123, 136
5:1–9:34	135
5:14b	97
5:17	64, 123
5:43	232
5:43-48	124
7:24-27	123
7:28	136
7:28-29	136
8:1-4	107
8:1–9:34	135
8:18	106-7
8:23-27	106-7
8:51	185
9:1-8	107-9
9:13	137
9:34–11:2	135
9:35	136, 137
9:35-38	135
9:36	137
10	75
10:1–11:1	135
10:5-6	64, 124
11:1	136

Matthew—cont'd

11:2-6	134-37
11:5	96
11:21-24	96
12:34b	97
12:35	97
12:39	109
12:46-50	104-6
13	75
13:11	123
13:24-30	123
13:34	63, 99
13:51	99
13:53	136
14:3-12	77
14:13-33	185
14:14	137
15:32	137
16:19	109
18	75
18:18 ff.	109
19:1	136
19:13 ff.	100
19:17-19	124
20:34	137
21:42	210
23	75, 124
23:3	123, 225
24–25	75
25:31-46	236
25:41-46	96
26–27	184
26:2	136
28:16-20	64
28:18	236

Mark

1:1 ....54-58, 60, 116
1:1–5:30 55
1:1-11 116
1:2 ff. 36
1:7 134
1:7-8 84-86
1:9 119
1:9-11 ....77, 82-86
1:11 ....57, 121
1:12-13 100
1:14 ....119, 156
1:14-15 ....232, 240
1:14–9:50 119
1:15a 96
1:16-20 185
1:21-28 77
1:21-34 ....135, 136
1:29-31 100
1:39 137
1:40-45 107
2:1-12 ....98, 100, 107-9
2:6-10 98
3:1-6 97
3:11 ....57, 116
3:11-12 119
3:20-30 97
3:27 97
3:31-45 104-6
4:10-12 225
4:11-12 99
4:33-34 63
4:34 ....99, 186
4:35-41 106-7
5:1-20 100
5:7 ....57, 116
6:17-29 77
6:20–8:3 78
6:30-52 185
6:45-52 100
8:11-12 109
8:30 119
9:7 ....57, 116, 121
9:9 63
9:51–18:14 78
10:1 ff. 119
10:29-30 96
10:47 ff. 119

Mark—cont'd

11:15-19 97
12:18-27 97
13:14 ff. 120
13:32 96
14-15 184
15:39 ....57, 116, 121
16:7 120
16:9-20 ....31, 65

Luke

3:1–4:30 78
3:7-9 85
3:7-18 85
3:15-18 84-86
3:21-22 ....77, 82-86
4:31-37 77
5:12-16 107
5:17-26 107-9
6:20–8:3 ....64, 71, 75
6:43 ff. 97
7:1-10 185
7:18-23 134-37
7:28 134
8:9-10 99
8:19-21 104-6
8:22-25 106-7
9:1-27 78
9:10-17 185
9:51–18:14 ....64, 71, 75
13:31-32 97
17:23-24 96
19:42-44 96
22–23 184
22:14–24:53 78
22:51b 100
24:27 210

John

1–12 202
1:1-18 202
1:18 202
1:19-34 134
1:21 ff. 63
1:32-33 185
1:34 202
1:36 202
1:41 202
1:51 202

John—*cont'd*

4:25 202
4:46-54 185
4:54–6:1 191
5 191
5:16 205
6:1 191
6:1-21 185
6:35 202
6:60-71 192
7:1 205
7:15-24 192
7:53–8:11 31
8:42-47 192
10:31 205
11:25 202
13–17 205
13–20 202
13:1 186
14:51 191
15–17 191
18–19 184
18:1 191
18:33-35 177
18:37-38 177
19:7 205
20:31 . . . . 191, 202, 203
21 191

Acts

1:7 ff. 130
2:14 ff. 128
3:12 ff. 128
4:8 ff. 128
4:12 . . . . 209, 240, 241
10:39 143
16:7 96
18:22-31 204
19:1-3 134

Romans

1:1 216
1:3 143
1:3 ff. 139
1:3-5 143
1:4 . . . . 95, 143, 156
1:14-15 213
1:16–3:20 142

Romans—*cont'd*

9–11 . . . . 160, 188
10:9 . . . . 156, 240
16:7 143

I Corinthians

1:1 216
1:2 240
1:12 146
1:18–4:21 142
7:1 19
8:1 19
11:23-25 . . . . 139, 143
12:1 19
12:28 216
13 . . . . 144, 176
15:3-4 95
15:3-5 143

II Corinthians

2:10 216

Galatians

2:16 143

Ephesians

2:20 142

Philippians

2:5-11 . . . 139, 143-44, 156, 232, 236

I Thessalonians

1:3 . . . . 143, 144

II Thessalonians

3:17 33

I Timothy

3:16 . . . . 121, 144

II Timothy

2:2 142
3:16 210
3:16-17 281

Hebrews

1:1-3 144
1:1-4 236

Hebrews—*cont'd*
  1 :5-13 121
  9 :14 39
II Peter
  1 :20-21 282

Revelation
  1 :1 178

Revelation—*cont'd*
  1 :4 178
  1 :9 178
  5 121
  22 :8 178

Psalms
  137 :4 252

Author Index

Aland, Kurt, 226
Athanasius, 218

Baldensperger, W., 205
Barrett, C. K., 185, 193, 201, 203
Barth, Gerhard, 125
Barth, Karl, 157-59
Bartsch, Hans Werner, 270
Baur, Ferdinand Christian, 26, 140, 145-49, 152, 154, 161, 180-81, 229-31
Beardslee, William A., 72, 138, 269-70
Beatty, Sir Chester, 40
Bodmer, M. Martin, 40
Bornkamm, Günther, 125, 162, 173, 227-28, 235, 244, 248
Bousset, W., 150
Briggs, R. C., 179
Brown, Raymond E., 196-97, 203, 207
Büchsel, F., 181
Bultmann, Rudolf, 88, 100, 155, 158-59, 162, 165-68, 170-71, 185, 190, 192, 199, 200, 240-42, 247-48, 260-63, 265, 270
Bultmann, Rudolf, and Kundsin, Karl, 88, 103
Butler, B. C., 72

Charles, R. H., 149
Colwell, Ernest Cadman, 36-37, 51
Comte, Auguste, 152
Conzelmann, Hans, 122, 126, 129-30, 162, 166-67, 186, 202, 205, 247
Cullmann, Oscar, 160, 245

Cumont, Franz, 150

Daube, David, 196
Davies, W. D., 153, 172
Deissmann, Adolf, 138, 150
Descartes, René, 255
DeWolf, L. Harold, 283
Dibelius, Martin, 88, 94, 128
Dodd, C. H., 170, 183, 192, 195-96, 200, 204, 244-45, 282
Doresse, Jean, 199
Dupont-Sommer, A., 150

Ebeling, Gerhard, 224, 267-68
Erasmus, 46, 50
Eusebius, 66, 76, 178, 213

Farmer, Herbert H., 283
Farmer, William R., 72
Feine, Behm, and Kümmel, 141, 179, 196, 206
Filson, Floyd V., 226
Foerster, Werner, 195
Fuchs, Ernst, 244, 267-69
Funk, Robert W., 269

Gaster, Theodor H., 196
Grant, Frederick C., 74, 80
Grant, Robert M., 205
Gregory, C. R., 38, 47
Grenfell and Hunt, 40-41
Gunkel, Hermann, 88
Guy, H. A., 80

Hegel, 147, 152, 229-30
Heidegger, Martin, 263, 266, 268

287

Heitmüller, W., 155
Held, Heinz Joachim, 125
Hofman, J. C. K. von, 159
Holtzmann, H. J., 70, 181
Hummel, Reinhart, 125
Hunter, A. M., 143, 172-73

Irenaeus, 23, 43, 60, 218

Jeremias, Joachim, 99, 249
Jerome, 55, 214
Jonas, Hans, 151, 198

Kabisch, Richard, 168-69
Kähler, Martin, 89, 114, 157, 234-35, 238
Käsemann, Ernst, 130-31, 162-63, 167, 171, 175, 207 242-44
Knox, John 162
Kümmel, W. G., 147-48, 175, 188-89, 207

Lachmann, Karl, 70
Leaney, A. R. C., 150
Lohmeyer, Ernst, 120
Lucian, 37, 46
Lüdemann, Hermann, 164-65
Luther, Martin, 23-24, 50, 160-61, 211, 215, 222, 225

Malachy, Jona, 72
Manson, T. W., 80
Marcion, 218
Marxsen, Willi, 120, 138, 141, 179, 226
Metzger, Bruce, 37, 39-40, 47, 52
Montgomery, Robert M., 80
Montgomery and Stegner, W. Richard, 103

Origen, 36, 43

Pannenberg, Wolfhart, 246
Papias, 66, 76, 213
Perrin, Norman, 132, 249

Pfleiderer, Otto, 153

Robinson, James M., 120-21, 176, 244, 249, 266
Rohde, Erwin, 150
Rohde, Joachim, 132

Schleiermacher, F. D. E., 177, 180
Schmidt, Karl Ludwig, 88
Schnackenburger, Rudolf, 202-3
Schulz, Siegfried 190, 192-93
Schürer, Emil, 149
Schweitzer, Albert, 114, 147, 153, 161, 169-70, 234-35
Schweizer, Eduard, 193
Simon, Richard, 25
Smith, T. C., 204
Souter, Alexander, 226
Stacey, W. David, 166-68
Strauss, David Friedrich, 149, 180, 228-31
Strecker, Georg, 125-26
Streeter, B. H., 74, 76, 78

Taylor, Vincent, 37, 88, 103
Tertullian, 43
Throckmorton, B. H., Jr., 40, 47, 60, 80, 110, 116
Tillich, Paul, 253
Tischendorf, Konstantin von, 38-39
Trilling, Wolfgang, 125

Vaganay, Leo, 37, 52
Via, Dan Otto, Jr., 99
Vielhauer, Philipp, 121-22, 128

Weiss, Bernhard, 70
Weiss, Johannes, 114, 168-69, 232
Wendland, Paul, 150
Westcott and Hort, 39, 46
Wilckens, Ulrich, 130
Wilder, Amos N., 99, 138, 268-70
Wrede, William, 89, 113-14, 119, 156, 161, 234-35